The Road to Nuremberg

THE ROAD

TO

NUREMBERG

Bradley F. Smith

Basic Books, Inc., Publishers

NEW YORK

Copyright © 1981 by Basic Books, Inc.
Library of Congress Catalogue Card Number: 80–68174
ISBN: 0–465–07056–6
Printed in the United States of America
DESIGNED BY VINCENT TORRE
10 9 8 7 6 5 4 3 2

To the Memory of Edith Barrie

CONTENTS

Acknowledgments   *ix*

Preface   3

CHAPTER 1
The Great German War on the Potomac,
August–September 1944   12

CHAPTER 2
Genesis of a Trial Plan   48

CHAPTER 3
Marching to Nowhere   75

CHAPTER 4
From Malmédy to Consensus   114

CHAPTER 5
From Yalta to London and Warm Springs   152

CHAPTER 6
Setting the Stage   190

CHAPTER 7
Conclusion   247

Guide to Frequently Cited Sources   263

Notes   265

Bibliography   287

Index   291

ACKNOWLEDGMENTS

My debts of gratitude for aid in the preparation of this volume are extensive. A number of archivists were very helpful, especially Agnes F. Peterson, Hoover Institution, Stanford University; Marilla Guptil, John Mendelsohn, Edward Reese, William Cunliffe, Robert Wolfe (Chief, Modern Military Branch), and Patricia Dowling (Diplomatic Branch), National Archives; James Miller and James Hastings, Federal Records Center, Suitland, Maryland; Harry Clark and Philip D. Lagerquist, Harry S. Truman Library; Jon Kepler, Dwight D. Eisenhower Library; David Crosson and Gene Gressley, University of Wyoming; Mary K. Hembree, Thomas Marvin, and John Martin, Justice Department; and Alice Prochaska, Public Record Office.

Professor D. C. Watt provided fruitful leads in London. Merritt Robbins, Ken Neary, and Jenny Wilkes read portions of the manuscript and gave helpful suggestions. Margaret and Leslie Smith helped with research. Charles Burdick caught a number of my missteps and was, as always, generous with his wisdom and sound advice.

Since the writing of this book tended to be peripatetic, a number of people gave me room or shelter including Helen La Chelle, Jenny Howarth, Lawrence and Lee Walker, Jenny Wilkes, and Josephine Lowe.

Travel and research grants extended by the Hoover Institution and the Mabel McLeod Lewis Memorial Fund of Stanford University for other projects allowed me to tuck in a few bits of work on this volume. Martin Kessler, Maureen Bischoff, and Libby Bruch, all of Basic Books, helped smooth out the final product.

The generosity of all these individuals was essential for the development of this project, but the responsibility and the gratitude are mine.

The Road to Nuremberg

PREFACE

We're all little people; we have our good days, [and] our bad days.

George F. Kennan

1977 [1]

Their presence in the dock at Nuremberg seems perfectly natural and obvious now. Dozens of photographs show them in two neat rows, with Reichsmarschall Hermann Göring seated on the aisle. Twenty-one rather drab figures, the remnants of the Nazi elite, waiting before the International Military Tribunal, which would set their punishment and certify the Allied triumph in the European theater of the Second World War. This scene is so firmly fixed in our mind's eye that it suggests the inevitability of justice and judicial retribution. Yet the Nuremberg trial did not have to be; it was not the product of some basic rule of the universe and it rested on no clear historical precedents.

The score had been settled at the end of previous wars by a variety of methods ranging from genteel handshakes to the slaughter of the innocents. In the early nineteenth century, the Grand Alliance had banished Napoleon to Saint Helena, and in 1919 the Germans had been required to carry out limited, and ultimately perfunctory, trials of a handful of war criminals. But before 1945 no group of victorious powers had ever established an international tribunal to prosecute their defeated enemies for alleged violations of criminal law.

Nuremberg changed all that. The trial of the Nazi leaders by the Big Four Allied powers (the United States, the Soviet Union, Great Britain, and France) transformed the way we look at the acts of warring governments and the consequences that we expect to follow victory or defeat. Since 1945, the whole world has come to view international conflicts not just as matters of morality and government policy, but as possible objects of international criminal prosecution.

This fundamental change was not produced merely through some trick of circumstance. The Allied victory in 1945 inevitably meant that most of the top Nazi leaders would face an unpleasant future, but the use of a trial, especially the kind of complex international proceeding employed at Nuremberg, was the result of a series of decisions made, not by fate, but by Allied officials.

What these decisions were, who made them, and how is the central theme of this volume. In pursuing answers to these questions, it might seem appropriate to range back over the history of international law and then, after recording the horrors perpetrated by the Nazis, to examine the response of the public and the press in the Allied countries. But such accounts have been given many times before, and though relevant, they miss the central locus of the decision-making process.[2] After we allow for the spirit of the age as well as for the legal background, ranging from the Hague conventions to the resolutions of the League of Nations, the central fact is that the Nuremberg trial system was created almost exclusively in Washington by a group of American government officials. The system was developed, altered, and redrafted during the last ten months of the European war and was then presented to the British, Soviet, and French governments for comment and concurrence at a four power conference held in London in June–July 1945. America's allies modified and shifted features in the United States plan, but its basic elements remained intact and were embodied in the London Charter and the indictments that became the legal ground rules for the main Nuremberg proceedings and for a series of subsequent trials of Nazi and Japanese leaders.

This, then, is a book about a special aspect of America's role in World War II; but there are few battles in it, no dashing generals, no gallant warriors. Its concern is with policy decisions and some of the men who made them. Franklin D. Roosevelt is here, as are Harry L. Hopkins, Henry Stimson, Harry Truman, and a large number of lesser-known figures, all struggling to decide what should be done with Hitler and his paladins. We will follow the course of their effort, from the fall of 1944 until the early summer of 1945, as they developed the plan for prosecuting the major Nazi war criminals, which came to be called the Nuremberg trial system. At that time, America was involved in the final phase of a bitter struggle that extended to nearly every corner of the globe. Allied with Britain, Soviet Russia, Nationalist China, and a multitude of smaller states, the American government was up to its neck in coalition warfare. America had become the main Allied workshop, "the great arsenal," as FDR had called it, for producing the weaponry necessary to defeat Nazi Germany, Italy, and Japan.

These tasks posed great challenges for the people and institutions of the United States. They also brought a crushing burden of work and responsibility to government leaders. Together with all the customary duties of government office, these men in 1944 and 1945 had to try to keep their focus on the main lines of wartime and postwar policy while every day brought new baskets piled high with papers and problems crying for attention. Beyond all this was the most awesome responsibility of all—the duty to confront and make decisions that would determine life or death for thousands, perhaps millions, of people. The orders that dispatched the aircraft to turn German and Japanese cities to ashes, as well as those that sent thousands of young American soldiers and marines to die on the beaches of Okinawa and Normandy, came from the desks of these men.

As a group, the Washington leaders possessed great abilities, not the least of which was the capacity to deal with the endless crisscross of policy matters that came before them. They also had their failings, especially class and ethnic prejudices, which on occasion blinded them. Yet they were not callous men, and in retrospect many of them seem to have been very special. No one reading the condolence letters that Secretary of War Stimson wrote to the grieving parents of boys who had been killed carrying out his orders can doubt the moral and emotional burden borne by the men of Washington in 1944–45.[3]

Thus, when the issue of war-crimes policy planning is removed from the frenzies and feelings of the times in order to place it in a clinical atmosphere for calm study, we greatly oversimplify the case. In the Washington of 1944–45, war-crimes policy was not primarily a matter of ruminating over postwar patterns of life and thought; it was an element in waging the most destructive war the world had ever seen. Furthermore, by taking this single thread from the tangled mass of planning activities dealt with by Washington officials, we make it seem much easier to resolve than it actually was. None of those then involved had more than small amounts of time and energy to devote to it. Yet if we are going to see the policy clearly, and grasp the factors that modified its evolution, it must be separated from the hundreds of other matters that were under consideration at the same time. By constantly reminding ourselves that this is a narrowed focus, we will minimize the risks of distortion, but some is still inevitable.

At times the reader, like the author, will be hard pressed to remember that this actually is a simplified version of the problem. The subject of war crimes was highly complex and touched on many controversial political and legal issues. In consequence, the plan did not move forward in one direction but, in response to the pressure of events and the fortunes of power politics in Washington, surged and twisted, on occasion curling back on itself like the course of a southern river. The description will also frequently be struggling to keep its head above water, and there will only be limited opportunities to examine the hidden motives of the most significant planners, or to explore the broader social and economic factors at work. The focus must be kept on the development of the plan, however, because this story has not been fully told, and until it is, no search for marginal psychological or economic nuances will be possible. Since we are concerned with the formation of a highly significant political-legal system, how and why the individual pieces came together in the way they did is a subject of major importance. These are the causal questions that have first claim on historical attention. They are also the most meaningful questions for lawyers, because any light that can be thrown on the *intent* of the Nuremberg fathers should ease the task of those evaluating the system's subsequent effects on international law.

Since the development of a policy for dealing with the major Nazi war criminals was both a political and a legal question, we are blessed with an abundance of source materials to help trace out the story. In addition to the notes, letters, telephone calls, and other forms of communication used by all political officials, legal draftsmen make heavy use of summary memoranda. Frequently circulated among the various officials concerned with a given project, such memoranda generate margin comments and countermemoranda, which provide an unusually rich record of a developing historical process. Now that government-classification restrictions have been relaxed, the most important pieces in this memoranda puzzle have been gathered from thirty-odd manuscript collections in Britain and the United States, and these are the basic materials on which this account is based.

We will spend some time examining these drafts, not only because they are splendid historical sources, but because they are the mode, the medium, through which the plan developed and assumed its essential form. Readers from the legal profession will probably never tire of looking at the issue in this way, but others, including some historians, will become nervous when confined for long periods in the offices of Washington bureaucrats. They crave to break free, and to move about among the causal forces of the "real" world, perhaps sitting with Churchill and Roosevelt at Quebec, or racing with Hodges's First Army to seize the bridge at Remagen. This volume has therefore tried to strike a balance in its description of the development of the plan, utilizing in addition to the draft memoranda* a broad range of other activating elements, such as conferences, personal encounters, and the impact of outside events, ranging from the Allied liberation of the concentration camps to the first reports of Hitler's suicide.

Before leaping into the maelstrom of Washington policy-making in the late summer of 1944, there are some general features of the 1940s *Zeitgeist* and of prior developments on the war-crimes question that need to be briefly noted. Certain attitudes bearing directly on the war-crimes issue, which were prevalent throughout wartime America, seem to have been especially pronounced among the Washington planners. The youth of these men had been dominated by World War I, and they were inclined to believe that this conflict had produced eternally applicable lessons about the nature of Germany and the best ways to deal with the problems of postwar adjustment. The events of the 1930s and 1940s seemed to have confirmed their belief by indicating that Germany had become dangerous again because the Allies had not done a sufficiently thorough job of purging the country after the First World War. The wartime Nazi record of aggression and atrocity greatly strengthened this general conviction and set the stage for a tough war-crimes policy.

A second general consideration, now a truism among historians, is that the American wartime government leaders, led

---

* For those who would prefer to tarry longer within the world of memoranda, a companion volume, which reproduces most of the significant texts in full, has been prepared: Bradley F. Smith, ed., *The American Road to Nuremberg: The Documentary Record* (Stanford, Calif., 1981).

by Franklin Roosevelt, sought to deemphasize political questions and thus prevent political divisions in wartime by delaying as many controversial issues as possible until the postwar period. Long-range political planning was not much appreciated in wartime Washington, and the war-crimes issue had to be forced upon American governmental leaders. Time itself, and the apparent imminence of victory in the fall of 1944, were the most important factors compelling Washington officials to act. But there were also pressures from those groups who spoke for the major victims of Nazi aggression and atrocities. The American Jewish Conference was the most notable example, but various spokesmen and associations of immigrant communities, especially those whose homelands were ravaged by the Nazi occupation, called incessantly for punitive action in the press, in Congress, and through every available public forum.[4] In addition, the various governments in exile (Dutch, Polish, Norwegian, and so on), which were headquartered in London, had from the beginning of the German occupation beseeched the Allies to announce a tough policy of war-crimes prosecution. These governments needed to certify their legitimacy and effectiveness by securing Anglo-American support for policies that would aid their people. Hoping that a stringent war-crimes policy would help to prevent the Nazis from perpetrating further atrocities, the governments in exile demanded a program that would deter the Nazis by its harshness. This demand, echoed by American Jewish and immigrant organizations inside the United States, increased the pressures on Washington.

But the British and American governments were cool to such ideas. They did not want to commit themselves to any political or legal program until the war ended; they were reluctant to give too much authority or recognition to the governments in exile, and they were paralyzed by the fear that if they threatened specific postwar punishment of German malefactors, the Nazis might retaliate by wholesale slaughter of Anglo-American prisoners of war. So Washington and London temporized, issuing vague threats of postwar retribution; and the Soviet

Union went its own way, calling for the punishment, and then initiating action, against "Hitlerite criminals" wherever they might be found. Not until the Moscow Declaration in November 1943 did the three Allied powers announce that the smaller fry among the Nazi war criminals would be taken back to the scenes of their crimes in the occupied territories and punished there. But the question of what was to be done with the major German leaders was still left unanswered. Then, between October 1943 and January 1944, London and Washington bowed to rising pressure and helped establish a United Nations Commission for the Investigation of War Crimes (commonly known as the United Nations War Crimes Commission—UNWCC), which gave substantial representation to the smaller powers and the governments in exile. The Soviet Union objected to the imbalance created by the inclusion of so many small states, especially the British Dominions, and refused to join. Nevertheless, the commission, meeting in London during 1944, went about the business of assembling lists of war criminals and tentatively debated broader aspects of the problem, such as the creation of special war-crimes courts and the possible inclusion of pre-1939 persecutions among prosecutable "war crimes."

As the Allied armies advanced and the horrors of the German occupation became better known, the demands and ambitions of the governments in exile on the commission increased. They wanted more authority and renewed pledges by the great powers that serious retribution would be exacted. The London and Washington governments, which had been nervously hedging in the commission during the first six months of its existence, gradually found themselves confronted by a rising tide of political pressure and public indignation. By August 1944 the Western armies had produced their great breakthrough in western France, and the Red Army was closing in on Nazi death camps in Poland such as Maidanek. Nazi Germany was reeling under massive blows from east and west, and the Anglo-American effort to delay consideration of the difficult war-crimes questions was under equally heavy attack from the United Nations War Crimes Commission, the British and American press, and an aroused public opinion.

Caught up in the general belief that victory in Europe was imminent, Secretary of War Henry Stimson noted in his diary on 23 August 1944 that "certainly the end seems to be approaching on a galloping horse." [5] Delay was no longer possible. With the War Department in the van, Washington policymakers were forced to scurry forth and produce a final occupation plan for Germany—one that would give precise meaning to the vague threats of full and just retribution that they had long claimed would one day envelop the leaders of the Third Reich.

CHAPTER 1

THE GREAT GERMAN WAR ON THE POTOMAC

August–September 1944

The difference is not whether we should be soft or tough on the German people, but rather whether the course proposed will in fact best attain our agreed objective, continued peace.

Henry L. Stimson
15 September 1944

At the time that VE Day fever swept over Washington, D.C., in mid-August 1944, little had been prepared for the time when Germany would lie prostrate, awaiting occupation. Here and there in the State Department and the Civil Affairs Division of the War Department, file drawers bulged with special studies on German institutions and plans for what should be done on specific postwar questions, such as reparations.[1] There had been some low- and middle-level consultation and coordination, and of course the corridors were ringing with emphatic pronouncements that at the end of this war there should not be another muddled armistice such as that of 1918. But in the late summer of 1944 no task force was at work on a comprehensive program for the treatment of postwar Germany; and, in fact, the question had apparently not yet been seriously considered at the top level of any department in the United States government.

The reason for this lack of preparation was simple: Nothing definitive had come down from the White House indicating what Franklin Roosevelt thought should be done with the remains of central Europe once nazism had been destroyed. The President was still stalling on this question, as he had been stalling since the United States entered the war in 1941. Repeatedly he had danced around the many recommendations, both foreign and domestic, that urged him to provide a picture, or at least a rough sketch, of what should be done with postwar Germany. On occasion he had been compelled to give some ground, tentatively agreeing, for example, to the proposal that Germany should be divided into zones of occupation, and also cautiously permitting the establishment of a nearly powerless inter-Allied commission (the European Advisory Commission) to discuss policy for Europe. By firmly reiterating his devotion to such tough positions as that of unconditional surrender, he had also implied that stringent measures were in store for the Germans; but this was only a broad hint, and nothing more. He apparently believed that it was wisest to put his main effort into preserving friendly relations with Churchill and Stalin so that a decisive victory could be won. Then, only after Nazi defeat was certain, and the actual situation in central Europe had become crystal clear, would the Grand Alliance, still alive and healthy, be able to go to work on the postwar fate of the German people. In the meantime, as Roosevelt told a reporter at a press conference on 29 July 1944, questions on postwar plans, such as those dealing with Nazi war criminals, were "a little premature." [2] The President then paused for a

moment, as if reflecting on how to capsulize his whole attitude toward the German occupation problem, and finally
added, "premature—that is a good word to use."

The word was useful to the President—whether or not it
stood for a sensible policy in the long run is another matter—
and it represented a stance that also took much planning pressure off the State Department and most other branches of
the government. Masterly inactivity seemed to work for everyone, except of course, for the U.S. Army command that had
to give directions to the forces that sooner or later would be
going into Germany. Once the Normandy invasion occurred on
6 June it took no prophet to foresee that it would probably
be sooner, and that Eisenhower and his aides needed to have
broad directives on the policies to be followed from the moment they first breached the Siegfried line. The army planners
do not seem to have been especially eager to take on the responsibility for developing what they called an "immediate
posthostilities" policy for Germany. They knew that it was
loaded with political perils, but they were stuck with the problem, and their experience with lack of preparation in an analogous situation was not encouraging.

In the summer of 1943, the Allies had waltzed into Sicily
and southern Italy with little or no prior planning and soon
found themselves responsible for the administration of a large
portion of the population and territory of a former enemy.[3]
Their advance then moved so slowly that what had initially
been envisioned as an interim phase, lasting days and weeks,
stretched out to become a way of life covering months and
years. Allied generals with little or no understanding of the
conditions in which they found themselves tried to deal back-
handedly with a multitude of political, economic, and social
problems, while reserving their main energies for combat with
the German army in Italy. The result was unedifying confusion
crowned by an authoritarian military hierarchy, deep suffering
of the civilian population, and a general lack of direction that
frequently bordered on chaos. The Allied military government

in Italy never could develop a guiding principle that worked; and, eschewing any hope of making ideological or political sense of the situation, it put military necessity first and restricted its actions regarding Italian civilians to those matters necessary to preserve the health and safety of the Allied forces and their lines of communication. In sum, the Allied occupation policy in wartime Italy became nothing more than a constantly shifting series of improvisations centered around the idea of preventing "disease and unrest."

If the occupation of Italy had been, and still was, difficult, it was reasonable to assume that a slowly advancing occupation of Germany might turn into a nightmare. Considering the stubbornness with which the Wehrmacht had contested every molehill in western and eastern Europe (until some of its fighting strength began to melt away in northern France during August 1944), the battle for Germany might well be long and bitter. Washington had no foolproof way to tell if German civilian morale was cracking, but the fanaticism with which elite Nazi formations, such as those of the SS, fought on was not a good omen. The abortive attempt on Hitler's life (20 July 1944) also seemed to be merely an isolated incident that the regime, led by the SS and the police, had mastered with ease. As long as this kind of war continued, an Anglo-American army advancing across Germany might well have not only a smashed economy and a battered transportation system in its rear, but a sullenly hostile civilian population driven on by a partisan army of Nazi fanatics who would contest every move made by the allied authorities.

We can now see that these fears were largely imaginary; when defeat loomed, even SS units calmly surrendered, and German civilians invariably and enthusiastically accommodated themselves to Anglo-American rule. In fact, Germany was the only central west European country in the Second World War that did not mount a popular resistance movement against any of its invaders. Although Washington was a confusing place in the late summer and early fall of 1944, partly because it had momentarily succumbed to a victory fantasy, the more serious miscalculations arose from a general Allied inclination to overestimate German resources and Nazi power during the last stages of the war. Both the Soviets and the Anglo-Americans were in part trapped by their own propaganda; they had denounced the evils and dangers of nazism for so long that they continued to give credence to Hitler's threats and claims of power long after most of their reality had evaporated. The U.S. War Department's fear of possible serious problems confronting an occupation authority in Germany was thus not a local affliction but part of a general disease that touched virtually every Allied policymaker. The unique problem facing the War Department was that it alone was required somehow to produce plans for the American zone of occupation that would meet both the supposed dangers lurking in Germany and the cloud of rosy optimism that was rapidly rising in Washington.

Understandably, then, during the summer of 1944 the War Department planners moved with considerable caution when they prepared their two occupation policy guides, the *Handbook of Military Government for Germany* and the *Interim Directive on Occupation Procedures,* which later evolved into Joint Chiefs of Staff order number 1067.[4] As much as possible they attempted to keep the focus on the initial stage of occupation and they tried to avoid making pronouncements regarding long-term policy goals. The planners were concerned primarily with laying out the most important steps necessary to maintain and restore the German administrative and economic system so that it could best serve the needs of the advancing Anglo-American army. They wished to give Eisenhower and his aides as much latitude as possible, but they had to indicate not only the areas where preservation and repair of the German system were vital, but also the points from which the most serious security threats might arise. Therefore the *Handbook* included long lists of Nazi party and police officials who were to be automatically arrested and detained;

such individuals were indicated not by name but by rank and position.

Many of those scheduled for automatic arrest did not actually represent any danger to the occupation authorities, because the lists of offices and positions had apparently been taken from an out-of-date U.S. Army manual on the Wehrmacht and its auxiliary forces. It included the leaders of such groups as the "Nazi Flying Corps," which had ceased to be viable organizations years before.[5] But allowing for the anomaly of such needless inclusions, the drafters of the *Handbook* had tried to prepare a rather tightly circumscribed list of approximately 250,000 men scheduled for automatic detention. Mainly leaders and officers from the rank of major and above were listed, while most rank-and-file members of organizations such as the Storm troopers (SA) were not included. Only the membership of the Gestapo and Security Service (SD) as a whole were scheduled for blanket detention, but no members of the regular armed forces were included because they would be given prisoner-of-war status. Even the enlisted ranks of the SS were excluded.[6]

The only serious qualifications to the general rule that those holding lower ranks in the Nazi governmental system were to stay at their posts were a proviso that the Nazi party (NSDAP) itself be dissolved, and a statement in the *Interim Directive* that read: "Adolf Hitler, his chief Nazi and Fascist associates and collaborators" as well as all individuals "suspected of having committed war crimes, including those who appear on lists drawn up by the United Nations . . . shall be arrested and held for future investigation and subsequent disposition."[7] In that last clause the U.S. Army planners slipped over the line to touch on the question of war criminals, but they did so cautiously and without giving any indication of what the future fate of such people should be.

In order for the army to obtain routine approval for its occupation plans in August 1944, it needed a run of good luck to keep political problems, such as that of war-crimes disposition,

from opening up a general policy debate. But the god of good
fortune was apparently busy elsewhere, and such a problem
began to emerge when the UNWCC and the British government moved to raise questions about a potentially explosive aspect of the war-crimes issue. The UNWCC had been debating
for months whether or not to include in its lists of war criminals those individuals who had committed atrocities against
enemy nationals on racial, political, or religious grounds—that
is, whether acts committed against German Jews, Communists,
and Jehovah's Witnesses, for example, should be classified as
war crimes.

From the early stages of the war London had feared that the
allies, faced with Nazi atrocities, would be tempted to bend
or break the traditional rules for prosecuting war crimes, and
thereby jump into an abyss of ex post facto law and wide-
open future precedents for the punishment of anyone that a
warring state found convenient to brand as a war criminal.
In an aide-mémoire sent to the State Department on 19 August, the British government took the view that the enemies'
persecutions of their own nationals were not war crimes in the
traditional sense, because this term was normally reserved
for instances where an official or a soldier of a belligerent country did something in violation of the rules of war to a soldier
or civilian of another country.[8] The British did concede, in a
roundabout way, that measures would probably have to be
taken regarding the atrocities that the Germans had committed
against their own nationals; and they tentatively suggested that
someday the Allies might exert pressure on whatever postwar
government existed in Germany to bring the culprits to justice.
But the London government was adamant that the UNWCC
—and by implication all other western Allied authorities—
should not go about extending or broadening the established
legal definition of war crimes.

If this message had arrived in Washington a few months
earlier, it would have caused little stir, and most probably it
would have found nearly universal approval. In May 1944 both

the State Department legal adviser, Judge Green H. Hackworth, and a State Department policy committee had gone on record to the effect that the enemies' persecutions of their own nationals, and all prewar persecutions of any kind, were "not war crimes." [9] In the spring of 1944, Roosevelt himself had notified the American representative on the UNWCC, Herbert Pell, that in the President's opinion, "no act" committed before the beginning of hostilities was a "war crime." [10]

Thus, the higher authorities in the American system, along with the British government, had been inclined toward a prudent and conservative policy on the question. The army's plan to order Eisenhower to go slow once he entered Germany, merely arresting Hitler and his top aides (if he could catch them), as well as those "suspected" of traditional war crimes and those on the automatic detention lists, seemed to go along with this view. But as we know, by mid-August the caution of many American leaders was being overcome by the notion that victory might be just around the corner, and one of the first points where this change of mood expressed itself was on war-crimes policy.

The State Department and the President—responding in part to a rising clamor in the press—were showing increased nervousness about the possibility that the top Nazis might suddenly take to their heels, and, like Kaiser Wilhelm in 1918, try to gain protection from war-crimes prosecution by finding sanctuary in neutral countries. In a cabinet meeting of 18 August, the President directed Secretary of State Cordell Hull to use all possible means to convince neutral governments not to grant political asylum to the Nazi leaders; and he also indicated that his mind was moving in the direction of more imaginative and innovative methods for dealing with war criminals. Roosevelt wondered aloud in the course of the discussion whether it might not be possible to thwart the flight of the Nazis by setting up extradition procedures based upon "charges of murder or conspiracy to murder [thereby] bringing Hitler and the other Nazis outside such law [of political asylum]." [11]

Obviously the President was not as determined as he had been
to stay safely within the customary legal procedures applicable
to war crimes, and therefore it is safe to conclude that by
mid-August a routine approval of the cautious positions taken
in the British aide-mémoire, and the American army's directives on the initial treatment of war criminals, was no longer a
foregone conclusion.

What halted routine approval of any aspect of the occupation
plans for Germany was a dramatic intervention at this point by
the Secretary of the Treasury, Henry Morgenthau, Jr. The
Treasury Secretary had spent much of early August traveling
through western Europe, ostensibly carrying out a fact-finding
mission in preparation for establishing a currency policy for
occupied Germany. But Mr. Morgenthau was also highly suspicious that officials in the War Department as well as other
branches of the American government were inclined to molly-
coddle the Germans, and at every stage of his journey he en-
countered new evidence that he thought confirmed his suspi-
cions. In the course of his flight over the Atlantic, one of his
Treasury assistants, Harry Dexter White, disapprovingly showed
him a copy of a State Department paper entitled, "Report on
Reparation, Restitution, and Property Rights—Germany,"
which had been prepared in late July by a special committee on
economic foreign policy.[12] Ironically, the report that had raised
Harry Dexter White's ire was prepared under the direction of
Dean Acheson, and in the postwar period both of these men
would be denounced by Senator Joseph McCarthy, and other
rightists, as "Reds" or "dupes" of the Communists. In August 1944, however, White and Secretary Morgenthau felt that
the Acheson paper was far too conservative, much too solici-
tous of German property rights, and did not go far enough in
striking at what they saw as the economic foundations of
nazism and German military power.

Once on the ground in England, another of Morgenthau's
aides showed him additional documents indicating that a "soft"
policy on Germany was in the making. Lieutenant Colonel

Bernard Bernstein, a Treasury representative assigned to military planning, had copies of some of the draft directives which Eisenhower's staff had been preparing in conjunction with Washington's work on the *Handbook* and the *Interim Directive*.[13] When Bernstein passed these materials on to Morgenthau, the Secretary thought he saw new evidence of a far too lenient economic policy, and he may also have objected to the relatively lax war-crimes provisions contained in the directives.

When he arrived at Eisenhower's headquarters in northern France, Morgenthau apparently objected to an indulgent occupation policy and in turn gained the impression that the general also believed that harsh measures were necessary. It is not now possible to determine precisely what Eisenhower said on this occasion. Harry Dexter White, who was present at the meeting, quoted Ike soon afterward as stating that he favored letting "Germany stew in its own juice."[14] A year later, when publishing his self-justifying account of the events of 1944, Henry Morgenthau quoted the general to the effect that tough measures were necessary because "the whole German population is a synthetic paranoid,"[15] a phrase which does even graver violence to the language than anything the worst critics of Eisenhower's English have attributed to him. In an unpublished letter written in 1950, the general himself expanded on the explanation that he gave in *Crusade in Europe*. Declaring that at the time of his talk with Morgenthau he had "not yet given the whole subject of occupation sufficient study to venture the formulation of specific recommendations," he nonetheless believed that the German war industry had to be destroyed, that the members of some Nazi organizations needed to be prosecuted, and that "certain individuals of Germany should be punished for bringing on the global disaster of World War II."[16] Whatever the general's exact words, it seems highly likely that when Morgenthau left Europe, he had good reason to believe that Eisenhower was on his side.

From the time of his return to Washington, Morgenthau threw himself into the task of convincing his cabinet colleagues that it was necessary to turn about and come out in favor of a stringent occupation system in Germany. An ardent New Dealer, friend, and Hyde Park neighbor of Franklin Roosevelt, the gregarious, affable, and generous Secretary of the Treasury was, in many ways, a kind and lovable man. He was also a tough bare-knuckle politician and veteran of over a decade of Washington's policy struggles. He knew how to fight, maneuver, reassure, and he was especially adept at sending forth Treasury assistants to lobby for his policies among subordinate officials in all the nooks and crannies of the Washington bureaucracy. It is fair to say that Henry Morgenthau was nearly universally liked as a person, but almost as universally feared, and somewhat distrusted, as a political combatant.

Now in the third week of August 1944, Morgenthau set out as the champion of a tough peace for Germany, not merely because he thought that such a stand was good politics, but because he believed that it was right. Like many moderate "assimilationist" Jews, Morgenthau had been slow to rally to the cause of an all-out effort to blunt Nazi atrocities and exterminations. Only during the previous year (1943) had the full force of the horror that was unfolding finally penetrated to his heart.[17] But once aroused, he became the Administration's strongest advocate of aiding the victims of Hitler's repression, and he also repeatedly called for the use of all available means to deter the Nazis from continuing their murderous policies. It was the Treasury Secretary who, in January 1944, had led the way, against strong State Department opposition, to guarantee the establishment of the War Refugee Board. This organization, staffed largely with Morgenthau's aides and allies, became his chief instrument, not only for extending assistance to refugees, but also for advocating the toughest possible war-crimes policy.

After all the horror and suffering that the Nazis had brought to the world, it seemed to Morgenthau that if the Allies turned around and gave the Germans an easy occupation system it would not only be the height of injustice and the nullification of all that he and the country had fought for, but it might also lay the basis for yet another round of aggressive German expansion and mass atrocities. Therefore the Secretary of the Treasury entered the fray against a "soft" peace with much of the spirit of a crusader, but he did so openly, and with no pretense of concealing his intentions or his fervor. On the morning of 18 August, the day after his return to Washington, he telephoned the ailing Secretary of State, Cordell Hull, and declared that not only was he—Morgenthau—in favor of a tough peace, but that on the basis of his talks in London, he believed that Winston Churchill was inclined to the same view. Then, before ringing off, Morgenthau told Hull straight out, "I am going to stick my nose in" to guarantee that the Allies imposed rigid terms on Germany.[18]

With that, the Treasury forces were off and running. During the next few days Morgenthau tried to enlist Harry Hopkins, President Roosevelt's closest and most trusted assistant, in the cause of a Carthaginian peace, and he seems to have had some measure of success.[19] At the same time, Harry Dexter White went to work on the chief of the War Department's Civil Affairs Division, Major General John H. Hilldring, the man primarily responsible for preparing the Army's occupation plans. In his talk with Hilldring, White stressed that Eisenhower favored tight controls on the Germans, and the civil affairs chief, apparently not grasping which way the wind was blowing, stated that he too believed that Germany should be shown little mercy.[20]

A few days later, on 23 August, Morgenthau had lunch with Secretary of War Henry L. Stimson and Assistant Secretary John J. McCloy, and he used the occasion to present them with his views on Germany.[21] He apparently not only summarized the general idea of deindustrialization but also outlined a range of measures so comprehensive and harsh that it even envisioned removing from Germany members of the Hitler Youth and other children infected by the Nazi virus. But like Hilldring before them, McCloy and Stimson apparently failed to grasp that this was not just an exploratory luncheon conversation, and that Morgenthau was deadly serious. McCloy seems to have hoped that the army could distance itself from responsibility for long-range policy problems in Germany, and he voiced the opinion that the War Department was chiefly concerned with the immediate postdefeat period.[22] For his part, Stimson seemed ready at this point to look with sympathy on anyone prepared to consider the need for serious planning about what should be done with Germany. He had just gone through another in a long series of frustrating meetings with the President in which he tried to get Roosevelt to make a final decision on German zoning and related matters; but all FDR had done was dally, fuss about minor details, and promise that he would settle all such questions when he met with Churchill at Quebec in September.[23] Thus, Stimson seems to have welcomed Morgenthau's concern about the German problem and may even have thought that he had discovered a useful ally.

In his diary the Secretary of War referred to their luncheon meeting as "a very satisfactory talk," [24] and he apparently did not grasp that he had led Morgenthau to believe he was interested in the long-range aspects of the German question but had not yet accorded them much thought.[25] Before the luncheon ended, Stimson readily, and imprudently, agreed to Morgenthau's suggestion that the President be asked to create a cabinet committee on Germany consisting of Morgenthau, Stimson, and Secretary of State Hull to advise the Chief Executive in advance of his scheduled meeting with Churchill.[26]

Round one therefore went so decisively to Morgenthau that not until the following day did the War Department chiefs begin to realize they might be in for a serious policy fight. At lunch on 24 August, Stimson met with John McCloy, Harry Hopkins, and William Bundy to discuss the German zoning problem and to begin exploring the possibility of keeping the Germans in line by means of a tough and comprehensive program aimed at war criminals. This was to be an alternative to Morgenthau's deindustrialization scheme. The idea was not developed very far on this occasion; although there was some discussion of taking harsh action against whole organizations such as the Gestapo, the question of trials was not seriously considered. All that Mr. Stimson concluded from the exchange of views was that "if shooting [was] required" it would have to be done "immediate[ly]; not postwar" and that "our officers must have the protection of definite instructions." [27]

With the cabinet scheduled to meet on the afternoon of 25 August, Stimson hoped to gain a march on his colleagues by arranging to have lunch with the President just before the cabinet session. But the Secretary of the Treasury was too quick for him. When Morgenthau accidentally learned via McCloy on the morning of the twenty-fifth that Stimson was scheduled to lunch with the President that day, and that Hopkins might also be present to discuss the whole German question, Morgenthau decided it was imperative that he get to Roosevelt first.[28] Although he knew that the army *Handbook* had not yet been approved by the higher authorities of the War Department, including McCloy and Stimson, and if he showed it to the President at this point, Stimson would probably be deeply angered, Morgenthau decided to go ahead anyway.[29] In the late morning Morgenthau saw Roosevelt, and by bringing with him a copy of the *Handbook* and a memorandum that purported to show, through selected quotations, that the army was preparing to pamper the Germans, he virtually guaranteed that a full-scale struggle over German policy would follow. Morgenthau had thereby also attained his major objective; Franklin Roosevelt was angered by what he saw as an army attempt to treat the Germans like a liberated, rather than a defeated, country.

The remainder of the day was made up of a series of hard trials for Henry L. Stimson. Harry Hopkins was apparently not present when the Secretary of War lunched with the president, and Stimson was unable to move the conversation much beyond idle chitchat.[30] Roosevelt seems not to have raised the issue of the army *Handbook*, but from all indications he also paid little or no attention to Stimson's urgings to treat Morgenthau's deindustrialization ideas with great caution. During the cabinet session that followed, the President agreed to the formation of a committee on Germany consisting of Stimson, Hull, Morgenthau, and Hopkins, but this time he made critical remarks about the *Handbook*.[31] Thus, although not yet decisive, the balance had tipped toward Morgenthau. The President was sympathetic to his view, and a committee had been established, over the strong objections of Hull, who loathed such committees, on which the State Department, the War Department, a White House representative, and Henry Morgenthau were all given equal representation to deal with what was essentially a question of military and foreign policy.

Considering the sharpness of the scuffle that had just taken place, and the bitterness that would be engendered by the ensuing conflict, it is warming to note that after the cabinet meeting Stimson and Morgenthau could put most of the rancor behind them and go off together on the same plane for a weekend with their respective families in New York. En route they had what Stimson called "a fairly satisfactory talk . . . on matters on which we are inclined to disagree, namely the use of over-punitive measures in Germany." [32] But on this occasion too, if there was a winner, it was apparently Morgenthau who, though still thinking that the Secretary of War's ideas had not developed very far, liked the notion, which he attributed to Stimson, of taking "all the members of the SS troops and put[ting] them in the same concentration camps where the Germans have had these poor Jewish people. . . ." [33] Thus Morgenthau was able to take the rough ideas that Stimson was developing as an alternative to the Treasury proposals and, by integrating them into his own program for a draconian peace, use even these for his purposes.

If 25 August had been a difficult day for Stimson, when he returned to Washington on the twenty-eighth, he was met by a near disaster. In the aftermath of the Friday cabinet meeting, the president had fired off a blistering letter to the Secretary of War in which the nicest thing he had to say about the *Hand-*

book was that it was "pretty bad." [34] "It gives me the impression that Germany is to be restored just as much as the Netherlands or Belgium" the president observed, and he inquired about who was responsible for its preparation, "and who approved it down the line." The concluding paragraph of the letter indicated that the President was apparently as determined as Morgenthau to give the German people a sense of what later came to be called collective guilt. It was not true, the President said, that "only a few Nazi leaders" were to blame for the horrors perpetrated by the Third Reich. The responsibility lay with "the German people as a whole" and therefore Allied policy must drive "home to them that the whole nation has been engaged in a lawless conspiracy against the decencies of civilization." [35]

For those like Stimson, who were inclined toward a more moderate and cautious occupation program, the propositions advanced by the President were, on their face, cause for grave concern. But the Roosevelt letter was in fact merely an embellished and expanded version of the memorandum that Morgenthau had given to the President on 25 August.[36] In his letter to Stimson Roosevelt claimed that the offensive passages he cited from the *Handbook* were the ones which happened to have "caught my eye," but he had actually just appropriated the selections from Morgenthau's memorandum. The President had seen the *Handbook*, but it is doubtful whether he had read any of it; Morgenthau's memorandum, and his verbal comments, were what had turned Roosevelt's mind so completely against the army's occupation plans. Although Stimson was deeply upset just by the content and tone of the President's letter, if he had known the whole story, he would have been even more alarmed. At this point, Franklin Roosevelt was completely at one with the Treasury Department on what should be done with Germany.

While Stimson was left partially in the dark about the situation, Morgenthau, of course, was not. He understood that Roosevelt had concluded—probably rightly—that without

Treasury Department intervention, the *Handbook*, now totally discredited in the President's eyes, would have become the foundation of American policy in Germany. Therefore, all Morgenthau had to do was supply a steady stream of new and harsh proposals for dealing with occupation problems. Urging his staff on with the remark that the President was now "hungry for this stuff," Morgenthau came up with increasingly bizarre suggestions for making the Germans suffer.[37] Expanding on an idea he had appropriated from Stimson, at one point he thought it would be a good idea if "this whole SS group" was deported "somewhere—out of Germany to some other part of the world . . . because you can't keep them in concentration camps forever."[38] By 4 September, a Treasury conference was seriously pondering what to do with children of SS men who happened to be under the age of six, since Morgenthau and his aides had already decided that the older children should suffer the same penalties of confinement and probable banishment that were in store for their parents.[39] At this very moment in Berlin, Himmler and Hitler were preparing to apply a similar principle: Making an individual's family responsible for his misdeeds by throwing into concentration camps the children and even distant relatives of those who had attempted to kill the Führer on 20 July 1944. Total war certainly does make strange bedfellows!

Compared with such aberrations, the alternate draft of the *Interim Directive*, which the Treasury Department completed on 1 September, seemed relatively moderate, but it still contained an ample measure of the harsh provisions that would later gain notoriety for the *Morgenthau plan*.[40] In addition to a program of deindustrialization that would have flattened the German economy, the Treasury proposal contained drastically expanded detention provisions that called for the arrest of the whole SS and SA, along with a large number of officials from the fields of education, law, and industry. Such proposals were anathema to American army leaders because wholesale arrests and economic dismantling would throw what remained of the

German economy and civil administration into chaos, just
when Eisenhower's advance would most depend on stability
and order in the rear areas. But beyond that, there was the
matter of departmental authority and pride, for here was the
Treasury Department actually suggesting that it should prepare
the definitive orders to Eisenhower for what the American
army considered one of the high points of the whole war—
the actual invasion of Nazi Germany.

Therefore, although War Department officials were in a tight
corner as they saw it, there was no choice but to fight, and in
the Secretary of War they had an imminently gifted and powerful champion. Seventy-seven-year-old Henry L. Stimson was
probably the most prestigious Republican political figure in
the nation, and certainly one of the country's most influential
authorities on foreign affairs.[41] For forty years he had been a
major force in American government. Beginning as U.S. attorney for the southern district of New York under Theodore
Roosevelt, he had served as Taft's Secretary of War, and then
as a colonel in the American army in World War I. During the
1920s, Stimson was a special emissary to Nicaragua and gov-
ernor general of the Philippines under Coolidge. From 1929 to
1933, he was Herbert Hoover's Secretary of State. Finally, in
June 1940, in a major break with the principle of partisan
politics, Franklin Roosevelt selected him to be Secretary of War.

Stimson had helped direct American policy—for good or ill—
at many critical junctures, including the Manchurian crisis of
1931. He was a passionate believer in military preparedness and
collective security, and when, in 1940, he agreed to join Roosevelt's cabinet along with his fellow Republican Frank Knox
(who became Secretary of the Navy), Stimson immediately
found himself in the forefront of those advocating rearma-
ment and aid to Britain. In the course of the struggle over isolationism, he did temporarily alienate some of the more conservative members of his own party, especially during the election
campaign of 1940. But after Pearl Harbor most of these wounds
were quickly healed, and to many Republicans it seemed that

Stimson and Knox, along with Wendell Willkie, had helped save their party from being permanently tarred with the brush of defeatism and isolationist folly.

As Secretary of War, Stimson was obviously one of the most powerful forces in the Roosevelt administration during the years 1940–1945. The great influence that he possessed in Republican circles made him invaluable in rallying support on Capitol Hill for Roosevelt's military and foreign-policy programs. He had greater international and diplomatic experience than any other member of the cabinet, including Secretary of State Hull, and abroad he was generally regarded as the most significant American civilian official after the President himself. But the core of Stimson's power lay in the pivotal post he occupied in Franklin Roosevelt's system to run the war. Since the President wished to depoliticize the conflict by playing down controversial issues and placing much of the decision-making responsibility in military hands, Stimson held the crucial post in the cabinet. It is not an exaggeration to say that Stimson's success in screening the army off from serious political controversy, while developing a close working relationship with the army Chief of Staff, General George C. Marshall, was one of the keys to the whole governmental system that operated in America during the Second World War.[42] Although Roosevelt still leaned heavily on his old "cronies," such as Hopkins, Morgenthau, and Judge Samuel I. ("Sam") Rosenman, most cabinet members and congressmen were forced to the sidelines. The President and Stimson, meanwhile (and to a lesser degree Knox, who was succeeded in 1944 by James Forrestal), worked with the Joint Chiefs of Staff to control the decision-making process for virtually all questions that even remotely touched on the direction and conduct of the war.

Thus when Morgenthau attempted to move the army aside and take charge of postwar planning for Germany in August 1944, he was not only contesting an important policy question, he was challenging the War Department's special right to steer wartime policy. Furthermore, he attacked Stimson and his colleagues at a point where their claim to supremacy was especially shaky, because occupation policy lay in the shadow zone between war and peace. Yet it would be a mistake to conclude that Stimson fought back against the Treasury Secretary solely for reasons of political principle or territoriality, because his response did bear some measured signs of personal antipathy.

For all of his prestige and influence, Stimson was no saint. An upper-class New York attorney, born to the purple, he had little doubt that he held a right to rule as he moved from Yale to Wall Street and on to Washington. Morgenthau's robust earthiness was not his style and the Secretary of War obviously bore a certain disdain for the marks of crude aggressiveness and new money that clung to Morgenthau. Stated baldly, Stimson was a social anti-Semite, as were the vast majority of old-family New York aristocrats in the 1940s. His diary entries include references to Morgenthau's "race" and his "Semitic" characteristics; [43] as the struggle over German occupation policy grew more intense, the number of such comments increased. But even here the case is not simple, for none of the remarks are pointedly abusive or bear the tone of an intentional desire to wound or insult. In a number of cases Stimson decried the fact that Morgenthau had taken the lead in advocating harsh peace terms. Specifically, he believed that this could rebound and provide ammunition for those who would attribute all stringent controls on Germany to a mere "Jewish" desire for revenge.[44] Still, a number of Stimson's diary entries make embarrassing reading, probably even more embarrassing than the records of some of the closed Treasury conferences in which Morgenthau mocked and threw snide insults at his opponents, including the aging Secretary of War.

Both men were accustomed to hitting hard, a wide chasm of class and heritage divided them, and they had a genuine and honest disagreement about what should be done with postwar Germany. It may therefore be more important to stress that with all the above qualifications duly noted, Stimson and Morgenthau actually seemed to have liked and enjoyed each other's company. For every nasty or patronizing remark that either of them penned, there is at least another in which each expressed his regard, or paid tribute, to the other fellow. Amid all the bitter pushing and shoving that characterizes serious political controversy, this is one of the few instances in which flashes of warm humanity and mutual regard actually show through.

Perhaps the revisionist historians with their emphasis on economic causation may be able to provide us with a clue as to how Stimson and Morgenthau could fight so vigorously, yet frequently turn the other cheek. While the center of the controversy did concern economic policy—the industrial future of Germany—both men were dedicated to the development and expansion of postwar American capitalism. The Wall Street lawyer and the New York banker were agreed on this economic objective, as well as a shared desire to attain other ends, such as long-term peace and security for the United States. What was at issue was the most suitable and effective means to attain these goals; and perhaps in politics as well as economics, if the focus is kept on means rather than ends, it may be easier to indulge in a bit of gentility and mutual affection.

But none of this probably gave much comfort to Henry Stimson in the last days of August and the first days of September. The ball was in his court and with the initial meeting of the cabinet committee on Germany scheduled for 5 September, he was under heavy pressure to come up with some viable alternative to the Morgenthau plan and to do it fast. During the week following receipt of the President's letter denouncing the *Handbook*, Stimson tried to find a system that would connect immediate detention of groups such as the Gestapo with a massive war-crimes prosecution, which, starting at the top with Hitler, could work on down through the Nazi chain of command. For suggestions and support, the Secretary turned to his closest aides and allies, including McCloy and Marshall. He thereby sent a message down into the hold of the Pentagon that all possible hands should be put to work on developing a formula that would unite organizational and individual prosecution—the first and most basic characteristic of what later came to be known as the *Nuremberg system*. With time so short, however, there was no way that such a complex system could be discovered and put in finished form soon enough. Stimson had to content himself with collecting as many testimonials as possible to the principles of mass detention and war-crimes trials while the War Department lawyers went about finding a way to tie them together.

Stimson received his warmest support from General Marshall and the judge advocate general, Major General Myron C. Cramer. Marshall believed that in the light of the recent revelations concerning the Nazi death camps in Poland—the Soviets had just overrun Maidanek, and in his discussion with Stimson, Marshall specifically mentioned the "Lublin mass murder"—there could be little objection to broad trials of organizations responsible for such atrocities.[45] In regard to both organization members and individuals responsible for specific war crimes, however, the army Chief of Staff stressed that summary execution should not be employed because some kind of judicial proceeding was essential in all cases. The general thereby reinforced Stimson's growing inclination to champion what would become a second basic premise of the "Nuremberg" approach—namely to use judicial procedures that dealt with all the culprits from top to bottom, rather than using a combination of "political" executions of the top Nazis and trials for the underlings. When the Secretary discussed the matter by telephone with the army's top legal officer on the morning of 5 September, General Cramer vigorously supported the view that all war criminals must be dealt with through trial, not by summary execution.[46] Cramer also declared that under military law it would be possible to simplify procedures in such trials and that mixed tribunals of civilian and military judges could be used.

But not everyone in the Pentagon was so supportive of the

trial approach, and some important officers, such as General Hilldring, were still out of step with the direction in which Stimson was heading. In an informal small meeting with Morgenthau and Harry Dexter White, it was Hilldring who suggested that the army just be given a list of "2,500 war criminals" and that American troops should then be ordered to shoot them on sight.[47] When Morgenthau remarked that Churchill wanted to give every soldier the authority to shoot those on an official war-crimes list, and that Stalin had "a list with 50,000" on it—exaggerations of both the British position and what Stalin had apparently said at Teheran—Hilldring raised no objections. Finally it fell to Morgenthau himself to remark that "American soldiers wouldn't shoot them. Somebody else would, probably." [48]

Thus on the eve of the first meeting of the cabinet committee on Germany, it was easy for Morgenthau to miscalculate and to underestimate the degree to which Stimson was prepared to stand firm in opposition to the Treasury proposals. This tendency was probably increased by the "pleasant" tone of a dinner meeting of Stimson, McCloy, Morgenthau, and White that occurred on 4 September. During the course of the dinner Morgenthau read out portions of the Treasury plan to the other guests.[49] According to Morgenthau's impressions,[50] the Secretary of War showed no signs of sharp hostility; but the Treasury Secretary did notice that Stimson was most interested in the war-crimes sections, and he had emphasized that some judicial proceeding utilizing the main elements of due process and the right to counsel was essential, although a public trial might not be necessary.

For his part, although he had been taken aback by what he considered Morgenthau's excessive bitterness toward Germany, and his general ignorance of world affairs,[51] Stimson went into the cabinet meeting of the committee far too confident. Not only was the war-crimes trial concept only a vague idea, lacking even full War Department support at this point, but Stimson had miscalculated the amount of assistance he would get from Secretary of State Hull. On previous occasions Hull had shown little sensitivity to the need to try war criminals,[52] but he had always stood shoulder to shoulder with Stimson on the importance of removing trade barriers and the need to promote worldwide economic interdependence. Stimson seems to have believed, therefore, that in a showdown on a plan keyed to deindustrialize Germany, Hull would automatically line up with him.[53] But Hull, who had seen the authority of his department seriously eroded during the preceding four years, and who was racked by illness in the fall of 1944, also found himself under heavy pressure to stand tall in favor of hard terms for Germany. Not only was the President tipping in that direction,[54] and the press crying loudly that the Germans must be made to pay for their crimes, but Morgenthau and his aides had been leaning hard on State Department officials during the preceding two weeks.

The American Jewish Conference [55] had also chosen this moment to send Hull a long memorandum reminding the State Department that United Nations leaders, including Hull and Roosevelt, had frequently proclaimed in the course of the war that the Nazis would be punished for the atrocities that they had committed against the Jews. With the end of the Third Reich apparently at hand, the American Jewish Conference wanted the State Department to declare unequivocally that Nazi actions against Jews would have a central place in the American war-crimes program, and that the nationality of Jewish victims—that is, whether they were technically enemy nationals—would be no shield against punishment of those responsible for the persecutions and mass killings. On 28 August, John W. Pehle, a close associate of Morgenthau's and executive director of the War Refugee Board, sent Hull an even more strongly worded memorandum.[56] He demanded that the United States government back up its previous declarations by doing everything in its power to make the UNWCC come

out in favor of the proposition that no matter what the nationality of the victims, all Nazi persecutions and atrocities
would be treated as war crimes.

By the time the cabinet committee on Germany met, the
State Department had set its course with the prevailing wind
and prepared a short memorandum that called for harsh economic measures against Germany and the development of a
procedure whereby Nazi war criminals could be perfunctorily
"tried and executed." [57] Stimson's diary records his "tremen-
dous surprise" [58] at the discovery that he alone opposed a Carthaginian peace, while Hull "was as bitter as Morgenthau
against the Germans." [59] Stimson struggled to convince his colleagues of the need for economic moderation—if for no other
reason, because it would serve the interest of American business—but it was all in vain. "We were irreconcilably divided" [60] on the issue of German deindustrialization, Stimson
later remarked. So deep was the division that no time or
energy remained to discuss the question of Nazi war criminals
or to determine what the State Department paper meant by its
cryptic expression that they should be "tried and executed." All
Stimson could salvage from the wreckage was an agreement
that Hull would send the State Department memorandum on
to the President, and that all the other members of the committee could send memoranda indicating their views "in respect to it." [61]

As soon as the meeting broke up, Hull did forward the State
Department paper to the President, while Hopkins merely
notified Roosevelt that with some minor reservations regarding
the form of expression, he agreed with it.[62] On the same afternoon a copy of the complete *Morgenthau plan* for Germany,
which had been under preparation in the Treasury for weeks,
finally went up to the White House. It included not only the
now famous, or infamous, "pasturalization" program of deindustrialization, but also a comprehensive war-crimes system
that included provisions for group detention, the creation of

labor battalions, and the summary execution, without hearing or trial, of the Nazi leaders.[63]

Before the day ended, the Secretary of War also sent his own memorandum to the White House. It was a short, eloquent plea for moderation, in which he advanced the thesis that only "through apprehension, investigation, and trial of all the Nazi leaders and instruments of the Nazi system of terrorism such as the Gestapo" [64] would the evils of the Third Reich be eradicated. By contrast, Stimson told the President, the proposal to flatten Germany economically, which had been developed by Morgenthau and supported in varying degrees by Hopkins and Hull, was bound to fail, because in the long run, "such methods . . . do not prevent war, they tend to breed war." [65]

Faced with a split cabinet—even in isolation Stimson was no one to trifle with—Roosevelt was apparently inclined to move carefully, and when the Cabinet Committee on Germany met with him on the next day (6 September), he was quite conciliatory.[66] He still had no use for any leniency toward the Germans, and when the question of who might be a suitable "czar" in the American zone of occupation arose, he passed over the names of Robert Murphy, and even Harry Hopkins, before he hit on Jimmy Byrnes as a man possessed of the requisite toughness.[67] Yet, while inclined toward reducing the Germans to a primitive economic level, Roosevelt was troubled by how such a program could be reconciled with his primary postwar goal in Europe of aiding British recovery. Thus, although the thrust of the meeting was still directed toward harsh measures to be applied in postwar Germany, Stimson was not "steam-rollered" [68] as he was afraid he might be; and in the end, Roosevelt indicated that no decision would be made on the basic issues for the time being.

The indecisive results of the committee's meeting with the President could not, however, disguise the fact that the divisions of opinion were very deep and that the conflict was destined to become increasingly acrimonious. Following the committee's session of 5 September, Hopkins and Morgenthau had shared their feelings of disgust that Stimson was "soft" on the Germans; [69] and there was an element of burning frustration in Morgenthau's report to his subordinates when relating Roosevelt's failure to solidly support the Treasury plan. [70] For Stimson, too, it was difficult to keep the conflict within the bounds of genteel rivalry. He noted in his diary that the session of 5 September was the most "difficult meeting" he had experienced "in all the four years that I have been here." [71] But the Secretary of War was able to keep his sense of humor, and during a discussion with General Marshall on the afternoon of 5 September he had a good laugh over the irony that as "the man who had charge of the Department which did the killing in the war," he "should be the only one who seemed to have any mercy for the other side." [72] While giving Stimson full credit for a stand that was both responsible and courageous, because it really was extraordinarily difficult to advocate moderation when American troops were fighting and dying against an opponent such as the Nazis, one should be cautious about simply making him the hero and Morgenthau the villain.

Clearly, Morgenthau's idea of deindustrialization was unwise from every point of view. Without an industrial base much of the German population, including invalids and children, who by no stretch of the imagination had played a part in the Nazi system, would have been condemned to suffering and perhaps even to death. The European economy, which had already been flattened by the war, would have been further disrupted. In any event, as the developments of the last thirty years—including, of course, those of the cold war—have shown, economic destruction was not the only way to deter Germany from resorting to aggressive warfare. The Morgenthau plan was thus not just wrongheaded in terms of the capitalist system, it would have been an act of political and economic folly under any conditions.

On a deeper level it is important to note the emotional and perhaps ethical merit that lay on Morgenthau's side. One of the reasons why Stimson found it possible to keep a cool head on the question of German peace terms was simply because, like many other American officials, he had not let himself directly perceive or feel the full brutal force of the genocidal system being used by the Nazis in the occupied territories. By walling off all considerations except those of military necessity, officials in Washington were temporarily able to sidestep many political problems and keep their eyes fixed on the measures that they believed would bring the quickest victory at the lowest cost in American blood.[73] But in practice this meant that they had to try to wage an amoral war—that is, a war in which ideological, political, and ethical considerations were kept from intruding on operational planning. Repeatedly Stimson and his colleagues had felt compelled to deny or turn their backs on appeals such as those which asked that raids in Nazi-occupied territories be scratched to spare "friendly" civilians; or that supplies intended for the military be diverted to aid the populations of the liberated areas. Of course, on some occasions the pressures were so great that the military necessity principle had been bent, if not broken, but these were exceptions.

By and large Stimson and the Joint Chiefs had held the military necessity line, and it was just their success in doing so that frustrated men such as Morgenthau and Pehle. It seemed to them as if official Washington, while talking in platitudes, was in actuality rarely willing to raise a finger for the victims of persecution or even to acknowledge openly that mass murder was taking place. In general they were right, and when in the fall of 1944, Stimson and his associates indicated that they were prepared to handle the problem of postwar Germany in the same practical and matter-of-fact manner in which they had prosecuted the war, it is little wonder that Morgenthau exploded. It is therefore one thing to charge that people such as Hopkins and Hull simply succumbed to the vengeance mood of the late war period after playing along with a policy of apolitical war making during the previous years. But it is not fair to put Morgenthau in this group. He may have awakened slowly to the frightful implications of a war in which military necessity was the highest law, but he had ultimately stumbled on part of the message; it is little wonder that he was ready to use almost any means to stop it from being projected into the postwar era.

During the three days between the first meeting of the committee with the President on 6 September and the second, which occurred on the ninth, a bitter but indecisive war took place between Stimson and Morgenthau. The Treasury Secretary initially tried a frontal attack, and in a conference with McCloy and General Hilldring on 7 September, he joined forces with Hopkins and some Treasury aides to force the War Department to agree that the *Handbook* needed revision.[74] But McCloy and Hilldring—the general had finally been brought around and was now towing the Stimson line—flatly refused to throw vast numbers of Germans into automatic arrest categories on the familiar grounds that it would create chaos in the army's rear area. Gradually, in the course of the discussion, McCloy and Hilldring took the initiative away from the Treasury people by stressing, on point after point, that in the "predefeat" period nothing should be done that would impede Eisenhower's advance into Germany. The old military necessity argument was working once more, and Morgenthau left the meeting having secured a few paper concessions, but little else.

On the following day (8 September) he was also unsuccessful in forging a really firm alliance with Secretary of State Hull. Although on the surface they seemed to agree on the general approach to the German problem, Hull was cautious, and Morgenthau believed the Secretary of State was "holding back" on him.[75] Morgenthau's efforts to work around and through the higher and lower levels of the various departments—"rooting around behind the scenes" Stimson scornfully called it[76]—was meeting increasing resistance at the State Department and elsewhere. The Treasury Secretary understood what was happening, and at one point he remarked that "of course underneath it all I think Cordell resents my being in on this." [77] But he kept pressing ahead anyway.

In the other camp Stimson was also busy lining up support. On the seventh he secured a blanket opinion from Marshall and his military aides that the army stood for "absolute rejection of the notion that we should not give these men [the Nazi leaders] a fair trial." [78] He also picked up the endorsements of a number of prominent people who rejected the idea of de-industrialization of Germany, including Marshall, Isaiah Bowman (one of FDR's economic advisors), and his old friend and colleague at the Foreign Policy Association, Hamilton Fish Armstrong. [79] But Stimson's greatest success in his own "rooting around behind the scenes" came when another of his old friends, and one of the most influential men in Washington, Justice Felix Frankfurter, declared his absolute opposition both to deindustrialization and to executing the Nazi leaders without trial. [80] By 8 September, Frankfurter was so busy helping Stimson to undermine Morgenthau's position that some leaders in the War Department began to fear he might commit some serious indiscretion. [81]

For those who may be inclined to see anti-Semitic factors as the primary driving force in the whole German policy debate, it is necessary to point out that by the first week of September, prominent "assimilationist" Jews were active on both sides of the controversy. Similarly, although the Secretary of War would soon be grumbling angrily because Morgenthau had been carried away by his "Semitic grievances" [82]—a rather remarkable way to characterize phenomena such as Maidenek and Auschwitz—he also continued his custom of frequently dining with Frankfurter. On 7 September Stimson praised the Justice for his statesmanlike attitude, although Stimson observed that Frankfurter "was a Jew like Morgenthau." [83] Thus anti-Semitism was definitely a factor, but it alone will not suffice to explain either the shape or the tone of the struggle.

By 9 September, the two sides had arrived at something close to a draw. Stimson had apparently gained some ground in the

previous three days, but a second committee meeting with the
President was nearly a rerun of what had transpired on 6 September. Again Morgenthau pushed hard, Stimson stressed responsibility, Roosevelt inclined toward Morgenthau, and then
at the last possible moment, the President pulled back and
failed to direct the committee to prepare the policy statement
that Morgenthau wanted.[84] Stimson and Morgenthau both
left the White House more frustrated and angry than when
they had arrived, grumbling that the President was primarily
concerned with trivia—such as whether the Germans should
be allowed to wear uniforms—or phantoms—such as the alleged danger of a revolution in France that might endanger the
American army's lines of communication.[85]

In fact, Roosevelt was worn out by the years of work and
responsibility. His health was failing, and he had just begun the
final two months of his last election campaign. The old charm
flashed now and then; but his masterful ability to improvise,
and to surround himself with the most varied advisors while
he played with one option after another, had gradually
turned into a welter of irrelevancies and an inability to make up
his mind. Stimson, alarmed by what he saw as not only the
President's inclination to come down on the wrong side of the
German question, but also by the obvious signs of illness,
weakness, and indecision, made one final effort to set things
right on 9 September by sending Roosevelt a calm and clear
memorandum in support of his position.[86] Again he explained
that deindustrialization would not work and that a trial of the
Nazi leaders was essential. Not only was it politically and
morally necessary to extend due process to the enemy, but the
record produced by such a trial would reveal the full story of
Nazi wickedness, and thus it would help to ennoble the Allied
war effort. By relaxing some of the usual procedural stringen-
cies, the court in such a trial would be able to work rapidly.
But the Secretary was forced to grant that he had come up
against one apparently insolvable problem. Wartime and prewar
actions against German nationals (including apparently the ex-

termination of German Jews) were not war crimes, and every foreign court would be without jurisdiction, just as "any foreign court would be without jurisdiction to try those who were guilty of, or condoned, lynching in our own country."

Stimson had anguished over this problem and had sent down to the War Department lawyers all available arguments in support of such prosecution (including the American Jewish Conference paper that had been forwarded to him by Hull) in hopes of finding an answer.[87] But no solution had been forthcoming, and Stimson was forced to admit this to the President on 9 September and again to Hull two days later.[88] It does credit to Stimson's honesty that he put the problem to Roosevelt so forthrightly, but the fact remains that this vacuum in the War Department approach meant that the President had no viable alternative to the Morgenthau plan as of 9 September 1944. Stimson was championing an attitude, or a line of attack, but he had no definite judicial instrument that could purge Germany quickly, efficiently, and to the satisfaction of the millions of people in the world who had been tortured and victimized by the Third Reich. Stimson had done the best he could, he had helped prevent formal acceptance of the Morgenthau plan, but he had nothing that would produce a clear victory. When the President left Washington to meet Churchill in Quebec on 10 September, there was no American consensus on what should be done with Germany. Without such a settled policy, Mr. Roosevelt was free to indulge his inclination toward Morgenthau.

The President walked into a situation where the scales were tipped in such a way that the Treasury's views, rather than Stimson's, would receive the readiest hearing. Churchill was not coming to Quebec primarily to settle the German question, but to get every ounce of help he could to aid Britain's postwar economic recovery. The Prime Minister was faced with the reality that when hostilities ended, his country would be on the edge of bankruptcy, and he wanted to use all the goodwill he had stored up in America to get the financial assistance to avert this disaster. As some of the remarks he had made during the policy struggle over Germany indicated, Roosevelt was also eager to find ways to assist the British.[89] But the man who was in the crucial position to say how this might be accomplished financially was not the President, and certainly not Stimson or even Hull; it was Henry Morgenthau, Jr.

When Roosevelt departed for Quebec, no top cabinet officials accompanied him, not even Secretary of State Hull. Along with the others, Henry Stimson was left in Washington to fuss and worry. He hoped that Felix Frankfurter's prediction would prove to be correct, and the Morgenthau plan would "fall to the wayside by its own weight." [90] But then in the late afternoon of 12 September, Roosevelt sent a secret telegram to Morgenthau directing him to be in Quebec on the fourteenth.[91] On the same 12 September, in one of the war's more subtle ironies, advance units of the American First Army crossed Germany's western border for the first time.

Morgenthau hurried to Canada, arriving in Quebec on the thirteenth, a day earlier than the one specified in Roosevelt's telegram. When Stimson learned that Morgenthau was in Quebec, he railed that the Treasury Secretary was so "biased" [92] that he was "a very dangerous advisor to the President at this time." For a moment Stimson and Hull toyed with the idea of convening the cabinet committee on Germany in the Treasury Secretary's absence in order to hammer out a more moderate program.[93] The Secretary of State was enraged that he had not been allowed to accompany the President and that Morgenthau would participate in the talks with Churchill.[94] Stimson even considered issuing the *Interim Directives* to Eisenhower on his own authority, because now American forces were inside Germany.[95] But upon reflection and after a night's rest, both these radical notions were abandoned. Instead, Stimson merely addressed another of those eloquent memoranda to the President, calling for the relinquishment of the Morgenthau plan, not only because it would not work, but because "it would be just such a crime as the Germans themselves hoped to perpetrate upon their victims—it would be a crime against civilization itself." [96]

Meanwhile, in Quebec, Morgenthau played his hand with considerable skill. He had long recognized that Britain's postwar economic plight would be a central concern in the Roosevelt-Churchill talks, and in the preceding weeks the Treasury had made a number of studies exploring possible ways to assist Great Britain.[97] Treasury aides of Morgenthau's had suggested that one method to improve Britain's position as an exporter would be to destroy the Ruhr industry of her German competitor,[98] a suggestion which fit into Morgenthau's plans for Germany. Building on this base, he presented the major tenets of his scheme to the British. On a first hearing, however, Churchill was apparently cool to the idea.[99] Then the American Treasury delegation managed to get the floor a second time, and the plan was advanced in such a way that it seemed to be intertwined with the question of whether lend-lease aid would be extended to Britain in the postwar period.[100] Still, Foreign Secretary Anthony Eden and other British officials raised objections to the notion of deindustrializing Germany.[101] But Churchill ultimately yielded, later noting that after all, Mr. Morgenthau was a man "from whom we had much to ask." [102]

Aside from a longing for lend-lease aid, British acceptance of Morgenthau's economic plans for Germany was facilitated by the Prime Minister and many other British leaders agreeing with Morgenthau that summary execution, not trial, was the best way to deal with the major Nazi war criminals. For over two years, the Lord Chancellor, Lord Simon, had been advocating that, due to the wide range of legal and political difficulties which would be associated with a trial, it would be better if the Allies disposed of Hitler and his aides by "political" execution, in a manner analogous to what the London government had done to Napoleon in 1815. For more than a year, Churchill had been championing this position in the cabinet. He had coupled it with the idea of a public announcement that anyone who assisted in the Hitlerian mass murders would be handled in the same way as the Führer. He hoped this might deter further Nazi atrocities,[103] but the cabinet repeatedly refused to support the idea of such an open threat for fear that it would produce reprisals against British POWs in German hands. Simon and Churchill would not give up however, and in the summer of 1944 they managed to secure a cabinet decision directing Simon to prepare a draft proposal favorable to summary execution. On 4 September, Simon completed the draft, which advanced a number of legal and political arguments to show that trials were inappropriate. It contended that the *Moscow Declaration*, stating that "the joint decision of the Governments of the Allies" [104] would determine the fate of the Nazi leaders, implied that the problem would be dealt with politically, not judicially. Simon concluded, therefore, that the best thing to do was simply to shoot a handful of the top Nazi leaders like Hitler and Himmler.

Judging on the basis of earlier and subsequent debates, the Simon paper probably represented a majority view of the cabinet, but it had not been laid before that body prior to the Quebec meeting. The regular officials of the Foreign Office also had not seen it before the departure of the British delegation for the conference in Canada.[105] Simon simply took a copy of the draft with him to Quebec, and in the course of the discussions he apparently laid it on the table with the Prime Minister's approval. Thus, while the British were considering the Morgenthau plan as if it constituted the established position of the Washington government, Roosevelt and his aides were examining the Simon draft as if it were official British policy.

When Secretary of War Stimson had first learned that Churchill and Roosevelt would decide the economic and war-crimes issues largely on their own, he confided to his diary the prediction that the results would probably be a disaster, because the two leaders were "similar in their impulsiveness and lack of systematic study." [106] Whether this was true prophecy or a self-justifying commentary added subsequently, it was right on the mark. On 15 September, after agreeing on postwar economic aid to Britain, Churchill and Roosevelt initialed a summary of the Morgenthau plan, which seems to have been drafted by the Prime Minister himself. Then after a brief discussion in which Roosevelt reportedly came out strongly "for shooting the Nazi leaders without trial," [107] the two leaders also accepted a short paper that read:

The President and Prime Minister have agreed to put to Marshal Stalin Lord Simon's proposals for dealing with the major criminals and to concert with him a list of names.[108]

With that, the Quebec conference was over, and apparently the American policy battle over Germany had ended too, with total victory going to Henry Morgenthau, Jr.

CHAPTER 2

GENESIS OF A
TRIAL PLAN

The criminality with which the Nazi leaders and groups are charged does not consist of scattered individual outrages such as may occur in any war, but represents the results of a purposeful and systematic pattern created by them to the end of achieving world domination.[1]

War Department Memorandum
11 November 1944

A cloud of gloom descended on the Pentagon in the immediate aftermath of the crushing defeat the War Department suffered in Quebec. General Marshall was "very much troubled," especially by the news that the President had approved the "shooting without trial"[2] of the Nazi leaders. Secretary Stimson predicted that if the Quebec agreements were carried out, they would "sure as fate . . . lay the seeds for another war in the next generation."[3] The Secretary was also racked by doubt about whether the President would be able to see the folly of the Quebec program; but in the following days his spirits gradually revived as he grasped at the hope that the Morgenthau plan could not actually be implemented.[4] When on 20 September an extremely conciliatory Henry Morgenthau provided the other members of the cabinet committee on Germany with his account of the Quebec events, he was still sharply attacked by Hull and Stimson.[5] The two Secretaries apparently raised all the familiar objections to the content of the plan and the unorthodox way in which it had been approved by the two governmental leaders. In addition they emphasized that the Anglo-Americans had placed themselves in a vulnerable position; they had taken a stand on the most fundamental issues regarding the occupation of Germany without inquiring about the views and wishes of the Soviet Union.

The Secretary of War's reviving confidence and good cheer were further buoyed by encouragement from his undauntable friend Felix Frankfurter and the comic pen of an anonymous official in the War Department. On 19 September Mr. Stimson was obviously amused and delighted to receive a memorandum from one of his aides that set forth a satirical alternative to the Morgenthau plan.[6] Under this scheme all of Germany was to be turned into one enormous workshop for making cuckoo clocks, but the population would not be permitted to possess any sharp or pointed tools for use in the manufacturing process. The beauty of the idea, according to the droll author, was that without such implements, the Germans would be unable to attack their neighbors with knives, saws, chisels, and the like; and it would also make cuckoo-clock manufacture virtually impossible. This would guarantee that there would be no German competition for the industries of other countries and, in one stroke, the rest of the world would be assured of peace and prosperity!

Justice Frankfurter's assistance to the Secretary was obviously more serious and businesslike than this, but his imperturbable optimism was at least of equal help to Mr. Stimson.[7] Always ready to find some bright spot on the horizon, in the third week of September Frankfurter was predicting that the British would soon come to their senses and quash the whole scheme approved at Quebec. With a keen eye for the core of Stimson's problem, however, the justice also noted that a comprehensive war-crimes trial plan, which would garner wide support and thus serve as a practical alternative to Morgenthau's grand design, had to be developed. Frankfurter even mentioned the name of a young attorney in the judge advocate general's office, Lieutenant Colonel Frederick Bernays Wiener, whom he thought might help the Secretary of War in developing such a plan.

Actually, by the time Frankfurter tendered this advice, War Department legal planners, not only in the judge advocate general's office, but also in the civil affairs division and the personnel branch (G-1), had been struggling for weeks to produce such a program. In mid-September, unbeknownst to anyone outside the inner recesses of the Pentagon, Lieutenant Colonel Murray C. Bernays—a distant relative of the man in JAG whom Frankfurter had recommended to Stimson—believed that he had succeeded. Bernays, like most of his colleagues, was a civilian attorney who was performing his wartime military service as a War Department legal specialist. His official position was chief of a catchall organization in personnel (G-1) called the special projects branch. In the course of the war Bernays had worked on a wide range of problems, including the treatment of American prisoners in German hands and the development of procedures to help protect them as the end of the Third Reich drew near. He had therefore been forced to give attention to the Nazi organizations most likely to mistreat American POWs, such as the SS and the Gestapo, and in regard to these as well as many other matters, he had been required to cooperate closely with the civil affairs division. It was natural therefore in early September, when the pressure was on to produce a broad and effective war-crimes program, Bernays would try his hand at developing a solution.

Bernays realized that the basic task was to produce a relatively simple procedure to deal with the major war criminals and organizations while retaining the basic elements of due process. In addition the colonel understood that something would have to be done about atrocities, including those committed before the war and the persecution of German nationals. Such acts were not technically war crimes, but were uppermost in the minds of Washington officials from Mr. Pehle to the President himself. In Bernays's words, a suitable system would need to produce "an international judgement," which rejected the thesis that "high interests of state" justified "national crimes"; at the same time it exposed the "menace of racism and totalitarianism" by driving home to the German people "a sense of their guilt, and . . . a realization of their responsibility for the crimes committed by their government." [8] If this was not done, and the broad sweep of Nazi "brutalities" went "unpunished," millions of people would feel that their sufferings in gaining victory had been in vain, and they would end the war "frustrated and disillusioned." [9]

After much toil and trouble, including discussions with his colleagues in personnel and the civil affairs division, Bernays produced a short six-page memorandum that was immediately approved by Major General Stephen G. Henry, the chief of G-1, on 15 September. (For those who appreciate ironies, this was the same day that Roosevelt and Churchill signed the Quebec agreement.) [10] Under the Bernays plan "the Nazi Government and its Party and State agencies, including the SA, SS, and Gestapo" would be tried before an international court, charged "with conspiracy to commit murder, terrorism, and the destruction of peaceful populations in violation of the laws of War." [11] In the course of the trial, evidence of anything that had been done by the Nazis "in furtherance of the conspiracy," including persecution of German and other Axis nationals, would be admissible. If the international tribunal found in favor of the prosecution and sustained the conspiracy charge, it would sentence the individual Nazi leaders before the court. It would then turn over to the civil and military courts of the Allied governments all members of organizations, such as the Gestapo. In the subsequent proceedings, all that was required for conviction by an Allied court was to show that the individual in question had in fact been a member of one of the organizations held to be criminal.

Thus appeared the first formulation of what came to be

known as the *Nuremberg* trial plan—the prosecution of the leaders and major organizations of the Nazi system for allegedly participating in a criminal conspiracy that embraced both wartime and prewar acts. Although many aspects of the trial system that was later used at Nuremberg were not included in Bernays's original proposal—most significantly there was no mention of charging anyone with "the crime" of preparing or launching an "aggressive war"—this memorandum was the first big step on the main road to Nuremberg. As such, it should be noted that a number of problems that gradually manifested themselves in the course of later developments were already implicit in Bernays's original idea. The plan was founded on the principle of a presumption of guilt based on mere membership in an organization, a concept which must—when stated as a general principle—make all civil libertarians wince. Furthermore, the idea of prosecuting on the grounds of a conspiracy charge inevitably created enormous difficulties, because conspiracy is primarily an Anglo-American legal conception with few parallels in continental and international law. Consequently, it would later not only confuse the German defendants and their attorneys, but it would baffle the French and Soviets from the beginning of inter-Allied negotiations until the last days of the Nuremberg trial.

The liabilities inherent in the conspiracy approach were not immediately recognized in Washington. No one involved in the war-crimes debate was very concerned about the specifics of European legal processes or even of the actual conditions that prevailed inside Nazi Germany during the last stages of the war. The whole war-crimes controversy in the American capital was marked by an inclination toward vague generalization rather than solid fact. As indicated earlier, most Washington officials had, understandably, little desire to look directly at the mass murders taking place in the Nazi death camps. They also were disinclined to closely examine who was making the genocidal decisions, and they had little or no idea how the Nazi killing system operated. From Morgenthau to Stimson to Bernays, they all tended to make general statements about "Storm-troopers" or the Gestapo, and in so doing they produced serious factual errors. That the SA was of no political importance in the Germany of 1944 was never clear to any of them, nor did they realize, for example, that the Gestapo did not operate concentration camps or death factories such as Birkenau. In late 1944 no one in authority in Washington would even have recognized the name of Adolf Eichmann, much less identified him correctly as the official in charge of deporting Europe's Jews to the death camps in Poland.

Part of this welter of confusion and ignorance was due to a lack of hard intelligence data, but it was primarily caused by the outlook of War Department officials. These men were mainly concerned with developing solutions to political problems as they manifested themselves in Washington, D.C., which meant giving the War Department leaders a viable alternative to the Morgenthau plan. That was the problem that had been posed, and that was what Bernays's proposal would brilliantly solve, once it made its way up the chain of command and into the hands of Henry L. Stimson.

But it is a truism about Washington that the official trans-mission of anything moves very slowly, and it is equally true that most walls in the American capital are thin. Therefore, while the Bernays plan crawled tortoiselike from one Pentagon office to the next, McCloy and Stimson were actually only left in need of deliverance for a short time. However, even in that interval, they made it clear that they had no intention of giving up without a fight. On 23 September, McCloy called together the JAG lawyers and told them to speed up their work pre-paring for war-crimes trials despite "the talk going around" Washington in favor of summary execution.[12] According to Mc-Cloy, Henry Stimson had made it clear that as long as he was Secretary of War, "there would be nothing of the sort done," and therefore the whole range of Germany's brutal acts, in-cluding those perpetrated "against Jews in Germany, both be-fore and during the war," would have to be brought inside a

judicial net. Once again the Soviet capture of Maidenek
loomed large, because McCloy specifically referred to "the recent atrocities in Lublin," as an example of what cried out for
prosecution.

In the course of this meeting, Lieutenant Colonel Wiener—
the man whom Justice Frankfurter a few days earlier had
recommended to Stimson as potentially very helpful—suggested that perhaps one way to head off the "talk around
Washington" favoring liquidation of the captured Nazi leaders
was to plant a question about it in the Secretary of War's next
press conference. In this way Stimson would be able publicly to
denounce it and speak out in favor of a trial.[13] McCloy thought
this was a splendid idea and directed the JAG officers to prepare both the plantable question and the answer that would
be made by the Secretary. But before Wiener and his colleagues could finish their work, the press showed, as it has so
often before and since, that it was perfectly capable of ferreting
out secret information. The New York Sunday papers that
came out the next day (24 September) carried stories about
the cabinet splits on the Morgenthau plan. On the twenty-
fifth the whole national press took up the cry, with Morgenthau
receiving heavy criticism.

Only six weeks were left before the election, and Roosevelt
suddenly found himself in a difficult spot. The situation was
immediately made worse when Nazi propagandists seized upon
the American press revelations regarding the Morgenthau plan
and used it to flay the German people with the threat that an
Allied victory would mean the total annihilation of Germany.
The more Goebbels screamed, the more some American press
observers contended that Morgenthau's idea would inevitably
lead to stiffened German resistance and higher Allied casualties. At this moment Morgenthau's luck gave out completely;
the Allied advance had ground to a halt in the fortified positions of the Siegfried line, and when the British attempted to
flank these defenses by a northern swing into the Netherlands,
the result was the disastrous reversal at Arnhem.

With that, all of the anti-Morgenthau wolves were loosed, and while the Treasury spokesman and the Secretary himself did their best to lie low, Franklin Roosevelt began to beat a strategic retreat from Quebec. In a memorandum that he sent to Cordell Hull on 29 September, the President emphasized that keeping Britain solvent was the most important goal. Then, while rather petulantly expressing his hope that someone would "catch and chastise" those responsible for the press leaks, he added that "no one wants to make Germany a wholly agricultural nation again," and "no one wants a complete eradication of German industrial capacity in the Ruhr and Saar." [14] Four days later (on 3 October) in a talk with Stimson, Roosevelt was forced to admit that the first press leaks had probably come from the Treasury itself, and he then declared he himself did not favor "pasturalization." Putting on his best velvet charm, he tried to push the responsibility completely onto Morgenthau, telling the Secretary of War, according to the latter's diary, that " 'Henry Morgenthau had pulled a boner' or an equivalent expression." [15] When Stimson, with his usual directness, pulled out a copy of the economic agreement made at Quebec, the President claimed to be "staggered" that he had initialed it.

This encounter marked the demise of the Morgenthau plan. Henceforth, if anyone was rude enough to refer to the President's role in the affair, he merely observed that he was "amazed" he had signed the Quebec agreement.[16] Franklin Roosevelt, badly burned on the Morgenthau plan, had become so circumspect by the third week of October that he replied to a State Department memorandum on occupation policy for Germany by declaring he disliked "making detailed plans for a country which we do not yet occupy." [17] With the President acting like a sphinx on the German question, Henry Morgenthau's plan, and his political leverage on this issue, had been destroyed. The initiative thus passed completely to the State and War departments, with the latter, as usual, leading the way. No sooner had Morgenthau's position begun to slip than the army's postdefeat directives, slightly revised to meet the strongest objections of the hardline critics, were cleared by the War and State Departments and dispatched to Eisenhower.[18] However, it was chiefly in regard to war-crimes questions that a new take-charge attitude was visible, with officers in the War Department pushing ahead on a number of aspects of the problem.

On 27 September the judge advocate general, General Cramer, forwarded to McCloy a series of recommendations regarding the use of international military commissions for trying war criminals in Europe and Asia.[19] Although this memorandum did not deal with many of the more delicate questions, such as prewar persecutions in Germany, it did set up a program for swift prosecution of traditional war crimes. Cramer recommended that the normal trial procedures and evidentiary systems used in military courts, which were already highly favorable to the prosecution, should be tipped even further in that direction. In war-crimes trials, "all evidence which has probative force in the minds of reasonable men" should be made admissible, and defendants would lose the right of appeal. All sentences, including death sentences, were to be "executed within 24 hours." [20]

In McCloy's office on this same day (27 September), the conspiracy/criminal-organization scheme developed by Bernays was given its first open hearing before representatives of the judge advocate general's office and other interested staff officers (the Secretary of War was, of course, not present).[21] After the presentation, McCloy charged his assistant executive officer, Colonel R. Ammi Cutter, with the duty of evaluating the proposal and making a report. Cutter was another able young civilian attorney—temporarily on duty in the War Department —who would blossom in the postwar period, ultimately serving as a justice on the Supreme Court of Massachusetts. Next to Bernays, he would be the War Department officer most deeply involved in the detailed shaping of the conspiracy/criminal-organization trial plan as it developed between September

1944 and May 1945. After his first survey of Bernays's work, Cutter characterized the plan as "ingenious," but he was troubled by the "fairly radical departures from existing [legal] theories" that it embodied. He was also concerned that the proposed "grandiose state trials" might give the defense an opportunity to make political martyrs out of Hitler and his aides.[22]

The conspiracy/criminal-organization plan had obviously not swept the field, but it had survived the first hurdle; and there was as yet no competing proposal available that dealt with the basic political and legal issues posed by the Morgenthau plan. Furthermore, Bernays was not just a passive or disinterested draftsman; he passionately believed that the solution he offered was the right one, and he worked diligently to line up support for it. Realizing that Cutter was not yet totally convinced, Bernays sent him every available scrap of paper which indicated that prosecution of groups such as the Gestapo was necessary and legally justified.[23] Ranging beyond the War Department, on 5 October Bernays also took the opportunity at a routine conference with Green Hackworth, the State Department legal chief, to put before him the essential features of his plan. Hackworth, who had been holding to a rigidly conservative definition of what constituted a war crime, had recently come under heavy pressure to find a more elastic interpretation which would meet the demands of groups such as the American Jewish Conference and the War Refugee Board. Having as yet been unable to hit on such a formula, Hackworth seemed highly, perhaps "enthusiastic[ally]" interested in the conspiracy/criminal-organization approach as a likely solution to his own difficulties.[24]

As Bernays moved gradually forward, assembling a coalition of adherents and sympathizers for his ideas, he was inadvertently assisted by the JAG lawyers who were trying to remove obstacles that stood in the way of their own program for streamlined trials of conventional war-crimes cases. On 4 October, the chief of JAG's war plans division, Colonel Archibald

King, forwarded a memorandum to G-1 that recommended amending the provisions of the *American Rules of Land Warfare* (FM 27-10), relating to an appeal to superior orders as a covering defense against conviction in military courts.[25] King wanted the provision modified so that it applied only to orders that did not require "the doing of acts which violate accepted rules of warfare or are otherwise clearly illegal." Although King advanced a number of arguments to support the need for this revision, the last and most heavily stressed was that "Axis war criminals" might appeal to the existing formulation in an effort to escape punishment. Since the British had already amended their *Manual of Military Law* in this sense, the JAG officer thought it only reasonable that the Americans do the same so "that we should not furnish the war criminals with ammunition." After a number of conferences and some substantial redrafting, a softer version of the King proposal was approved by War Department planners on 31 October. The *Rules of Land Warfare* were revised, and another barrier to the conspiracy/criminal-organization plan, as well as to the other, more modest, war-crimes trial scheme, fell away.[26]

By October, if a proposal on war criminals did not advocate trials, then it was given short shrift in the War Department no matter how wise or authoritative it might appear to be. On 6 October, the head of the Office of Strategic Services (OSS) and a friend of the president, General William Donovan, sent McCloy a report on "Problems Concerning War Criminals," with a covering note claiming that this "was the story" on the war-crimes question.[27] The report was long, detailed, and thorough, but it unfortunately implied that in light of the many legal difficulties involved, the top Nazi leaders could best be disposed of by political rather than judicial action. Thus hopelessly tainted, it was immediately filed and never played any part in the development of American war-crimes policy.

With the War Department so firmly committed to the judicial principle, it would seem that a trial plan, or a series of such plans, should have moved ahead rapidly, but McCloy's office was still cautious. By mid-October both Cutter and McCloy were inclined to separate the traditional war-crimes cases from the political/legal complexities attendant on the issue of the major criminals.[28] They also decided to leave JAG with most of the responsibility for developing cases in the former category of prosecution. But in regard to the major criminals, they could not quite bring themselves to approve Bernays's proposal, yet they also did nothing to develop any alternative. So the conspiracy/criminal-organization scheme gradually took on the appearance of being the de facto procedure to deal with the major war criminals and organizations, and just as gradually, the burden of proof shifted from its supporters to its critics.

No one at this time called upon Bernays to make another general defense of his proposal, but when anyone objected to an aspect of it, he did try to answer them. In a meeting of 19 October, for example, some JAG officers voiced doubts about whether a finding of conspiracy against an organization by one court could, under American law, be taken as proven in a case before another court. If this negative view was correct, then it might not be possible to simply transfer the international tribunal's conspiracy ruling to hearings of individual organization members in American military or civil courts. In reply, Bernays offered to make a slight modification in his original proposal, conceding organization members the right to challenge the general conspiracy ruling in their individual trials.[29] Even so, the burden of proof would be on the defendant; and unless he challenged successfully, a finding of organizational complicity made in the first trial would be allowed to stand. This response by Bernays did not actually meet the problem posed by JAG, for the real issue was not where the burden of proof should fall, but whether a conspiracy finding could be conveyed from one court to another under American law. To propose that it could was analogous to contending that if a court found an organization such as the PTA to be engaged in a criminal conspiracy, then another court could routinely send members to prison without showing individual guilt, unless someone managed successfully to challenge the original ruling.

This was one of the weakest legal arguments that Bernays would advance during the many months in which he was called upon to ward off all kinds of criticisms of his plan. But in mid-October, no one pressed the attack any further; JAG's question, as well as Bernays's answer and the plan itself, were left in a limbo while everyone waited for a decision on whether or not the conspiracy/criminal-organization approach would become the basic War Department trial program. Since that question was not answered in McCloy's office, it would ultimately have to be supplied by a personal judgment of the Secretary of War.

Precisely how much information about the plan had passed along the grapevine to Stimson by this time cannot be established. But he knew quite a bit, and there were rumors—apparently erroneous—that he shared some of JAG's doubts regarding the legality of transferring a ruling from one court to another.[30] Certainly, if he had reservations about specific features of the plan, these did not dampen his ardor for the general idea of holding trials. Throughout October he made use of his social and political connections to promote his belief in judicial disposition, not summary execution, as the only appropriate way to deal with the Nazi leaders. On 9 October at a social gathering, he got around the requirements of formal diplomacy and strongly advocated the idea of trials in a discussion with the British ambassador, Lord Halifax.[31] The next day Halifax offered to transmit Stimson's "own thoughts on the subject" to London, and he requested "a short note" so that he might get "the point right." [32] Stimson, in turn, passed Halifax's request on to the Assistant Secretary with a wry comment that this was "a job" for McCloy's "war criminal experts." [33] A draft for a Stimson reply to Halifax was prepared. After noting that War Department planning was still "in the preliminary stage," it went on to provide a summary of Bernays's scheme for a conspiracy/criminal-organization trial.[34] Presumably because he did not want to ruffle feathers in the State Department, Stimson ultimately decided not to send anything in writing and "verbally" passed on his views to the British ambassador.[35] But the incident is symptomatic of the mood in the War Department, for although no one beyond the level of the personnel branch had as yet approved Bernays's plan, it was nonetheless used to indicate to others the "direction" of the department's thinking.

Whether Stimson actually went ahead and told Halifax about the plan in detail cannot now be established. It seems rather doubtful, as there are no indications of such a conversation in the British Foreign Office records. But by mid-October the Secretary of War had hit on another reason why some form of organizational prosecution was necessary, especially one that could be used against secret-police units. Disturbed by reports of Soviet secret-police action in the areas of Eastern Europe being occupied by the Red Army, and desirous of avoiding a full-scale diplomatic confrontation over the matter, Stimson came up with the idea of publicly prosecuting the Gestapo in a kind of show trial to discredit all secret-police organizations, including the Soviet Secret Police (OGPU). This was a rather naive echo of the grand, progressive days when Teddy Roosevelt and Wilson could arouse public opinion by using antitrust actions to expose the evils of big business. But Stimson was deadly serious. On 23 October he confided to his diary that the use of an organizational trial to undermine secret-police operations everywhere had become his new "gospel."[36]

The timing of these comments is important, for on the following day (24 October) Bernays made a formal presentation of the conspiracy/criminal-organization plan in Mr. Stimson's office. Although Stimson was apparently not altogether clear who Bernays was—indicating in his diary that the colonel came from JAG [37]—he instantly grasped the essential features and advantages of the plan. According to an account penned

eight months later by Bernays, he had only a brief opportunity
to mention the need to strike at the basic crime, "the Nazi
plan for total war." Bernays characterized it as "a conspiracy
of gangsters who had taken over a complaisant or conniving
Government for their own criminal purposes," when Stimson
intervened to take charge of the discussion and set out his own
arguments in support of Bernays's proposal.[38] The Secretary
then waxed eloquent on the importance of going back to "the
basic conspiracy," which would make possible the proof of
"the real crime and reach the maximum number of criminals."
Stimson championed the cause of the plan so enthusiastically
and so well that at the close of the meeting, Bernays apparently took his courage in hand and complimented the Secretary on having "stated my case better than I could have stated
it myself." [39]

Bernays's presentation of the plan exerted a strong new influence on Henry Stimson. In the words of the Secretary's diary,
these events pushed his thought "further along the line which
it has been following in connection with dealing with the German secret police and the forms of secret police among other
nations." [40] After the meeting he rushed off to tell General
Marshall about his reflections on the relationship between a
trial of the Gestapo and control of the OGPU, tracing out for
the general the main features of Bernays's conspiracy/criminal-
organization plan.[41] That evening, while dining with McCloy
and the American ambassador to the Soviet Union, Averell
Harriman, Stimson pumped the ambassador on particulars of
the Soviet secret-police system.[42] On the following day he
went after Harry Hopkins, whom the War Department was
always trying to court for fear that Morgenthau might somehow recover and the army's right to determine immediate
occupation policy could be threatened anew. But this time
Stimson had no enthusiasm for discussions about Morgenthau
or occupation policy or administrative procedures. All he
wanted to drive home to Hopkins was the central idea—now
that he had an operative plan in his pocket—that a broadly based

war-crimes trial was necessary "so as to make a dramatic record of the whole Nazi system which we have been fighting." [43] By 27 October Stimson's missionary enthusiasm carried him beyond the narrow confines of the American government; on that day he emphasized to both John G. Winant, the American ambassador to the European Advisory Commission, and Sir Arthur Salter, secretary to the British Ministry of War Transport, that he favored the idea of "a big trial for conspiracy." [44]

It was an excellent moment for an American advocate of a conspiracy trial to extend the discussion into the realm of inter-Allied relations, for another of the great powers had just made its support for a trial very clear. From at least November 1942, Stalin and Molotov had repeatedly stressed that the U.S.S.R. wanted the Nazi leaders put before a court rather than simply shot. But the Anglo-Americans failed to get the message straight, in part because of the cloudy incident at Teheran during which Stalin apparently advocated the raw execution of 50,000 German officers.[45] Additional confusion had arisen in the fall of 1944 because of the contradictory opinions the Russians expressed about the Morgenthau plan. On 28 September 1944 Mr. S. S. Sobolev, the vice-chairman of the Soviet delegation to the Dumbarton Oaks Conference (which was laying the groundwork for the United Nations) told a State Department official that "Mr. Morgenthau's type of thinking was not acceptable to the Soviet Government." [46] But one week later, on 5 October 1944, Andrei Gromyko remarked to Harry Dexter White that the Soviet Government stood "very close . . . to what is spoken of as 'the Morgenthau plan.' " [47] No one in Washington was sure what either of these remarks implied about the Soviet attitude toward the treatment of war-crimes in Morgenthau's scheme. And they were at least as confused about how to reconcile Soviet support for a trial with Stalin's remark about the elimination of thousands of Wehrmacht officers.

Their distress on the latter point would be permanent, and Anglo-American leaders would be haunted by uncertainty and a sense of foreboding about what Stalin actually meant by the word "trial." But from the last week of October 1944 on, they could no longer doubt that it meant something different than summary execution.

Meeting with Stalin in Moscow, Churchill was told point blank that the Soviet leaders rejected a political disposition of Hitler and the other top Nazis, and they would insist on a trial if death sentences were to be imposed.[48] On 22 October, the Prime Minister so informed Roosevelt, and his message produced the impression in Washington that the British had lost their enthusiasm for the Simon plan.[49] Actually, even before his meeting with Stalin, Churchill had decided to go slow [50] because of the recurrent fear of reprisals against Allied POWs in German hands. However, without any indication from Washington that FDR had backed away from the deals made in Quebec, Churchill saw no need to completely abandon summary execution and decided instead to merely put the idea on the shelf. "I consider that we should let this matter lie until there is a triple meeting," [51] he told Eden on 24 October, and that is exactly what he and the British government did. Nothing of importance was done in London on the major war-crimes question during the remainder of the winter of 1944. The Americans did not understand that the Simon plan had merely been placed on hold, and that the British Foreign Office would continue to pursue its conservative and highly cautious policies regarding traditional war-crimes prosecutions.

Misjudging the true situation in London, the American leaders, led by Stimson, interpreted the events of October to mean that the Quebec agreements were dead and that the way was clear for a vigorous espousal of a broad and innovative trial system. To clear the way, a meeting of the minds between the War and State Departments was necessary, and on 27 October Stimson made the first move in that direction. After allowing the memoranda of the American Jewish Conference and the War Refugee Board to lie about for seven weeks, Stimson chose this moment to reply to the State Department request for an opinion. He used the opportunity to champion the trial approach, and to acquaint Hull and his colleagues with the conspiracy/criminal-organization proposal.[52] Although cool to some of the propositions advanced by the American Jewish Conference, Stimson reiterated his support for a general war-crimes program, and in passing he tipped his hat to the preparations that JAG had made to deal with crimes perpetrated by the Axis against American nationals. Regarding the broader question of atrocities that might not technically be war crimes, Stimson again noted the importance of striking at organizations such as the SS and the Gestapo, and observed that this could perhaps be done through Allied military courts inside occupied Germany.

But the Secretary of War put his emphasis on the advantages of going at the problem by a different route, namely through Bernays's conspiracy scheme. He described Bernays's plan in detail, and while granting that it had not yet been "considered fully" or "officially approved" in the War Department, he nonetheless sent a copy of Bernays's original memorandum to Hull. In addition, Stimson urged the State Department not only to "consider the proposals at this time," but to send a representative to confer with G-1 about the conspiracy idea, "at your convenience." [53] If any question remained that Stimson was anxious to move the proposal to the highest reaches of the U.S. government, it was dispelled by his final statement; he was not only sending this ten-page letter to Hull, but he was also forwarding a copy to Secretary of the Navy James Forrestal, because of the interest which his Department has "in these matters." [54]

On the same day that Stimson brought up his big guns to open the way for the plan, Bernays himself offered to "assume the task of sparkplugging" [55] a committee of War, Navy, and State Department representatives that would put the proposal in finished form. Bernays's enthusiasm and ambition were boundless, and he apparently thought that once such a committee acted, it would be possible to move right along to the

initiation of "informal talks with the British." Considering
that even within the War Department not a single organization
except the personnel branch had formally approved the plan,
and that the crucially important judge advocate general's office
had not made any official pronouncement regarding it, Bernays
had obviously moved far ahead of himself.

But there actually were strong signs indicating that the plan
might move ahead rapidly. A meeting to see whether the War,
Navy, and State Departments would accept it in principle was
scheduled for 9 November, and even before that meeting
occurred, McCloy was working to incorporate the plan's major
components into the War Department's occupation policies.

On 2 November, for example, Colonel Cutter, speaking for
McCloy, informed JAG that before its paper on so-called
"routine" war crimes could be submitted to the Joint Chiefs
of Staff, "it should be supplemented by a general explanation
of the conspiracy theory of prosecution for the guidance of the
committees which are to consider the paper." [56]

The mood in the Pentagon was tipping ever more decisively
in Bernays's direction, and on the eve of the three-department
meeting, only one potentially troublesome obstacle appeared
on the horizon. A British aide-mémoire had arrived in Washington on 30 October. It addressed itself to another group of
proposals that had recently been placed before the UNWCC.[57]
The latest UNWCC debate concerned a recommendation that
an international war-crimes court be established by treaty, and,
in addition, that mixed military tribunals be created to deal
with supplemental war-crimes problems. The Foreign Office
emphatically rejected the idea of a treaty court, and it asked
the United States to second its contention that such a court
was unnecessary and would be hopelessly difficult to establish.
The aide-mémoire did cautiously concede that international
military tribunals might be of some value if they were established by the Allied military authorities in Germany during
the occupation period. But even this was a marginal consideration for the British, who appeared cool toward any extension

of the concept of war crimes or any innovative judicial systems. The aide-mémoire put supreme weight on the statement that "the present view of His Majesty's Government is that they would wish to try by British military courts persons accused of having committed war crimes against British subjects or in British territory." [58]

The positions taken by the British in this paper did not, on their face, clash directly with the main tenets of the conspiracy/criminal-organization theory. No one in the War Department was advocating that a court be established within the UNWCC, and the American government was as anxious as the British to keep in its own hands the prosecution of war crimes that had been committed against its nationals. But the conservative tone exuded by the British message, when combined with the sharpness used in spurning the treaty-court proposal, should have been sufficient to indicate that on this issue, the British and American governments were moving in opposite directions.

The possible existence of some such problem was not entirely lost on the War Department. On 4 November Cutter informed Bernays that an informal conference ought to be held by personnel and JAG to develop recommendations for Secretary Stimson's reply to the British aide-mémoire.[59] But there was no particular note of urgency in this request, and neither Cutter nor Bernays seems to have taken it very seriously. On the eve of the three-department meeting on war crimes, they were in no mood to go looking for potential problems in messages from London. As the agenda for the 9 November meeting,[60] which presumably had been prepared by Cutter, clearly indicates, they thought that the corner had been turned, and they were about to obtain a green light to put the conspiracy/organization idea into finished form. All they wanted to do was move the proposal past the representatives of the three departments and then get on with the business of drafting a formal paper.

The agenda itself is the best evidence we have for their

view, although it reads rather like the directions for one of
those children's board games, where one uses special instruction
cards to get to the magic castle. First it called for the chairman of the meeting, John J. McCloy, to quickly summarize
the war-crimes problems, and then to turn to point 2c, which
was entitled, "Solution: Conspiracy Theory." After outlining
the main features of the plan, McCloy was supposed to take
up the question of possible courts—mixed military tribunals,
national courts, a treaty court, and so on—and then jump down
to point 3b, which read, "Solution: For proof of major conspiracy, a highly simplified treaty court." Not until the very
end of the game were the other players to be given an indication that not every war-crimes difficulty would be automatically eliminated by these proposals. The British aide-
mémoire was still not mentioned, but the last item on the
agenda did concede, under the innocuous heading of "Problems
Reserved for Further Study," that there were questions such as
the ratification of a treaty by the Senate, and the securing of
Allied approval for the American plan, which might take some
thought and extra labor. Yet even here, the main thrust was
not on caution, or reconsideration of the basic idea, but on
pushing it even further; among the items to be given additional
study was the question of "whether starting [a] war of aggression is itself a crime or whether the particular method in which
this war was started was a crime." [61] To the extent that this
agenda was representative of the prevailing feeling among the
War Department staff, it was one of supreme confidence, with
a ready eye for new worlds to conquer.

John J. McCloy was an artist at winning in Washington
committee meetings, and when the representatives of the three
departments began to assemble in his office on 9 November, he
quietly pushed aside the game-plan agenda and decided to play
it by ear.[62] He was faced by a number of officials whose names
should now be familiar to the reader: Generals Cramer (JAG)
and Henry (Personnel), Colonels Bernays and Cutter, plus the

deputy judge advocate general, Major General John Weir, and
the Deputy Chief of Personnel, Colonel R. W. Berry. In addition there was a large contingent from the navy and a sizable
group from the State Department, led by Mr. Hackworth and
the American ambassador to the European Advisory Commission, John Winant. But the State Department representatives
arrived at the meeting late, and in the interim, McCloy immediately raised the question of the British aide-mémoire
while expounding on the virtues of the conspiracy/criminal-
organization plan. Perhaps he hoped to take some of the sting
out of the issue before Hackworth and his colleagues entered
the discussion. Whatever his intentions, the approach worked.
Even after the State Department group was present, no one
contested McCloy's view that the intricacies of the UNWCC
court proposal were probably "largely responsible for the Foreign Office's adverse report." Any doubters were apparently
calmed by his observation that the British had left the door
open for mixed military tribunals.

Having skirted the most serious problem at the beginning,
the Assistant Secretary set the direction of the meeting by declaring "he understood" the American policy was to punish
not only war crimes in the conventional sense, but also "crimes
against humanity." When this statement brought forth no
negative reaction from the group, McCloy was ready to let the
reins lie slack for a bit. He commented briefly on a simplified
treaty court, and Mr. Hackworth added that a mixed military
tribunal might also be used. Both men agreed that prosecution
of the Nazi organizations was, in Mr. Hackworth's words, "desirable"; and both assumed that a trial based on the conspiracy
theory would take place, whether before a treaty court or a
mixed military tribunal.[63] A few technical legal reservations
were registered by a subordinate State Department official, but
Colonel Wiener immediately rushed forward and brushed these
aside.

With the stage thus set, McCloy asked Bernays to outline

his plan, and the colonel did so with gusto. In the course of his presentation he became so enthusiastic that he remarked the plan was intended to prosecute "the conspiracy to commit a war crime or the international war crime (if it is one) of starting the war in violation of the Kellogg-Briand Pact." Thus, even at the moment when the proponents of the scheme were trying to make it look as safe and respectable as possible, the gigantic and controversial issue of aggressive war was allowed to peep out of a proposal designed to strike at mass atrocities. But no one raised serious objections to anything, and much of the rest of the meeting was taken up with various testimonials to the conspiracy theory, as well as with pro and con arguments on the merits of a simplified treaty court and of mixed military tribunals. Near the close of the discussion, Ambassador Winant did remark that in subsequent planning little reliance should be placed on the Kellogg-Briand Pact because "people in Europe haven't much respect for it," but this statement was treated like a side comment and given no further consideration.[64]

Naturally it fell to McCloy to summarize the results of the session, and he did so in a way that reflected the confident, not to say arrogant, attitude that had taken possession of the supporters of the conspiracy/criminal-organization plan. He answered his own rhetorical question about what was "the U.S. policy on war crimes?" by declaring that "it was pretty clear (regardless of what the British view might be) that the United States feels that a broad program of prosecution is necessary as a matter of policy," and that the time had come to embody this view in a formal memorandum. The members of the group routinely gave their assent to this proposition. They further agreed that the War Department should bear the responsibility for drafting such a paper, merely "discussing it in the course of preparation informally, and to the extent deemed desirable, with the Navy and State Departments." Once completed and approved by the three departments, it would be signed by the three Secretaries and dispatched to the President. McCloy declared the paper would make clear that:

It was the State, War and Navy Departments' view that the United States was to take part in these prosecutions even where the crimes to be prosecuted were not committed against U.S. nationals. . . . that the memorandum to the President should point out the various considerations which gave support both to the treaty court idea and to the proposal to operate through mixed military tribunals. . . . the President should be informed about the conspiracy theory and its proposed application and that provision should be made for a research group to investigate the files on the alleged conspiracy's development and make sure (before prosecution on the conspiracy theory was discussed widely) that the evidence was available to prove the conspiracy.[65]

Perhaps in light of what has already been said, it is not surprising that McCloy's projections did not even stop on this side of the Atlantic. Assuming that the paper would ultimately be approved by the President, he told the group that it could then serve as the basis for American discussions with the United Kingdom, and if these talks resulted in an agreement which had "a sufficiently realistic view-point" then "it would be reasonable to suppose the U.S.S.R. would be prepared to acquiesce." [66] Considering there were already indications available that the Soviets might be more inclined to a grandiose conspiracy/criminal-organization trial than the British would be, this was a rather peculiar diplomatic scenario. But none of the seventeen representatives present voiced the slightest demur or raised a doubt about any of the points made by McCloy in his long and weighty summary of the results of the meeting. Therefore, McCloy, Bernays, and their associates had every right to come away from the Assistant Secretary's office that day believing they had scored a complete victory and had been given a mandate to prepare a policy paper whose acceptance was virtually assured in advance.

Bernays, perhaps assisted by Cutter, must have begun work

almost immediately. The five-page paper was drafted in two days and then put in final form and circulated to the relevant officials, within and without the War Department, two days later. The paper, entitled "Memorandum for the President from the Secretaries of State, War and Navy," began by citing statements and declarations of United Nations leaders (the references came from the paper prepared by the American Jewish Conference). It indicated the Allies had committed themselves to a broad program of punishing war crimes. It then tried to show that implementing these measures would not be easy due to the enormous scale of Nazi atrocities and because prewar actions and persecutions of Axis nationals were not customarily considered war crimes. At this point the memorandum brought forth the conspiracy theory, summarizing its major features and suggesting that it offered a solution to the atrocity problem. The door was left open for a subsequent decision on whether aggressive war should be added as an element in the conspiracy. The crucial sentences declared that the "outrages" were "the results of a purposeful and systematic pattern repeated by them [that is, the Nazi leaders] to the end of *achieving world domination*." [67] [Italics added]

Turning to the question of procedure, the memorandum laid out the system whereby the Nazi leaders, as individuals and as representative defendants for the organizations, would be judged in an international trial. Without indicating the possible difficulty in transferring a finding by this tribunal to American courts, the memorandum simply asserted that the rulings would be applied to the members of "criminal" organizations in the courts of the several United Nations. But regarding the importance of a judicial proceeding, and the nature of the court before which it should take place, the memorandum was not so reticent. It stressed that a trial was essential, primarily because it would produce a record that would convince future generations of the monstrous evil that was Nazism. While not explaining the considerations upon which this decision was based, the memorandum also strongly recommended that a simplified treaty court would be preferable to any other kind of tribunal. In an anticlimactic and cautious final clause, the paper declared the conspiracy-trial system would not preclude the routine prosecution of any individual who had been guilty of committing a war crime against an American national.

Again, it is not difficult to point to serious shortcomings in this memorandum. The issue of aggressive war was not squarely confronted, and the problems inherent in transferring a conspiracy ruling from an international court to an American civil or military court were not dealt with at all. Furthermore, no concessions had been made regarding the doubts about a treaty court expressed by Mr. Hackworth (despite McCloy's assurance that there would be), and the memorandum failed to make any reference to the possibility of using mixed military tribunals. This point lapped over onto the memorandum's most noteworthy deficiency: It did not even mention the British aide-mémoire or the various indications received in Washington that the London government had no sympathy for a treaty court or an innovative war-crimes policy.

Since the purpose of this paper was not only to present the case for the conspiracy/criminal-organization proposal, but also to provide guidance for the three Secretaries and the President on sensitive points in the war-crimes problem, these were serious omissions. Nonetheless, placing the primary emphasis on these failings would be to miss the importance of the memorandum of 11 November as a milestone on the road to Nuremberg. Prior to the memorandum's appearance, Bernays's idea had been merely a theory without distinct form or substance, wafting in and out of the policy discussions taking place in the Pentagon and elsewhere in Washington. As an idea it might be found agreeable or promising in principle, but there was no possibility that it could either be carefully examined or ultimately given formal approval. But once the draft of 11 November appeared, all this changed. With a definite proposal now on the table, the fate of the Bernays plan would be decided in a scramble of drafts and counterdrafts, revisions and amendments, which would spread over three of the highest departments of the American government and, in the closing weeks of 1944, would move on to the White House itself.

CHAPTER 3

MARCHING TO
NOWHERE

Everyone makes the most elaborate plans, and counter-plans (on paper), how to run different parts of the world. It all turns out in practice, of course, quite different.[1]

Sir Alexander Cadogan

Henry Stimson was not called upon to give his formal approval to the November 11 war-crimes draft immediately; the various War Department branches first needed to have their say regarding it. But in the third week of November, the Secretary enthusiastically threw himself into the task of convincing important officials that the conspiracy idea was the right approach for dealing with the major German war criminals. Stimson passionately believed that conspiracy prosecution was an appropriate and effective way to strike at complicated legal and political obstacles facing the government. He had made one of his first marks in public life, while a federal prosecutor under Teddy Roosevelt, when he convicted the sugar trust for conspiring to defraud the government of required duty payments. By making holes in the port scales, the sugar trust had managed to have its imported sugar underweighed, and the tariff duty was consequently lower.[2] Stimson succeeded in proving there had been a criminal conspiracy stretching from the top of the sugar trust to the bottom, and that this conspiracy had produced the famous "17 holes" in the port scales.

Now in November 1944, Stimson put this lesson before some of his most powerful colleagues and associates, endeavoring to persuade them that there were obvious and useful analogies between the case of the "17 holes" and a trial of the chief Nazi war criminals. On the nineteenth Stimson advanced this argument in a talk with the British ambassador, Lord Halifax, and John Maynard Keynes (the latter in Washington as part of the British delegation to the Dumbarton Oaks Conference). Two days later (21 November) the Secretary laid out much the same case for President Roosevelt. When speaking with the British officials, Stimson emphasized that the beauty of conspiracy prosecution was the flexibility of evidence allowed; it could produce "a full and public record of the whole evil system of Nazism." [3] Similarly, in his talk with the President, Stimson stressed that a great conspiracy trial of the Nazi leaders, like that used in the case of the "17 holes," "with all of the actors brought in from the top to the bottom would be the best way to try it and would give us a record and also a trial which would certainly persuade any onlooker of the evil of the Nazi system." [4]

The two British officials and the President seem to have been impressed with the political and propaganda benefits that the documentation of such a comprehensive court proceeding might engender. Stimson quoted John Maynard Keynes to the effect that it was "vitally important to make such a record of the great evil." [5] Apparently Keynes even went so far as to concede that "individual executions of the leaders" [6] of Hitler's Reich would not produce such a record. But as representatives of a government that was as yet undecided but wary of a great trial and inclined toward summary execution, both Keynes and Halifax met Stimson's urgings with a generous measure of circumspection and silence.

At least on the surface, Stimson's idea received a warmer reception from the President; the Secretary's diary declares not only that Mr. Roosevelt was "greatly interested" in the proposal, but that he had given "his very frank approval" to it.[7] A number of factors suggest, however, that one should be cautious about accepting these indications of presidential enthusiasm at face value. Stimson's own diary entries show he had suffered from the harsh criticisms that the President had leveled at him during the struggle over the Morgenthau plan, and he had perhaps become excessively appreciative of any sign of approval or favor from Mr. Roosevelt.[8] Significantly, the Secretary ended the entry on his 21 November talk with the President by happily noting he had not been criticized for his advocacy of a conspiracy prosecution; rather, during the whole discussion Mr. Roosevelt had been "very nice about it." [9] Obviously it was in the President's interest to smooth any lingering hurt feelings of his powerful Secretary of War. With the Morgenthau plan dead, it cost him nothing to give a sympathetic hearing to a proposal that might offer a way to deal effectively with part of the German occupation problem. The election crisis was past, Mr. Roosevelt had won a fourth term, and he could now safely indulge his "tough mood" [10] regarding the Germans by giving a hearing to every idea that recommended punitive policies for postwar Germany.

Furthermore, Franklin Roosevelt shared the common American characteristic of viewing many political and social processes in conspiratorial terms. While the British tend to see conspiracy only as a legal procedural device, Americans are more inclined to hold that conspiracies are of major causal importance in the processes of social change. Not only is this true of the radical Right—which easily finds alleged plots by Communists, blacks, or Jews at the root of every conceivable social problem—but the power of conspiratorial thinking cuts across the whole social and political spectrum of American life. Appeals to the necessity of punishing and controlling the conspiratorial plottings of big business—the malefactors of great wealth—are the hard currency of American progressive politics, and Franklin Roosevelt was as well steeped in that tradition as any chief executive in recent memory. Rarely did he speak at any length about his political opponents, whether within the narrow limits of partisan politics or in the broader field of opposition to the New Deal and his foreign and wartime policies, without some hint or suggestion being dropped that he was opposed by dark forces who were trying to work their conspiratorial will against the best interests of the American people. Conspiratorial explanations surely fitted neatly into his thought, and in this connection it is important to remember that in August 1944, it was Roosevelt himself who first suggested the possibility of charging the Nazi leaders with conspiracy to commit murder as a means of forcing neutral governments to deny political asylum to Hitler and his aides.[11]

Even so, this still falls far short of demonstrating that in November 1944, Franklin Roosevelt had given his complete or "frank approval" to a conspiracy trial of the top Nazis. Interested he surely was, and probably also sympathetic. Although gradually losing his strength, he nevertheless intended to play his cards with caution. In the course of the fall it had become clear that a winter, spring, and perhaps even another summer campaign would be required to beat Hitler's Third Reich to the ground, and there was thus no compelling reason to make a quick decision on the fate of postwar Germany. Whether sick or well, Roosevelt had not lost his awareness of how things were done in Washington, and he appreciated that when speed was not essential, there were benefits to be reaped from allowing a proposal to be tested in the bureaucratic maze of the American capital. Cabinet members differed in economic and ideological persuasion, and every department of government was internally divided into factions and cliques, which had formed not only along the lines of principle and technical specialization, but also around personal differences.[12] A slow-moving bureaucracy could be counted on to prevent any hasty action, and with every Washington office crammed to the ceiling with lawyers, it was a foregone conclusion that all remotely relevant precedents would be cited, and every possible

adverse legal consequence registered, before anything as ambitious as an international conspiracy-trial plan could find its
way up to the President's desk.

Therefore, as long as it was unnecessary for him to actively
push the proposal, Franklin Roosevelt found no difficulty in
standing back to see if Henry Stimson's ideas could find their
way through the sticky wickets of his own, and his colleagues',
departments. If the conspiracy plan survived all of this, it would
probably be safe and sound and could be expected to work
reasonably well. For his part, it was also easy for Stimson to receive the President's vaguely encouraging remarks with a light
heart. He was not the one who would have to bear the
burden of actually trying to secure the plan's approval.
McCloy, Bernays, and Cutter would have to do the dirty
work; and although McCloy was a tough competitor, probably
none of the three fully grasped the formidable nature of the
task they faced. This was probably merciful, because in November and December 1944, they would spend endless days revising, retreating, regrouping, and redrafting, far removed from
the lofty heights where a President and a Secretary of War glibly
make policy pronouncements and resolve problems with a few
words and waves of the hand.

From the moment they began to push the 11 November war-
crimes prosecution plan forward, nothing seemed to go well for
McCloy and his aides. After extensive preparation, McCloy had
a memorandum prepared on 18 November that detailed how
the conspiracy/criminal-organization approach should be incorporated into the Joint Chiefs of Staff's basic occupational directive for Germany (JCS 1067). No one actually rejected this
memorandum, nor was it violently attacked, but it failed to
find any warm support. In fact, nothing much happened to it,
and throughout December McCloy kept trying fruitlessly to
maneuver it through the lowest level offices and committees of
the Pentagon.[13]

The first formal response to the 11 November memorandum
that reached McCloy's office from another department was not

totally negative, but it was far from positive. Speaking for the
navy, Mr. R. Keith Kane, a special assistant to Secretary Forrestal, suggested that the question of traditional war crimes
should be separated from the issues surrounding other German
atrocities, and the latter could then be left exclusively to the
State Department.[14] Consequently, Mr. Kane declared that
the memorandum of 11 November should not be sent to the
President with the signatures of the three department Secretaries (War, Navy, and State); but he did allow that the conspiracy trial idea might merit further study by the War and Navy
Departments, if it was to be applied solely to recognized violations of the rules of war. This position was a reasonable one
from the Navy Department's point of view because that department would have no occupational role to play in Germany,
and in any event it had never exercised the influence on broad
wartime policy that the War Department had enjoyed. But
for McCloy and his aides, Kane's letter could have posed a
serious threat to the prospects of the conspiracy/criminal-
organization plan. To trim the plan's application back to traditional war crimes would be to forgo its main purpose—use of
a judicial procedure to punish crimes against humanity in a way
that would break the back of Nazism and make Germany
less dangerous in the future. Therefore, McCloy, Bernays, and
Cutter turned a blind eye to the most threatening features of
Mr. Kane's letter and concluded that he was merely saying the
Navy was not interested in any aspect of the problem except
for traditional war crimes.[15] Having convinced themselves
that this was so, they proceeded henceforth to ignore that department and went ahead to see if they could make the con-
spiracy/criminal-organization plan wash as a joint War and
State Department proposal.

They had some grounds for optimism on this score, because
when the State Department's response to the 11 November
draft arrived in McCloy's office on 16 November, in the form
of a letter from Mr. Hackworth, it was generally positive.[16]
Hackworth accepted the main points of the draft and devoted

most of his letter to suggestions for minor rewordings, which he thought would make the paper more precise and more acceptable to the president. Near the end of his letter, however, Mr. Hackworth drew attention to two features that he felt posed serious problems. In Hackworth's view the draft contained a fundamental confusion, if not a contradiction, on the nature of the conspiracy it sought to punish. At one point the memorandum stated that the conspiracy involved "the commission of atrocities which the United Nations have pledged themselves to punish" [17] and at another point it declared that the Allies would prosecute a conspiracy aimed "at world domination." Mr. Hackworth quite rightly indicated that the conspiratorial focus in these two statements was not identical, and this confusion was especially important because, as he noted, "a conspiracy for world domination could hardly be denominated a crime." Essentially Mr. Hackworth had asked whether the main focus of the prosecution should be on crimes against humanity or on aggressive war, but that question would plague the planners and Nuremberg prosecutors until the final days of the trial.

Mr. Hackworth's second serious criticism of the memorandum touched on an issue that pointed to more immediate difficulties. The 11 November draft had called for an international court to be established by treaty. Although not directly raising the specter of the problems such a treaty might encounter in the U.S. Senate—everyone involved understood in light of Woodrow Wilson's experience that this might be a high hurdle to cross—Hackworth brought forth two strong arguments against the treaty approach. First he declared the President must be informed that the British government opposed establishing a war-crimes court on the basis of a treaty. Mr. Hackworth had concluded, quite rightly as it turned out, that the British aide-mémoire of 30 October, which had rejected a UNWCC treaty court, indicated a general British hostility to proceeding against war crimes through a treaty. Mr. Hackworth's second objection to the treaty provision arose from the contention that it would be possible to base the court on a treaty and at the same time develop the whole program with enough secrecy to avoid German reprisals against Allied prisoners of war. Hackworth dismissed such hopes as totally unrealistic; no general treaty could be negotiated in full secrecy, and the ratification process, especially in the United States, put all hope of secrecy out of the question. He therefore suggested to McCloy, as politely as possible, that it would be politically wise to have a "mixed military tribunal" [18] hear the case, and thereby avoid all the difficulties associated with drafting, negotiating, and ratifying an international treaty.

On balance, Mr. Hackworth's criticisms were so reasonable, and were advanced in such a conciliatory form, that they alone should not have occasioned much concern for McCloy and his aides. But when Hackworth's letter was placed alongside another significant commentary on the conspiracy/criminal-organization plan, the Assistant Secretary of War had legitimate grounds for worry. After weeks of delay, the judge advocate general, Major General Myron Cramer, had finally addressed a memorandum to McCloy on 22 November, giving his office's appraisal of the *original* paper that Bernays had written.[19] (Cramer's comments were not addressed to the 11 November draft, but to the introductory paper that Bernays had prepared on 15 September.) The judge advocate general's office was two months in arrears, and its foot dragging would be a continuing source of controversy and confusion in the months to come. Most of Cramer's letter repeated what he had been saying since early September—namely that there should be a trial rather than summary execution of the top Nazis—but in addition, with one fundamental qualification, he gave an indirect and cautious endorsement to the conspiracy/criminal-organization approach. Cramer's significant reservation expressed the conviction—already raised earlier by JAG lawyers—that under prevailing American law, no civil or military court could accept the findings of another court, whether national or international, as binding upon it. This meant in practice that the streamlined secondary trials Bernays had envisioned cranking out rapid convictions of criminal-organization members could not, as things stood, take place before American civil or military courts.

According to Cramer's opinion, and he was the chief legal officer of the United States Army, existing law would necessitate that in every secondary proceeding held in an American court, the whole record of the major court process would have to be put into evidence, thereby laying the basis for great delay and endless legal challenges by the defense. The way out of this difficulty, in Cramer's opinion, was to insert provisions into the planned international treaty declaring that the transfer of the finding of the major court to the lower courts of all the Allied nations was legal. Then when the U.S. Senate ratified the treaty, the transfer provision would have the effect of constitutional law and would be binding on lower courts. Cramer granted that this amounted to an extreme step, one that went "beyond anything now known in our criminal law," but he also felt it was not "repugnant to natural justice." [20] In any case, without such a provision, the conspiracy/criminal-organization system envisioned by Bernays appeared to be legally impossible.

In light of the diametrically opposed views of Cramer and Hackworth on the question of a treaty court, as well as a tidy list of lesser points requiring changes or rewrites, the time had definitely come for a revision of the 11 November paper. On 23 November, Bernays and Cutter completed a substantial redraft, and on 27 and 29 November, modest additional alterations were made.[21] Aside from minor readjustments and rephrasings, the major changes introduced into the paper concerned the focus of the conspiracy and the treaty-court problem. Instead of pointing toward twin conspiracies, one to commit atrocities and the other to dominate the world, the revised draft sought to weave the two together by claiming the Nazis had conspired to:

achieve domination of other nations and peoples by deliberative violation of the rules of war as they have been accepted and adhered to by the world, the violation of treaties and international conventions and customs, and mass extermination of peoples.[22]

Although the language and form of expression employed in this passage were far from crystal clear, the intent of the authors is obvious. They sought to keep the primary focus of the conspiracy charge on war crimes and atrocities, while leaving the door ajar for the possible inclusion of additional charges related to a war of aggression. That this was their purpose is revealed by an additional passage, added midway through the paper, which asserted that the conspiracy/criminal-organization prosecution system would not only "afford a fair trial to those charged with atrocities," but would also "submit to the judgment of an appropriate tribunal the conduct of the Nazis in bringing about and carrying on the war." Thus step by step, the idea of prosecuting a conspiracy to wage an aggressive war was being worked into the basic trial plan.

Important though this development was, the most extensive revisions inserted into the late November drafts were aimed at easing the difficulties associated with the use of a treaty court. The new formulation made clear that the judgment handed down by the court of the major trial would be binding on all secondary courts, as Cramer had suggested. The 23 November draft declared that the first court proceeding would "determine the facts of the conspiracy in a manner which would thereafter be treated as establishing those facts in proceedings against the individuals, groups and organizations dealt with in the judgment and against the members of any such organizations." All that the courts in secondary trials would need to do was identify the members of such organizations, "appraise the degree of participation of each person in the conspiracy," and then set appropriate punishment.[23] Given this bald declaration of the transferability of a judgment from one court to another, the new draft had little choice but to recommend that a treaty basis for the trial system be established. Consequently, Mr.

Hackworth could only be granted a few palliatives rather than any important changes of substance.

However, within these limits Cutter and Bernays did their best to give something to the State Department legal specialist. In a section of the memorandum intended to provide the President with a balanced picture, they mentioned all the objections to a treaty court that Hackworth had raised, plus the possibility that negotiation and ratification of a treaty might produce long delays. The two colonels also acknowledged that under certain circumstances a trial system might be established without a treaty through an "executive agreement on the governmental level or by agreements between United Nations military commanders," and in a show of great restraint they did not note that using an executive or military agreement might create problems in transferring a judgment to secondary courts. Yet after a routine pause had been made at all these bases, the memorandum still returned to make the same recommendation: The United States government should aim at the creation of a treaty court.[24]

Significantly, this revision revealed that when McCloy and his associates had to choose between criticism from inside the War Department in the person of General Cramer, and criticism from outside the department in the person of Mr. Hackworth, they made an in-house decision and came down on the side of General Cramer. Put in another, but related, way, they were more inclined to free the memorandum from the kind of legal attack made by General Cramer than they were to heed Mr. Hackworth's advice that, practically speaking, the safest course would be the elimination of a treaty court, which was likely to produce political trouble. Even though the advocates of the conspiracy/criminal-organization plan ran into serious difficulty almost immediately after they leaned toward Cramer rather than Hackworth, it is still not reasonable to say with historical hindsight that they merely made the wrong decision. So many critics—inside and outside the War Department, armed with both legal and practical political objections—were lying in wait

that there really was no simple, and safe, way to turn in late
November 1944.

McCloy made a serious error that compounded the difficulty,
however, by failing to consolidate his position once the basic
decision had been made. Prudence suggested a pause at this
juncture to elicit formal agreement for the late November draft
from the various War Department factions and interest groups,
especially from JAG. If this had been done successfully, it should
then have been possible to secure a declaration from Secretary
Stimson that the conspiracy/criminal-organization plan was the
established war-crimes policy of the War Department. With his
back thus secured, McCloy would have been in a much stronger
position to gain agreement for the plan from other departments.
But this meant running the draft back through the ponderous
and pettifogging machinery of JAG, which had taken two
months to grind out an opinion on Bernays's original short paper of 15 September. McCloy apparently could not bring himself
to face all this again, and he decided instead to immediately
take his chances with the other departments. On 4 December
copies of the revised draft were sent to Mr. Hackworth, Attorney
General Francis Biddle, and Harry Hopkins at the White
House.[25]

By circulating the revision of the conspiracy/criminal-organi-
zation plan outside the War Department in early December,
McCloy managed to combine the worst of both worlds. The
content of the document—especially the treaty-court provisions—were sure to produce criticism from other departments.
Without the formal approval of JAG or a clear declaration that
the plan was War Department policy, there was nothing to
prevent opposition or controversy that developed outside from
flooding back into the department and setting off a war-crimes
policy conflict. As if this was not serious enough, a series of new
high-level executive appointments, made in the course of December, increased the difficulty of obtaining interdepartmental
support for the plan.

Apparently the President had concluded that the White

House should play some role in the development of war-crimes policy even though Mr. Roosevelt himself was unwilling to intervene directly; and Harry Hopkins, overworked and ailing, was unable to keep a firm grip on this complex problem. Characteristically, in an administration that relished divided authority and overlapping jurisdictions, the President did not meet the issue by appointing one White House official to oversee war-crimes policy. Instead he took the matter out of Hopkins's hands and gave it to two other special assistants, Judge Samuel I. Rosenman and Ambassador Joseph E. Davies. The appointment of Rosenman turned out to be a strong plus for McCloy and the other advocates of the conspiracy/criminal-organization proposal. The judge was one of FDR's favorite speech writers, his special legal counsel, and although not one of Roosevelt's most intimate cronies—he did not belong to the cufflinks club *—he was definitely part of the inner circle of White House staff members.[26] Rosenman was also a very hard worker, and a man possessed of the skills required for a top White House official—he had the right contacts and he knew how to get things done.

Within days of joining the ranks of those charged with overseeing the development of war-crimes policy, Rosenman met with McCloy, Cutter, and Bernays, and in the course of those sessions, he became an enthusiastic convert to the proposition that a trial based on a conspiracy/criminal-organization approach should be the bedrock of the American war-crimes program. In future months, some of the original inner group of war-crimes planners would feel that Rosenman was rather too inclined to make minor revisions; and on critical occasions, he was too willing to compromise on basic elements of the plan when faced with strong opposition. But from December 1944 until the appointment of Robert Jackson as chief U.S. war-crimes prosecutor in May 1945, Rosenman was the senior official in the American government who labored most assidu-

* The old boys group that had been with FDR from the earliest days of his political career.

ously in the cause of what came to be called the Nuremberg trial plan.

Mr. Roosevelt's second appointee as a White House trouble-shooter on war-crimes problems, Ambassador Joseph E. Davies of *Mission to Moscow* fame, was a less happy choice, not only for McCloy and his staff, but for all those seeking to hammer out a clear and effective U.S. policy on war crimes. Although Mr. Davies did not immediately insert himself into the war-crimes policy controversies, he would before long, and his very presence increased the complexities and uncertainties. Opinionated and freewheeling, with more than a touch of flamboyance, Davies had boundless confidence in his own judgment and in his ability to determine the wishes and meet the needs of foreign governments, especially those of Great Britain and the Soviet Union. A lawyer and financier with long service in the Democratic party and reasonably close to President Roosevelt, he enjoyed friendly, if rather presumptuous, relationships with Churchill and Stalin. Davies was Washington's best-known, and probably most naive, wartime advocate of intimacy with Soviet Russia. He was also impatient with the regular run of Washington officials, contemptuous of the unimaginative, and thus more successful in dramatizing the positions he favored than in actually pushing them along until they became part of official American policy.[27]

The manner in which Davies became involved with the war-crimes question is a classic, if slightly confused, example of the unorthodox and slapdash way in which he operated. In Davies's own account of the selection process, Acting Secretary of State Stettinius approached him on 16 November 1944 with the suggestion that he make a trip to London, and perhaps to Moscow and Paris as well, in order to look into war-crimes problems, because, as Davies quoted Stettinius, the question was "all messed up." [28] The inclusion of this short slang phrase, carefully bracketed by quotation marks in a summary of Davies notes, is typical of the condescending way he dismissed officials whom he considered to be slow-witted. But one must be careful in accepting at face value any statement contained in the ambassador's papers. In the postwar period, Davies rewrote many of his diary entries and notes to make them coincide with the enhanced portrait of himself he wished to present in the memoirs that he began, but never finished.[29] Therefore this short diary passage (perhaps doctored), with its rather snide jab at Stettinius, is itself a signpost pointing toward the ambassador's reputation for arrogance and marginal reliability.

When we turn to Stettinius's own account of the affair, we encounter another rather unpleasant feature of the ambassador's demeanor and reputation. Nothing approximating Davies's version shows up in a memorandum that was sent to the President at the time by the Assistant Secretary of State.[30] In fact, it appears from this source that it was not Stettinius, but the ambassador who initiated the contact; and Davies did so because (in Stettinius's words) "he had not been to England during the war" and had "a desire to take a trip there for a short period." [31] Now it would be both imprudent and unfair to conclude from this that Mr. Davies involved himself in the war-crimes question merely because he wanted to obtain a free plane ticket to England or because his ego demanded the satisfaction of being sent on another special mission. As will be indicated shortly, Mr. Davies had not strayed far afield when he opined that Edward Stettinius lacked a towering mind, and it may well be that the Assistant Secretary's account of what transpired is garbled. But it is difficult to believe that even Stettinius would have contended that a highly regarded diplomat such as, say, Joseph Grew or George Kennan, would have made the kind of remark he attributed to Davies.

What we are confronting here—at the very least—is an instance of the reputation for frivolous and manipulative behavior that Washington officialdom ascribed to Davies, and it makes little difference whether the Davies or Stettinius account is closest to what actually happened. The two sources combine to suggest that the ambassador was a dynamic maverick who would be unwilling to stay within narrow bureaucratic limits and was unable to exercise much tact. As such, he was magnificently unsuited for any post of importance related to such a complicated and sensitive problem as war crimes.

Yet when, on 11 December,[32] Ambassador Davies received President Roosevelt's authorization to carry out a special mission to review the war-crimes question, this did not exhaust the list of new appointments that greatly complicated the effort to gain approval for the conspiracy/criminal-organization plan. For many months, Cordell Hull had been so gravely ill that he had often been unable to function as Secretary of State; and throughout the fall of 1944, although Stettinius had periodically been pushed into the breach as Acting Secretary, the department definitely lacked strong leadership and clear direction. On 1 December 1944, Roosevelt was finally forced to act, accepting Hull's resignation and appointing Stettinius as permanent Secretary of State. The only significant consequence of this action, however, was that it formally sanctified the weakness in the Department of State and left little hope that the situation would be rectified in the immediate future. Stettinius was a hesitant and vacillating leader with little experience in foreign affairs, and his tenure as secretary could not bring a revival of the Department's influence and power. Another of the businessmen whom Roosevelt had drawn into the government under the banner of patriotic service during a time of international crisis, Stettinius was a friendly man without a base of power on Capitol Hill or among New Deal Democrats. In a wartime Washington dominated by strong and aggressive personalities, the new Secretary of State seemed as out of place as a goldfish in a tank of barracudas. To be considered soft and hesitant in such a setting was to be devoured or transformed into a powerless nonentity. Indicative of the fate that awaited the new Secretary, who had by this time spent four years in Washington holding various State Department posts, was an offhand remark by Henry Morgenthau at a January 1945 Treasury conference, when he referred to Stettinius as, "what's his name."[33]

Whether under Hull or Stettinius, the State Department had

become a center of political weakness. This fact, combined with the confusing dual appointments of Rosenman and Davies, not only dimmed the prospects for a rapid acceptance of the conspiracy/criminal-organization plan, it also meant that if any element of the plan raised strong foreign-policy complications, the State Department would be unable to take the lead in resolving the difficulty. In late November just such a bitter controversy did erupt when the question of aggressive war burst out into the open. The issue first became visible inside the State Department's realm of diplomatic discourse, but due to the department's leaderless drift, the aggressive-war question very quickly slipped into the territory of the War Department, where controversies over war-crimes matters cut much deeper.

As had happened in similar situations in the past, it was an action of the UNWCC that compelled the American government to consider the question of whether preparing or waging a war of aggression was a crime punishable under international law. A proposal had been before the commission for months, urging the governments of the United Nations to declare that aggressive war was a crime, and that the Nazi leaders would be punished for their part in the aggressive invasions of European countries between 1938 and 1941. During the fall of 1944, the proposal was hotly debated in a subcommittee of the commission, but a final vote had been deferred until the representatives of the various Allied nations obtained instructions from their home governments. In early November, the American member of the commission, Mr. Herbert Pell, cabled Washington for instructions, and on 15 November, the virtually headless State Department turned to the War Department and asked for guidance in instructing Pell.[34]

When this query reached McCloy's office, he referred it to G-1 for an opinion. G-1 immediately concluded that Pell should be instructed to stall, because common sense indicated it was better to get the conspiracy/criminal-organization plan adopted before tackling the imflammable aggressive-war question. McCloy endorsed the G-1 position, on 24 November so advised Secretary Stimson, and forwarded to him a draft reply to be signed and sent on to the Secretary of State. The reply, which was signed by Stimson and sent to State on 27 November, urged that Pell be instructed to employ every effort to put off a vote by the commission, "because this Government is not at present prepared to express an opinion on this matter." [35] As the War Department letter indicated, delay was necessary since "the question involves not only the preparation and launching of an aggressive war, but also the extent to which the Axis powers planned to conduct their belligerent operations by means and methods in violation of the laws of war." This line of continuity in turn linked the aggressive-war question to the conspiracy/criminal-organization proposal, and as Stimson's letter to the Secretary of State stressed, that issue was "pending in your Department and mine."

Some delay was essential, but the War Department did not propose that the whole aggressive-war question be permanently shelved. If some breathing space could be secured, Stimson wanted to make use of it to give the State Department and the judge advocate general's office an opportunity to investigate whether the planning and waging of aggressive war could be prosecuted as crimes. If anyone harbored doubts that the Secretary of War himself was deeply interested in the whole question, they should surely have been set right by a handwritten note that Stimson added to the bottom of the letter, which read:

I regard this matter as so important, that I request an opportunity for the expression of my personal views by the Sec'y or in his absence the acting Sec'y.

                                                              H.L.S.[36]

Even without this sentence, a minimum of political acumen was necessary to recognize that Stimson's heart and soul were involved in the aggressive-war question. He was a passionate believer in the proposition that only the rule of law, upheld by the great powers, could limit or end aggressive war. As an old progressive, he held firmly to the view that the force of an aroused public opinion was essential to compel governments to abide by any moral strictures or international agreements that banned aggression. It was Stimson, after all, who in 1931 had advanced the doctrine that nonrecognition of Japan's seizure of Manchuria would help to undercut the political benefits Tokyo hoped to garner from her conquest. Even after witnessing ruthless Axis expansion and wars from 1931 to 1944, he had lost none of his belief that somehow the positive power of the public conscience could limit or stop aggression. To Stimson's mind, the world's people were never so awake to the horror and danger of war as they were in the closing phase of World War II; with the record of Nazi brutality and aggression there for all to see, this was the best possible moment to prepare international measures that would rid the world of aggression.

Once the aggressive-war issue had been raised in November 1944, Henry Stimson's sympathetic concern was likely to produce some discussion of the matter both inside and outside the War Department. Since the criminal prosecution of the Nazi leaders for planning and waging aggressive war touched on many controversial legal and political considerations, such discussion could easily degenerate into the kind of heated and angry exchanges that John J. McCloy had hoped to avoid. All that was necessary to set off a serious quarrel over war crimes within the War Department in late November was for some official, one who could command a hearing, to come out strongly in favor of aggressive-war prosecution.

On November 28, the lightning rod made its appearance in the person of Colonel William C. Chanler, deputy chief of the War Department's civil affairs division. Chanler's official duties had a natural connection to the war-crimes question and his position carried some clout, but the colonel was far more important than a simple deputy division chief. In civilian life he was one of Stimson's legal protégés, his Long Island neighbor, a member of Stimson's law firm (Winthrop, Stimson, Putnam and Roberts), and a close personal friend.

Mr. Stimson was a man who liked to stand firmly on the rules of protocol and official address. When sending memoranda to his closest associates, he might on occasion use a salutation such as "Dear Jack" for the Assistant Secretary of War, but he was very careful to address all military officers, even reserve officers, by their proper rank. He himself liked to be addressed as colonel in recognition of his military service during the First World War. Perhaps here and there exceptions occurred, but the broad sweep of his official correspondence indicates that he tried conscientiously to keep his relations with every military officer, from lowly staff captains up to General Marshall himself, within the established forms of rank and position. With every officer, that is, except Colonel Chanler, who is routinely referred to as "Willi" or "Willi Chanler" in the Secretary of War's memoranda and in his diary.[37]

In late November and early December, "Willi Chanler" prepared two memoranda on war-crimes problems, which, predictably, produced considerable stir among War Department officials. The shorter of the two, which Chanler sent to McCloy on 1 December, need not detain us long,[38] although it brought forth energetic rebuttals from McCloy and Bernays.[39] Chanler had misunderstood a basic tenet of the conspiracy/criminal-organization plan, assuming that it was intended to prosecute prewar persecutions as if they were traditional war crimes. Believing this was unnecessarily innovative, Chanler recommended that occupation courts be allowed to deal with the problem instead. Bernays and McCloy both rushed forward to set the deputy division chief straight, and in the process McCloy declared that prewar atrocities would be fitted into a broader conspiracy charge because Hitler's "mass extermination of the Jews was only one of a number of military measures" used by the Nazis to carry out their operations in a "most economic manner."[40] To imply that large-scale exterminations had occurred before the outbreak of the war, and

to characterize the *Endlösung* (Final Solution) as an eco-
nomical "military measure," were so historically inaccurate
as to be near caricature. But this kind of tunnel vision was
endemic to the approach used in the conspiracy/criminal-
organization plan and as it turned out, Chanler was willing to
go along with it. He graciously acknowledged his error, re-
canted, and henceforth toiled in the ranks of those committed
to the implementation of the plan.[41]

This quick switch was easy for Chanler to make, because
for him the question of prewar persecutions was merely an interesting side issue. The matter which lay close to his heart was
the need to discover some method whereby the trial of the
Nazi leaders would produce a judicial precedent that helped
to ban the preparation and waging of aggressive war. His major
memorandum, entitled "Can Hitler and the Nazi leadership be
punished for their Acts of Lawless Aggression, thus Implementing the Kellogg Pact and Outlawing War of Aggression?" was
"informally" sent to Henry Stimson on 28 November. Stimson
immediately commented that although it was "a little in advance of the progress of international thought" it was so "interesting" and "thought provoking" that McCloy should send
copies to all those War Department officials concerned with the
war-crimes question. With that, the fat could not be kept
from the fire.[42]

The central argument of Chanler's memorandum, copies of
which were wending their way through the Pentagon by 30
November, was that the Kellogg-Briand Pact, or Pact of Paris
(1928), in which over sixty nations renounced war "as an instrument of national policy," had in fact produced a fundamental change in the legality of war. Chanler did not contend
that the pact itself made launching a war a crime; he knew most
legal authorities held that since the agreement had not established any sanctions or penalties for those launching a war, the
pact had not, on its face, made the initiation of war criminally
punishable. What Chanler did assert, however, was that once
the pact was signed, those who initiated war in violation of the

agreement lost their rights as lawful belligerents in their relations with neutral governments. In support of that position he
cited a resolution of the International Law Association to that
effect made in Budapest in 1934 and a statement by Henry
Stimson to the House Foreign Affairs Committee in 1941. At
that time the Secretary of War brought forth this argument to
justify the proposition that neutral America had a legal right
to send lend-lease aid to Britain.

Building on this foundation, Chanler went a step further. On
the basis of common sense he claimed that if an aggressor state
had lost its legal right as a belligerent in relation to neutrals, it
surely had also lost the protections of legal belligerency in regard to the country, or countries, it had attacked. "If this is so,"
Chanler wrote, then when the "armed forces of a signatory
state" invade "a neighboring signatory state," they "stand on
no better footing than a band of guerrillas who under established International Law are not entitled to be treated as lawful belligerents." [43] The people killed in such actions would
then not be casualties in a legal military action, but simply
innocent murder victims. And if aggressor armies were not lawful belligerents, they forfeited all the customary shields of
military-belligerent status; as killing bands outside the law,
they were subject to prosecution under the domestic statutes
of the countries where the killings had occurred.

Therefore Chanler proposed that after the war ended, one or
two of the countries that Nazi Germany had invaded—he suggested Poland or Czechoslovakia, the latter a poor choice because no armed clash had occurred there—should demand
"that Hitler and his associates be delivered to them for trial"
on the grounds that they had ordered forces to enter these
countries to kill citizens, destroy property, and so on, "in violation of the domestic law of the countries invaded." Who-
ever, at that moment, actually held Hitler and "his associates"
in their custody would then be forced to decide whether or
not to turn them over to the Czechs and Poles. Chanler believed that to make that decision, some court, perhaps an ad

hoc United Nations tribunal, would have to "hold hearings in the nature of an extradition procedure," and that in such hearings the Czechs and Poles would successfully show that Nazi Germany had breached the Paris Pact and was consequently not a lawful belligerent. What was to happen at this point—who would really put Hitler on trial, and what the charges would be—was soon lost amid much vague hypothesizing about United Nations courts and conspiracy trials.

The colonel was actually not much interested in the trial of Hitler; it was the international extradition hearing that most concerned him. Above all he wanted a "judicial interpretation of the Kellogg Pact [made] to the effect that any person or group of persons who engage in such a course of conduct as that followed by the Nazis in connection with the present war are violators of the Pact and as such are common criminals." If the Allied governments accepted his arguments and held an extradition hearing, Chanler believed they "would get around the great stumbling block which has stymied all previous attempts to outlaw wars of aggression." Since they would not require a new treaty to define aggression, it would be easy to establish the main elements of such a definition through a judicial finding "analogous to a common law precedent." [44]

Chanler ended his memorandum with the optimistic prediction that such a precedent would deter future aggressors, and he coupled this hope with a strong declaration that America and other United Nations would only resort to armed struggle in self-defense. Much of this seems gloriously naive today, but at the time it was written, these statements surely helped to heighten the memorandum's impact on Chanler's War Department audience. There was a broad and deep feeling throughout 1944 America, even among knowledgeable and hardheaded government officials such as McCloy and Stimson, that the current challenge to international security, which had so sorely tried the nation, had been caused exclusively by the dictatorial powers, and that democratic states could be counted upon to protect the peace. The belief in America's special democratic mission and higher morality was alive and well, and as the end of the war approached, the dream that the United States would somehow find a way to ennoble the sacrifices of this war by discovering a deterrent to future conflict was revived. Signs of this sense of moral mission had also whispered through the early drafts of Bernays's war-crimes paper, and there too, the desire to condemn aggressive war had kept arising out of a trial procedure that was ostensibly aimed at punishing those responsible for Nazi atrocities.

In addition to the broad appeal he touched upon by articulating the general desire to avert future wars, Chanler had raised an issue dear to the hearts of Stimson and all prominent Republicans: He offered a possibility of putting new life and meaning into the Kellogg-Briand Pact. Frank Kellogg had been Stimson's predecessor as Secretary of State, and although he had not been a strong advocate of collective security, or even very instrumental in developing the agreement of 1928, the pact had come to be associated with Kellogg's name and the era of Republican domination of national government in the 1920s. To many progressive Republican leaders such as Stimson, who had been forced for years to endure unflattering descriptions of their party as a band of grasping capitalists and ignorant isolationists, anything that offered a prospect of ennobling the Republican party's recent past was highly welcome. If the Kellogg-Briand Pact could become the basis for a new American-sponsored method of controlling aggressive war, many Republican idealistic, patriotic, and partisan dreams would be vindicated, even if it were within the bosom of the Democratic administration of Franklin Roosevelt.

A final consideration that gave Chanler's suggestion a special punch was its heavy reliance on the use of court procedure to cope with what was essentially a problem in international relations. It is important to remember that most of the War Department officials who were concerned with enemy atrocities and the related matter of dealing with postdefeat Germany were trained as lawyers. Most of them saw trial proceedings rather than international negotiation as the most direct and effective way to get things done. The whole administration, in fact, virtually all Americans then (and now) eyed diplomats and international politics with extreme suspicion but extended far greater respect and confidence to judicial procedures.

A number of factors thus combined to guarantee that Chanler's proposal would generate wide interest and some significant support within the War Department. But there were also present in Secretary Stimson's domain considerations that inevitably produced trouble for Chanler and the others supporting bold steps to control aggressive war. Foremost among them was the simple fact, which will be a major leitmotif of this story, that although most lawyers would trust courts more than diplomats, the legal profession tends to be very cool toward abrupt change or significant deviation from existing practice. However one might dress up Chanler's proposal, or any other plan that proposed to try the Nazi leaders for preparing or launching an aggressive war, it would still be a sharp break with precedent and would run head up against the prevailing view of the law held by most international lawyers. The predilection of legal conservatives to block change was reinforced within the War Department by a growing mood of opposition to the innovations that had been advanced by the personnel branch and championed by the office of the Assistant Secretary of War. Bernays, Cutter, and McCloy had stepped on the toes of some powerful people and had moved too fast between September and December for many War Department officers.

Furthermore, McCloy had been imprudent when he failed either to smooth ruffled feelings or to secure a departmental consensus in favor of the conspiracy/criminal-organization plan before promoting it in a number of other departments. In the fourth week of November, Bernays had already discovered that there were sharp limits to the innovations he could now get across simply by urging that a given change would facilitate war-crimes prosecution.[45] On 22 November the colonel tried to put forth a revision of field manual 27-10 (*The Rules of Land Warfare*), which would have banned the execution of hostages by U.S. Army commanders. Bernays argued that the exclusion of this provision from the American manual would prevent Nazi war-crimes defendants from citing it in their own defense. Although JAG had earlier led the way in amending the manual so that superior orders were no longer recognized as a covering defense, this time JAG joined the operations and civil affairs divisions in totally rejecting Bernays's proposal. No one except Bernays wanted to tie the hands of American theater and occupation commanders by eliminating their right to execute hostages, and the colonel's appeal to the importance of assisting war-crimes prosecutions therefore fell on deaf ears.[46]

McCloy read this situation accurately, sensing that in addition to the specific facts at issue here, there was a mood of legal caution present in JAG and also a tendency for many senior officers in that department to harbor resentment against the personnel branch. But on this occasion, McCloy did not try to appease General Cramer and his staff. Instead, on 29 November the Assistant Secretary prepared a memorandum, which was signed by the deputy chief of staff, Lieutenant General Thomas T. Handy, on the following day, that stripped JAG of exclusive control over enemy war-crimes questions. The order placed overall authority for war crimes in McCloy's hands, with the actual work divided so that JAG was left only with preparing and trying cases of customary war crimes committed against Americans, while the responsibility for developing general war-crimes policy was given over to G-1 personnel.[47] The loss of its traditional position as the office charged with exclusive authority to deal with war crimes was, of course, bitterly resented in JAG. That resentment led to an increased hostility toward legal novelties, and an even more intense desire to teach the war crimes upstarts and the Assistant Secretary of War's office a legal and political lesson.

When the aggressive-war question rose to the surface of War Department debate in early December 1944, it gave JAG a perfect opening to strike at legal innovation because the issue was controversial and JAG did not even have to struggle to pick up allies on this question. Within ten days of the appearance of the Chanler paper, another of Mr. Stimson's old friends and advisors, Mr. G. Harrison Dorr, circulated a memorandum through the department pillorying the idea that the Kellogg-Briand Pact could be used as the groundwork for trying the Nazi leaders as simple murderers with no shield of lawful belligerency. Mr. Dorr had first served Henry Stimson as a federal lawyer prior to the First World War and, out of a sense of loyalty and friendship, had returned to act as a special assistant to the Secretary of War in the 1940s. His views could therefore be expected to carry weight with the Secretary.

The memorandum that Dorr sent to McCloy on 9 December swept aside Chanler's arguments by declaring that there was nothing in the wording of the pact, in "the discussions leading up to it," or in subsequent treaty or court actions to support the contention that a state which launched an aggressive war had forfeited the protections of lawful belligerency.[48] Furthermore, by extending the rules of the Geneva Convention to the troops of Nazi Germany, the Allies had strongly suggested that they considered them to be covered by the customary rights accorded belligerents. Rather than take the wild leap Chanler recommended, Dorr thought it would be better to acknowledge frankly that international law had not advanced as far as Chanler thought. If no "practical way" could be found to prosecute aggressive war through the legally convincing arrangements of a formal treaty, then the United States might consider striking at it simply by using "our power as conquerors" to apply whatever "moral standards" we wished. If the ultimate goal of American policy was to prevent the repetition "of such conduct [as Hitler's] in the future," then Dorr thought it would be preferable to act with force rather than "to dress up such action in the guise of the application of existing principles of international law," for such a method "might be attacked in the future as legalistic legerdemain." [49]

Dorr's idea—if one is faced with an unprecedented legal problem it is better to use naked power than to bend prevailing custom and practice—is a notion that has appealed to amateur war-crimes strategists before and since, but it found few echoes at the Pentagon in 1944. Although military lawyers, like other lawyers, have little desire for innovation, they care even less for replacing judicial processes with summary execution or the rule of force. America's senior military commanders had no more enthusiasm for Mr. Dorr's suggestion that they assume the unilateral responsibility of punishing the Nazi leaders for preparing an aggressive war than they had when Henry Morgenthau advocated that they should settle the score for Hitler's crimes against humanity. War Department officials who were conservatively inclined apparently did find it agreeable that Mr. Dorr had helped to cut the legal ground from beneath the feet of Colonel Chanler and other innovators. But they rejected his advocacy of the mailed fist just as they turned away from what they saw as Chanler's legal radicalism.

More to the taste of the legal conservatives was the position taken by Brigadier General Kenneth C. Royall in a paper that he sent around the War Department's legal-opinion circuit on 14 December.[50] Royall was the army's highly regarded deputy fiscal director and would later serve as Secretary of the Army after the Second World War. McCloy had asked for his opinion on the conspiracy/criminal-organization proposal in hopes of finding a basis for broad support in the department, which would help to offset the obstructionism of JAG. But the plan backfired; although Royall did agree with the idea of prosecuting "criminal" organizations, he rejected almost every other feature of Bernays's plan. The general recommended instead that the Nazi leaders be tried before a military commission, which would not consider prewar atrocities or any "German acts in starting the war." The cautious Royall reluctantly conceded that military commissions might try cases where the German government had persecuted its own citizens during the war, but only if the postwar civil courts in Germany moved "slowly or ineffectively." [51] Under no circumstances was he prepared to grant that any Allied court should be concerned with the aggressive-war issue.

McCloy's effort to undercut JAG therefore totally failed, and with the conspiracy/criminal-organization plan and the aggressive-war prosecution proposals both wounded by the on slaughts of Dorr and Royall, the time was most opportune for a counterstroke by JAG. On 18 December that office sent through the War Department a twenty-page draft paper entitled, "Is the Preparation and Launching of the Present War a Crime?" [52] Although this paper had received only the "unofficial" approval of the chief of JAG, General Cramer, it had been prepared by one of the department's top legal brains, Lieutenant Alwyn Vernon Freeman—a man who would soon become a highly respected legal advisor to the American Government—and the paper actually expressed the views of generals Cramer and Weir.

A formal legal memorandum, complete with copious citations from the international legal literature, the Freeman paper methodically demolished the contention that aggressive war could be prosecuted on the basis of prevailing international law. Beginning with the statement that prior to World War I "it was a generally accepted principle of international law that every state had a right to resort to war—a right that was inherent in its sovereignty," Freeman declared "the burden of proof" rested on those who contended that the legal situation had changed since 1914. The lieutenant felt that no such case could be made, however, because in the previous thirty years war making had not become "a criminal offense," its "commission" had not been prohibited, and no "penalty or sanction either against the State collectively, or against the persons responsible, individually" had been established by "a positive norm of the law of nations." Freeman then ticked off the major declarations and treaties that were cited by Chanler and other advocates of aggressive-war prosecution, especially the 1927 League of Nations resolution on aggressive war, a 1928 resolution of the Pan American Conference, and the Kellogg-Briand (Paris) Pact of 1928. While granting that especially the latter made "resort to war" unlawful, Freeman contended that it "by no means follows that aggressive war is made a crime." [53]

The crucial point of his paper was that under international law, a violator of an agreement did not customarily suffer criminal penalties. Rather, "the usual consequence of the violation of an international obligation is the duty to make reparation for the damage suffered." The purpose of the Kellogg-Briand Pact, and the other resolutions, could not be to make government leaders subject to criminal sanctions because "the language used is the language of compact, not crime," and its context was one of "contract, not punishment." Freeman consequently declared that there was no legal basis for sending anyone to jail or the gallows for starting World War II. Even though "this result may be unfortunate; it may be immoral; it may be considered as socially outrageous," it was still, in the lieutenant's opinion, the "only conclusion compatible with existing principles of positive international law." Then, in an added swipe at the legal innovators in the War Department, Freeman also flatly rejected the whole conspiracy/criminal-organization approach to war crimes, because conspiracy was not a crime under international law, and in any event, "the greatest conspiracy in the world has nothing to do with the legality of the war, or with the criminal responsibility of its authors."

While Lieutenant Freeman believed he had obliterated the legal underpinnings of both the aggressive-war and conspiracy/criminal-organization plans, he was forced to admit that the political problems that had given birth to them were very real. World opinion in 1944 would simply be unable to accept a conclusion that the Nazi leaders should escape without punishment. Referring back to the UNWCC debate on whether or not aggressive war should be considered criminal, Freeman reiterated that if the commission went on record to the effect that it was, the UNWCC would be discredited "among lawyers." But he also granted that if the general public, "which was not concerned with the legal aspects" of the question, ever learned that the Allies did not hold the Nazis criminally responsible for the war, this information would "be met with outraged protests" because the people of the world believed what had happened was "plain mass murder." This was a dangerous admission, and Freeman's position was not much strengthened by his supplemental comments on how to cope with the difficulty.

In regard to the dilemma faced by the UNWCC, Freeman thought the commission should keep quiet and dodge the issue until the Allies worked out "other methods" to deal with the difficulty. This was the course that McCloy, Stimson, and the State Department had actually chosen to follow, but they tended to look toward the conspiracy/criminal-organization idea for the ultimate solution to the problem, while Freeman rejected that approach too. The lieutenant claimed the problem was solvable, and in passing drew attention to Hans Kelsen's notion that the Allies might take care of all their legal troubles in occupied Germany by assuming full sovereign control of the country, thereby securing a legal mandate to do whatever they wished. But pleading lack of space, Freeman did not follow up this idea or any other alternate answer to the political difficulties posed by the Nazi war-crimes question. His memorandum therefore inevitably left the impression that he had succeeded in battering the only proposed solutions while skipping right around the basic problem.[54]

The political hole left in Freeman's memorandum provided the proponents of the conspiracy/criminal-organization plan and aggressive-war prosecution with an ideal point of attack. Colonels Bernays and Chanler immediately joined forces "in thoroughly disagreeing" with the JAG paper,[55] and Bernays remarked acidly that it had "the perverse quality of arriving at the wrong conclusion on the basis of ample material to support the right" one.[56] Colonel Chanler zeroed in on Lieutenant Freeman's admission that he did not have immediately at hand an answer that would satisfy the lawyers and the public on the aggressive-war issue. "I suggest that this is a clear indication that there must be something wrong with that view of the law," Chanler noted caustically, and he went on to complain that the JAG paper had not dealt directly with his idea that the Kellogg-Briand Pact had deprived the Nazis of the shield of lawful belligerency.[57]

But the most important consequence of the handful of memoranda that Bernays and Chanler wrote answering Dorr, Freeman, Royall, and other assorted critics was that they were forced to more openly embrace the cause of legal innovation.[58] While noting that some international legal authorities such as Quincy Wright (who would be a legal advisor to the American Bench at Nuremberg) and Clyde Egleton supported the "Budapest Resolutions," which declared that under the Kellogg-Briand Pact an aggressor forfeited his belligerency rights in relation to neutrals, Chanler granted that the most respected international legal authorities such as Jessup, Borchard, and Hyde held the opposite view.[59] This admission did not incline Chanler to give up his basic point, however. Instead, in a pair of memoranda written shortly after Christmas 1944, he fired a general barrage at international law and its practitioners, contending that " 'international law' is not 'law' in the ordinary sense at all" because little of it rested on statute or was subject to court action. "What they call the International Legal System," he wrote, is little more than a body of declarations "which these professors" have "built up largely on their own and their predecessors' writings." [60] What they "would now probably say had become the accepted custom and usage of nations" should not, according to Chanler, bind the Allied governments hand and foot simply because "certain procedural steps may not have been followed."

While granting that the legal situation was clouded, Chanler emphasized two central considerations that pointed toward action—namely, that various international treaties and resolutions did declare "that a war of aggression is no longer lawful," and secondly that the defeat of Nazism and the prosecution of Axis war criminals opened up real opportunities for legal reform.[61] Chanler was therefore willing to do almost anything to obtain a "judicial determination as to the consequences of the Kellogg Pact" at the end of World War II. He welcomed "a real and tangible change in international law" because it would be a "drastic and revolutionary change . . . to *act* as if aggressive war was criminal." "We have been trying to bring about that change for over 20 years" Chanler told his War Department colleagues. "Here is our chance. Don't let it slip by." [62]

The conflict over the criminality of aggressive war, which had turned Chanler, and to a lesser degree Bernays, into flaming advocates of radical alterations in international law, also produced a number of other significant consequences. First, by dramatizing the innovative inclinations of men such as Bernays and Chanler, it inclined more conservative officials to oppose the conspiracy/criminal-organization approach they espoused. Secondly, the deadlock that resulted from the battle over aggressive war split the War Department and further sharpened hostilities between JAG and the McCloy/G-1 group. In the process, the strategy that McCloy and his aides had employed at the time of the late November redrafts was reduced to a shambles. Those drafts had included a major concession to General Cramer on the issue of a treaty court and had concomitantly failed to follow Mr. Hackworth's suggestion that emphasis be placed on political prudence. By mid-December, due to McCloy's decision to push ahead ruthlessly, and the divisions created by the aggressive-war question, there was no longer the slightest hope that JAG would help to obtain general concurrence for the conspiracy/criminal-organization plan. If the proposal was going to be approved through anything remotely resembling a normal bureaucratic procedure, support would have to be generated from outside the War Department. Since the drafts circulated on 4 December had made little or no effort to meet the inclinations of other departments, and the plan also now had the aggressive-war albatross hanging around its neck, the prospects were certainly not bright.

Considering all this, the first meeting that McCloy's staff held with Judge Rosenman on 12 December went rather well, and the judge's general sympathy for the proposal touched off another burst of wild optimism in the personnel branch. Bernays even prepared a formal transmission letter, which was intended to accompany the draft plan across the desks of the Secretaries of War and State and on to the President.[63] But this was just so much whistling in the dark. The real question was whether Stettinius—not to speak of Ambassador Davies—would be so enthusiastic about the plan that JAG's resistance could be overridden, and the conspiracy/criminal-organization plan could go on to the President as a recommendation of the Departments of War, State and perhaps Justice. The most obvious obstacle that stood in the way lay in the confusion and incapacity that characterized the State Department under Stettinius. Even when Stimson indicated that he might be prepared to transcend the lower-level bureaucratic confusion and take up the whole war-crimes matter with Stettinius himself, the State Department could do little but fumble and mumble. On 20 December Stettinius asked Mr. Hackworth for guidance on what he should say if Stimson directly raised the issues of prewar German atrocities and aggressive war.[64]

Hackworth replied two days later that the first issue was covered by the conspiracy/criminal-organization plan that had been "largely agreed upon" between the State and War Departments, and he implied that the Secretary should have no reservations about accepting that.[65] The aggressive-war issue was more complicated, Hackworth said, not only because views on its criminality "differ widely," but because Stimson was likely to "favor treating the launching of the war as a criminal act." It was possible, the State Department legal advisor suggested, that an aggressive-war count might be tucked away within the conspiracy/criminal-organization plan, but he advised

Mr. Stettinius not to involve himself with the matter. In his final recommendation Hackworth suggested that if the aggressive-war question arose in a high-level discussion, the Secretary of State should say that if the War and Navy Departments felt "a criminal charge" of aggressive war might "reasonably be made," and "particularly if the Attorney General feels that there would be justification," then the State Department "would be prepared to go along with them." [66]

It would be difficult to find many instances when a high level State Department official recommended such total departmental self-abasement on a matter of serious foreign-policy import. Hackworth was telling Stettinius to totally surrender the initiative to Stimson and Attorney General Biddle. Yet Stettinius wrote down Hackworth's precise words—including the crucial phrase that the State Department would "go along" if the others wanted to declare aggressive war a crime—in the crib notes he prepared for use when, like a school boy, he might have to talk to formidable cabinet members such as Forrestal, Stimson, or Biddle. [67]

State Department influence and capacity to initiate policy had simply been obliterated. Although the specifics of what was going on within that department were probably unknown to John J. McCloy, ultimately he must have come to realize that little or no help would be coming from that direction. Surrounded by critics within his own department, and unable to gain help from State, in late December the Assistant Secretary of War began to act like a trapped man. On the twenty-second, he even sent a copy of the late November conspiracy/criminal-organization draft to Henry Morgenthau, Jr.—an act that suggests an attack by the Greek furies or a mood of near hopeless abandon. [68]

However, the next and near-fatal blow to the conspiracy/criminal-organization proposal did not come from the Treasury. Before Morgenthau and his colleagues could begin to bombard the plan, the Justice Department launched its own more deadly assault. On 29 December Assistant Attorney

General Herbert Wechsler, friend and confidential advisor to
the Attorney General, circulated a short memorandum highly
critical of the whole War Department trial scheme to Biddle,
McCloy, Rosenman, and Davies.[69] Wechsler was troubled by
all the basic features of the plan. He doubted whether conspiracy was a relevant charge, organizational prosecution an
appropriate method, and an international treaty a suitable
means to deal with the Nazi war criminals. The Assistant Attorney General believed it would be necessary either to cut back
the legal innovations in the plan, or go forward and spell them
out in a treaty less vague and abstract than the one recommended by the War Department.

Wechsler's first inclination was to replace the woolly notion of conspiracy by the more sharply pointed legal device of
prosecuting participants as accessories in a criminal plan. But
the alleged Nazi plan that was to be prosecuted would then
have to be narrowed, and many of the charges proposed in
the War Department scheme, including those related to aggressive war, prewar persecutions, and acts committed against
German nationals, would have to be jettisoned. Wechsler also
wanted to dump the idea of trying the major Nazi leaders and
the organizations in a single case because he thought it would
trivialize the proceedings. In any event, the occupation authorities could work out administrative procedures for gathering up
the organization members if they really wanted them.

With the case thus limited, a treaty would not be necessary,
and it would then be possible to avoid a diplomatic hassle with
Great Britain and a ratification conflict in the U.S. Senate.
However, if the American government decided it wanted to go
after the Nazi leaders for aggressive war, prewar atrocities, and
so on, Wechsler granted that a treaty would be necessary to
create the required legal foundation. Such a treaty, in his
opinion, should not only specify certain acts as crimes but take
the next step, and declare the Nazi program and the leaders
of the Third Reich, "who had participated in its design or

execution," to be criminal. This way the case would be "kept within reasonable limits," [70] since the court would have to determine only the relative guilt of individual Nazi leaders and organizations and not the criminal nature of the historical events of the 1930s and 1940s.

Given the critical situation in which the advocates of the conspiracy/criminal-organization plan found themselves in the last days of 1944, Wechsler's memorandum should have been a very serious blow to their hopes, even if the Assistant Attorney General had only been giving his own opinion and speaking on his own authority. But a document from the files of the Justice Department indicates that much of Wechsler's dim view of the War Department plan was shared by his chief, Francis Biddle. The short one-and-a-half page note, apparently dictated by the Attorney General on 5 January 1945, declared there should be no prosecution of prewar actions or of acts committed against German nationals, and that the conspiracy approach should be dropped.[71] Biddle doubted the law of conspiracy was technically applicable to the problem or if conspiracy was a criminal offense "under international law." In addition, he thought that a conspiracy prosecution would cast far too broad a net. If the War Department scheme was actually put into operation, Biddle believed even the lowliest German soldier could then be deemed a party to the conspiracy, and the Allies would be faced with the problem of what to do with tens of millions of criminals. Biddle's inclination was to believe that by stressing broad categories and abstractions, the War Department plan had turned the problem upside down, and it would be wiser "to determine whom you wanted to get at and how many before determining the mechanisms of punishment." [72]

There is a classic double irony surrounding these sharply critical comments of Wechsler and Biddle. Within a month, the former would be helping touch up the War Department draft, making it more acceptable to senior members of the United

States cabinet, and the latter would be joining Stimson and Stettinius in approving the plan and forwarding it to the President. Within a year, Biddle would be seated in Nuremberg as the senior American judge hearing this very case, and by his side would be Herbert Wechsler, acting as one of his most respected legal advisors. There is even a touch of comedy hovering around Biddle's recommendation that the planners keep their focus on practical problems, especially that of determining who should actually be punished, because in 1945 the Attorney General went along with the other Washington officials, totally ignoring his own advice.

Yet these ironic and comic elements would gain their force only in later days. The year 1944 ended with the supporters of the conspiracy/criminal-organization plan blocked or beaten on nearly every front. After six weeks in which the plan had repeatedly been examined, debated, and revised, only to be challenged once more, not a single government department had formally approved it. The Justice Department was against it, the Treasury opposed every form of trial plan, State was impotent, and the Navy had stood aside. Even within the War Department, the senior officers of JAG were now universally hostile. The corollary proposal that the Nazis should be prosecuted for launching an aggressive war, and that this should somehow be connected to the conspiracy/criminal-organization plan, had been met by even more general opposition, especially inside the War Department. Careful deliberation had occurred and all the bureaucratic channels and methods normally used to secure approval for a program in wartime Washington had been tried, but after three-and-a-half months of struggle and effort, McCloy and his assistants had come up against stone walls. Even Bernays was forced to admit in a classic bit of understatement that the plan had not made "very satisfactory progress." [73] The government's verdict in 1944 was that the conspiracy/criminal-organization plan should be shelved, and that what we have come to know as the Nuremberg trial plan should never have existed at all.

But in January 1945, events far away in the forests of Belgium and on the shores of the Black Sea gave a twist to the decisions of the Washington bureaucracy. After all of these Washington memoranda and conferences, the conspiracy/criminal-organization plan was revived, and the Nuremberg trial system was born at Malmédy and on the way to Yalta.

CHAPTER 4

FROM MALMÉDY
TO CONSENSUS

Why don't I do this—call up McCloy and ask him whether he
wouldn't come over here, and we'd like to have a little discussion
with him, and I could learn as we go along. How would that be? [1]

Henry Morgenthau, Jr.

January 1945

During the early stages of the Battle of the Bulge, some seventy
American prisoners were gunned down near Malmédy, Belgium,
on 17 December by members of the First SS Panzer Regiment.[2]
It is difficult today, thirty-five years after the event, to appreciate the emotional impact the Malmédy killings had on American popular opinion and on the views of those who controlled
the U.S. government in December 1944 and January 1945.
German armed forces and SS units had carried out such mass
killings of military prisoners and civilians every day for years in
eastern, and to a lesser degree, in western, Europe. On many
occasions the number killed and the brutality of the executions
far exceeded what was done at Malmédy. Americans had been
disturbed by reports of such killings, in fact that was one of the
reasons why the conspiracy/criminal-organization prosecution
system had been developed in the first place. But as long as
the slaughter had taken place far away, and the victims had
been Russian POWs or Italian civilians, most Americans had

not fully accepted that the Nazis deliberately carried out millions of killings in cold blood and that this killing system could directly touch them.

A combination of skepticism regarding atrocity propaganda and a sense of superiority that cushioned Americans from what they saw as the harsh and brutal realities of European life helped to keep Nazi atrocities abstract and statistical. Then came the shock of the Battle of the Bulge, the humiliating reversals, and with the Panzers rolling westward once more, the chilling possibility that Hitler might really have turned the tables again. On the heels of the first news of the German advances, reports reached Supreme Headquarters Allied Expeditionary Force (SHAEF) headquarters on 16 December that the Nazis were employing all kinds of ruses, such as advancing in American uniform, which clearly violated the laws of war. Two days later (18 December), SHAEF received the initial message from the American First Army that SS troops had shot large numbers of American POWs "with machine pistols and machine guns." [3]

During the third week of December, when the national press put the initial fragmentary reports on Malmédy before the American people, cries of anguish and demands for the punishment of those responsible arose all over the country. It was as if the combination of yet another defeat—when defeats were no longer supposed to happen—and the reality of a Nazi atrocity committed against Americans threw the whole nation off balance. So great was the shock that four years later, in 1949, when Auschwitz and the atomic horrors were the common knowledge of every school child, a United States senator in close touch with the popular psyche could declare that "there is nothing that any of us can recall in recorded history that approaches the unwarranted type of mass slaughter that occurred at Malmédy." [4] Such exaggeration was surely not universal, but American opinion had been shaken by Malmédy, and the depth of the popular shock was real.

Malmédy also greatly influenced the highest levels of the

executive branch of the United States government. Even before the Germans had launched their offensive, the War Department was becoming increasingly worried that the Nazis might use American POWs as political hostages. On 15 December, the day before the German attack in the Ardennes, McCloy, Stimson, and their advisors had conferred on what should be done if, at the time the Nazis were "cornered," they threatened to "murder POWs." [5] Within a few days of the Malmédy incident, Stimson had shifted a portion of his anxiety to an examination of what the Germans had allegedly done during their offensive in the Bulge. Nine days after Malmédy, the Secretary of War noted in his diary, "it seems to be clear that their troops have been guilty of many violations of the laws of war against us." [6] Four days later, on the thirtieth, he summarized a conversation with Lord Halifax in which he told the British ambassador "we now had the facts" that gave "confirmation of the massacre of our troops by the Germans." [7] On New Year's Eve, during a conference with the president, Stimson said the army had "confirmation of the massacre of 150 [sic] of our troops by the SS divisions and had identified the German troops as being the First Regiment of the First SS Panzer Division." [8] By early January 1945, the Malmédy fever was burning so hot in the Pentagon that when Murray Bernays came to criticize the position on war-crimes prosecution taken by Herbert Wechsler, the worst thing he could think to say was that "under Mr. Wechsler's plan it might be impossible to convict a single member" of the First SS Panzer Regiment who had "participated in the slaughter of our men, taken as prisoners of war near Malmédy, Belgium." [9]

Therefore, it was something close to a foregone conclusion that Malmédy would help to heighten Washington's interest in developing an effective program to deal with Nazi war criminals. But it was the fact that the atrocity had been committed by a unit of the military (*Waffen*) SS that was the cutting edge for Malmédy's role in rallying support for the conspiracy/ criminal-organization plan. Seventeen years after the event, when Francis Biddle attempted to explain why he, along with others, reversed themselves in January 1945 and decided to support the War Department plan, he claimed that "what chiefly influenced our judgment . . . was the shooting of American officers and soldiers after their surrender at Malmédy by an SS regiment, *acting under orders*." [10] [Italics added] Especially interesting is Biddle's inclusion of the phrase, "acting under orders," for in actual fact no one in Washington in January 1945 had any way of knowing whether what happened at Malmédy had been done by a local German commander on his own initiative, or if he had been following a command of his superiors. Decades of investigation, and a series of hearings and trials, have still not conclusively answered the question of whether or not SS *Obersturmbannführer* Peiper and his men were literally executing a definite plan of systematic terror at the Belgian crossroad on 17 December 1944. [11]

The important consideration here, however, is that the highest leaders of the American government immediately jumped to the conclusion that the Malmédy killings were not an isolated atrocity but were part of a definite plan. For months many of them had been considering a prosecution proposal based on the existence of a Nazi plan or conspiracy to dominate Europe (or the world) by using organizations such as the SS and the Gestapo to commit atrocities and spread terror. Within this context, and enveloped by a great popular outpouring of emotion over the Malmédy incident, men such as Francis Biddle found it impossible to follow their own dictums that the best thing to do, while staying calm, was to "determine whom you wanted to get at . . . before determining the mechanism of punishment." [12] Instead of looking at Malmédy on its own merits—or lack thereof—they were swept along to see it as a telling instance of what the War Department draft called the Nazis' "purposeful and systematic conspiracy to achieve domination of other nations and peoples by deliberate violation of the rules of war as they have been accepted and adhered to by the nations of the world." [13]

Malmédy became the energizer that put life and emotional conviction into the American leaders' conversion to the conspiracy/criminal-organization plan. What gave this conversion a sense of urgency was that when the new year of 1945 dawned, only five weeks remained before the President was scheduled to meet with Churchill and Stalin. Among the many matters likely to be discussed at that meeting was the treatment of the major Nazi war criminals, and as we know, all attempts to determine American policy on that question had been stymied by the end of 1944.

The ideal way to break the deadlock and get the policy-making machinery moving again would have been to prompt the President to give some sign of his sympathy for the conspiracy/criminal-organization idea. This was not altogether easy, however, because Franklin Roosevelt had succeeded, during the three months that had elapsed since the beginning Morgenthau controversy, in keeping under wraps his views on nearly all aspects of the fate that should enfold postwar Germany. He had held Morgenthau's ideas at arm's length and generally ignored Stettinius. He had met Stimson's various declarations about conspiracy, analogies with the "17 holes," and German atrocities in the Ardennes with good-natured platitudes. But as the date for the Big Three conference drew closer, the President's tendency to avoid all serious problems became a grave national liability. No member of the cabinet was able to move him very far; Harry Hopkins was too ill to provide much of a lead, and men like Joe Davies lacked the necessary authority or steadiness to cope with the ailing Roosevelt's talents as an artful dodger.

Inevitably, the responsible officials in the executive branch had to marshal all of their energies and resources to hammer out policy positions on the most important questions facing the Big Three, such as the future of Poland and the conditions under which the Soviet Union would enter the Pacific theater of war. Many potentially serious issues were pushed to the fringe and ignored. Attention needed to be focused on working out positions on the gravest and most complicated problems, and such positions had to be acceptable to the President. What seems to have saved the subject of war-crimes policy and the conspiracy/criminal-organization plan from being shoved aside was the presence of Samuel Rosenman in the White House. He was apparently the one who kept working on the President, pushing the cause of the conspiracy/criminal-organization proposal while awaiting a suitable occasion to entice Mr. Roosevelt into signaling that he favored the plan.[14]

On 3 January 1945, for the first and last time, the President finally put himself on the record regarding the war-crimes question, ostensibly because he was concerned about the status of the UNWCC and its American representative, Mr. Herbert Pell.[15] The unfortunate Mr. Pell was a former New York Democratic congressman, possessed of a doglike devotion to the President, who was constantly at odds with the cautious and reserved officials in the State Department. Mr. Pell was energetic, possessing a touch of crude combativeness, and actually eager to do something inside the UNWCC that would contribute to the punishment of war criminals.[16] However, his appeals to Washington for instructions and for authority to take some initiative on the commission were invariably met by refusal or replies of transcendant evasiveness. When, for example, he asked State Department officials in early December 1944 if they would be good enough to outline the basic American policy on war crimes so that he would have some grounds on which to act, he was told by Mr. Hackworth that, "nothing definite and final could be said at this time regarding any phase of the subject on which you have asked for instructions." [17]

Of course, December 1944 was a time of great uncertainty in American war-crimes policy, but it would have taken a man of infinitely greater patience than Mr. Pell to stay at his UNWCC post in the face of such cold and insensitive treatment. Whatever Mr. Pell's strengths and weaknesses, he was neither bland nor passive, and immediately after receipt of Mr. Hackworth's reply he rushed back to Washington, met with the Secretary of State, and when Stettinius failed to satisfy him as to why he was being left in the dark, he asked to see the President on 9 January. This imminent meeting with Pell prompted Roosevelt to send a memorandum to Stettinius on 3 January, asking for a "brief report" on the status of the UNWCC and the American stand on punishment of Hitler and the other "chief Nazi war criminals." [18] But before the memorandum was sent to the State Department, someone among the White House staff—probably Judge Rosenman—let his influence be felt, and the President added two highly important sentences.

The charges against the top Nazis should include an indictment for waging aggressive and unprovoked warfare, in violation of the Kellogg Pact. Perhaps these and other charges might be joined in a conspiracy indictment.[19]

Nearly everything about these two sentences is peculiar. Their origin is unclear, and they do not fit very well with the rest of the memorandum. The emphasis on prosecuting aggressive war appears to come out of the blue, especially because of the bald statement that follows, tying it directly to violations of the Kellogg-Briand Pact. Equally strange is the lack of any direct reference to prosecution of criminal organizations or of a conspiracy to commit war crimes and other atrocities. Why the memorandum was written this way we shall probably never know, nor are we likely to gain much information about why Franklin Roosevelt agreed to sign it and then assiduously avoided ever putting another line on paper that might indicate he supported either conspiracy prosecution or the trial of the Nazi leaders for violating the Kellogg-Briand Pact. The memorandum of 3 January stands like a solitary and mysterious beacon, for with all the uncertainty that surrounds its origin and content, its effect was immediate and clear. Nearly every high official in the American government took it to mean that the President had given his general approval to the War Department plan.

Judge Rosenman immediately scheduled a meeting in his office for 5 January, at which time the representatives of the various departments concerned with war crimes—War, State, Justice—as well as the President's special representatives—Davies and Rosenman himself—were to offer their criticisms and suggested revisions of the War Department's November war-crimes memorandum.[20] Realizing that the conspiracy/criminal-organization plan had been saved and that a moment of decision was at hand, McCloy called his own meeting for 4 January. The Assistant Secretary hoped to smooth out the differences in his own realm so that the War Department would be able to speak with a united voice on the following day. On the morning of the fourth, Cutter, Bernays, and General Weir of JAG trooped into the Assistant Secretary's office, where they were joined by McCloy and Mr. George L. Harrison, an old friend and advisor of Mr. Stimson's, who often acted as a symbolic stand-in for the Secretary of War.*

From the moment this group assembled, it was clear that McCloy, Cutter, and Bernays were in for difficulty as the frustration and anger that had been bubbling within the judge advocate general's office now boiled to the surface.[21] Reversing the position of support that General Cramer had cautiously given in November, General Weir categorically rejected the whole conspiracy/criminal-organization scheme, contending that it could not be used effectively to prosecute prewar atrocities or actions that had been taken against enemy nationals. In any event, America's allies would never agree to the idea. Throughout the morning, Bernays, Cutter, and on occasion McCloy himself attempted to break down General Weir's opposition, but in vain. After lunch McCloy took over the main effort to turn the general around, yet he too had little or no success.

---

* Although Mr. Harrison did not exert much influence on this occasion, an indication of his symbolic importance is provided by the fact that 3 months later, whenever Secretary Stimson was unable to attend, Mr. Harrison acted as chairman of the so-called "Interim Committee" concerned with American atomic bomb policy.

After six hours of inconclusive haggling, McCloy reluctantly declared he would be unable to "present a common War Department view" on war crimes in the forthcoming meeting with Judge Rosenman and the other interested government officials. Instead, according to the notes that Bernays made during the meeting, the Assistant Secretary claimed he would have to limit himself to putting forth "the views of the Secretary of War," as he—that is, McCloy—understood them. Yet Bernays's notes also indicate that even as McCloy avowed he would only be voicing Mr. Stimson's opinions, he kept referring to the proposal for a trial based on the conspiracy approach as if it were the settled policy of the War Department.

On only two issues did the Assistant Secretary sound notes of caution and reserve—whether or not a treaty court should be used, and what was to be done about the problem of aggressive war. McCloy had reversed himself on the first of these, holding now that a treaty court was undesirable, presumably because after two months of battering in the bureaucratic wars, he had concluded that the practical difficulties associated with a treaty were insurmountable. Yet at the same time, the Assistant Secretary had been unable to discover an alternate solution to the problem, earlier posed by General Cramer, that without a treaty it would be impossible to transfer a conspiracy finding from an international trial to secondary proceedings before American courts. Caught on the horns of this dilemma, McCloy was prepared to dodge the issue and leave the treaty-court question open for the time being.

The posture on aggressive war that the Assistant Secretary adopted at the 4 January meeting was characterized by an even more pronounced degree of pragmatic temporizing. He acknowledged that the Secretary of War was "definitely inclined to take the position" that "launching an aggressive war . . . should be declared a crime." McCloy himself again waltzed around the pretense that he was only espousing Mr. Stimson's views, and he instead came out for a peculiar compromise position that had just been worked out by JAG and the personnel branch. After two weeks of wrangling, the two organizations had reached an understanding based more on expedience than legal principle. The JAG chiefs agreed they would not make the aggressive-war prosecution criticisms contained in Lieutenant Freeman's memorandum a matter "of record at this time," [22] and in return Bernays would recommend only the prosecution of a restricted type of aggressive war. The deal was closed in a memorandum on aggressive war that Bernays and one of his assistants had completed immediately prior to this crucial meeting in McCloy's office. [23]

The memorandum advanced an interpretation of international law so elastic that it would have justified criminal prosecution of those responsible for virtually any kind of military assault. Declaring that "customary usage and treaties" merely "disclose the principles of conduct which are from time to time accepted by states," it claimed that international law "more than any other law . . . grows and develops with the growth and development of the public conscience upon which it is founded." [24] Predictably, the memorandum used this as a basis to proclaim that by the year 1945 the "public conscience" had made launching an aggressive war a prosecutable crime. It cited resolutions—such as those of the League of Nations (1927), the Pan American Conference (1928), and the Kellogg-Briand Pact—as well as opinions—of Henry Stimson, and the British and Soviet legal specialists, Hersch Lauterpacht and A. W. Trainin—to support this contention. [25]

At this point the memorandum abruptly shifted focus, and while citing the Hague *Rules of Land Warfare* (Convention IV, 1907) and the Geneva Prisoner of War Convention (1929) as examples, it asserted that even when international conventions, such as these two, did not contain specific criminal sanctions, they were still enforceable through criminal court proceedings. This contention was based on a strained bit of analogous argument, since the provisions of the two conventions cited had actually been taken over and included in the military codes of the signatory powers, thus making them enforceable in each country's regular civil or military courts. The memorandum obviously wished to gloss over the holes in the analogy in order to maintain that the Kellogg-Briand Pact should be enforced through court actions against aggressors, just as Hague IV and the Geneva Convention were applied against those who used dumdum bullets or mistreated prisoners of war.

But there was an even more important reason why the memorandum focused attention on the Hague conventions. The major concession that JAG had made in the aggressive-war controversy was to concede that if one state attacked another without a declaration of war, the attacker was violating a provision of Hague Convention III, and was therefore criminally punishable. This position was remarkably unrealistic, because Hague III no more contained criminal sanctions than did the Kellogg-Briand Pact, and in contrast to the other Hague agreements and the Geneva Convention, it had not been made part of the criminal law of the signatory powers. Furthermore, the notion that if the leaders of a government pause for a moment to make a declaration of war on their way to rape their neighbor the attack is legal, while to omit such a declaratory gesture is to make it illegal, and make the leaders subject to criminal prosecution, breaks new ground in the realm of political-legal hocus pocus. No one of note, before or since, has ever claimed that Hague III could serve as the foundation for aggressive-war prosecution. But the JAG leaders were apparently so desperate to find a means of moderating at least a part of the proposed war-crimes program that as a face-saving device they tried to limit aggressive-war prosecution to instances in which the Nazis had attacked without respecting Hague III's injunction.

Absurd or not, they made their point, and the Bernays memorandum of 4 January concluded by turning its back on its case that all aggressive war was criminal. Instead, it declared anticlimactically that "the launching of the present war was a crime" only "against certain of the United Nations . . . because of the manner and circumstances in which it was done." [26] If any doubt remains about whether this was the essential quid pro quo for agreement within the War Department on aggressive-war policy, it is removed by the final statement John J. McCloy made at the departmental meeting of 4 January. The Assistant Secretary declared that during conferences on the conspiracy/criminal-organization plan with representatives from other departments, he would say the War Department was still studying if aggressive war as such, "no matter how instituted," was criminal. He would also say the department's position was that an aggressive war "launched without a declaration of war" was clearly a crime, and the Nazi leaders should therefore be prosecuted for any attacks thus initiated. [27]

At first glance it might appear that the legal innovators in the department had been checked at this meeting. A sharply limited aggressive-war formula had been adopted, and JAG's refusal to endorse the conspiracy/criminal-organization plan forced McCloy to stop saying that he was advancing a plan approved by the War Department. In actuality, these checks were more apparent than real, because it had been demonstrated to Bernays and his associates during the meeting that on most points McCloy and Stimson were on their side. The supporters of conspiracy/criminal-organization also knew JAG had seriously undermined the strength of its intransigent opposition by agreeing that a restricted form of aggression was criminally prosecutable. Therefore, when the interdepartmental conference on war-crimes policy opened in Judge Rosenman's office, after a few days' delay on the morning of 8 January, Bernays, Cutter, and McCloy were in a strong position. Although a representative of JAG was presumably present, the other three participants—Wechsler, Hackworth, and Rosenman himself—acting as if they had absorbed the lessons of Malmédy and the imminence of the Yalta conference, enthusiastically supported the idea of a conspiracy/criminal-organization prosecution based on the contention that aggressive warfare was criminal. [28]

JAG's hope of limiting aggressive-war prosecution to cases where there had been no declaration of war, as well as its opposition to the whole Bernays approach, was lost in the shuffle. The tone of the meeting is revealed by the acceptance of the War Department draft of late November as the basis of discussion. At the end of its deliberations the group gave the task of redrafting and strengthening that memorandum to a two-man committee made up of Bernays and Herbert Wechsler.[29] No JAG representative was included in the drafting group; and since Wechsler, along with his chief, Francis Biddle, had done an about face and was now among the strongest advocates of the plan, it was a foregone conclusion that the new draft would be a forceful presentation of the views embodied in that proposal.

The Bernays-Wechsler draft, completed on 13 January, was half again as long as that of 27 November. Substantially reorganized and rewritten, the new memorandum was less a document presenting a problem than it was a polemical position paper, marshaling arguments in support of the conspiracy/criminal-organization approach. It began by chronicling Nazi atrocities and crimes, and it enumerated the major groups of German organizations and leaders deserving punishment. In the post-Malmédy spirit it targeted the SS as "chief among the instrumentalities" that should be prosecuted.[30] After briefly summarizing the practical difficulties involved in any traditional prosecution of Nazi crimes due to their scale and complexity, it also cited the legal problems raised by the questions of aggressive war, prewar persecutions, and the actions taken by the Nazi government against German nationals. Following this five-page exposition of difficulties, the memorandum presented a somewhat modified form of Bernays's original conspiracy/criminal-organization plan as the only appropriate answer to the problem. The most significant legal modification was placing less emphasis on the specifically Anglo-American concept of conspiracy and more emphasis on prosecuting the Nazis for the "formulation and execution of a criminal plan," the illegality of which, the draft averred, was "common to all legal systems." [31]

This legal adjustment, as well as a number of minor re-wordings, was probably the work of Herbert Wechsler, but the primary substantive changes were surely Bernays's. The 13 January draft is especially noteworthy because, among all the various versions of the conspiracy/criminal-organization scheme that were produced in 1944–45, it came out most categorically in favor of using a treaty court and of vigorously prosecuting aggressive war. This memorandum championed the idea of a treaty court; it held that such an international compact was "evidently the most desirable instrument in which to formulate the applicable substantive law and the procedure to be followed[,] as well as to establish the court." Furthermore, the memorandum conceded that without a treaty, it was doubtful if the findings of the main trial could "be made binding in subsequent trials" of criminal-organization members "without amendatory legislation in the United States, and possibly in other countries as well." However, the clinching argument in favor of a treaty was acknowledging that in its absence there was grave doubt "that it would be legally possible to include as a constituent element of the charge the launching of aggressive war," and "the elimination of this offense, lying as it does at the root of the other crimes, would . . . represent a serious weakening of the general plan." This statement was far more than a rhetorical flourish. The 13 January draft repeatedly stated that aggressive war was the primary target of the prosecution, and at one point it declared that the long series of Nazi war crimes and atrocities should be seen as actions implementing the "broad criminal plan of aggressive war." [32]

It is worth noting that the unqualified advocacy of aggressive-war prosecution that Bernays championed in this draft inverted the emphasis contained in his original proposal. The G-1 plan of 15 September had been aimed chiefly at prosecuting Nazi war crimes and crimes against humanity so that members of the main Nazi organizations would be caught in the Allies' trial net. In that proposal there had been a hint of aggressive-war prosecution, but nothing more. Similarly, in his original plan, Bernays had not even raised the question of whether or not a treaty would be necessary to establish the legal basis of prosecution or if a judgment would be transferable within the American court system. Only after these issues had been put forth by others—aggressive-war prosecution by Colonel Chanler and the need for a treaty by General Cramer—did Bernays begin to wrestle with them; and not until 13 January did he come out strongly in favor of both proposals. His conversion to the cause of aggressive-war prosecution owed much to the long debate on the issue that had occurred in the War Department. But it was also surely affected by Secretary Stimson's support for the idea, and perhaps even more, by the 3 January statement of the President to the effect that a plan for prosecuting aggressive war on the basis of the Kellogg-Briand Pact would receive his approval.

Together with the fact that Bernays's thinking had simply grown until it embraced the importance and political expediency of the aggressive-war and treaty-court issues, there is also a touch of personal excess in his decision to lay such emphasis upon them in the 13 January memorandum. When on 4 January he had been faced by JAG's categorical opposition and McCloy's caution, he had reluctantly compromised and agreed to accept the limited aggressive-war formula that restricted the charge to incidents when no declaration of war had been made. But after the 8 January meeting in Judge Rosenman's office, where JAG seemed a tiny and impotent opposing force, he immediately scrapped the compromise and in the 13 January draft put maximum emphasis on a broad aggressive-war prosecution.

Bernays's handling of the treaty-court issue indicates the same inclination to go at least one step too far, for although he was probably nudged in this direction by Herbert Wechsler, the colonel knew full well that Mr. Hackworth was opposed to the idea and, even more important, that a strong statement in favor of a treaty court would certainly conflict with the current views of John J. McCloy. The Assistant Secretary's enthusiastic support was the bedrock that Bernays had to stand upon if he were to gain ultimate approval for his plan. Yet in the euphoria of the second week of January, he chose to place the strongest and most blatant emphasis on the two features of the plan—aggressive war and a treaty court—that were most likely to illicit determined opposition not only from his ardent critics, such as the leaders of JAG, but also from his warmest supporters, Hackworth and McCloy. Thus, much of the responsibility for unleashing the last festival of angry and determined opposition to the conspiracy/criminal-organization scheme that burst forth in mid-January must be attributed to Bernays's reluctance to compromise and his tendency to overplay his hand.

However, Bernays obviously did not create the opposition, he only provided it with a highly suitable opportunity to surface once more. The old opposition of legal conservatives and those made jealous, or long irritated, by Bernays's successes, had been waiting and grumbling throughout December 1944 and the first half of January 1945. All they needed was to gather up powerful allies and locate a weak point in order to go on the war path again. Even before Bernays and Wechsler's completed redraft—blessed by a cursory glance from McCloy—was sent around the War Department offices, and to Rosenman, the State and Justice departments, and Joseph Davies, the ambassador was showing increasingly clear signs of joining the opposition.[33]

Davies had apparently not been present at the meeting in Rosenman's office on 8 January, but it was easy for him to see the general direction that war-crimes policy was taking. On 10 January, when he finally met with the President to discuss the subject, he concluded—probably correctly—that Franklin Roosevelt did not have very strong feelings one way or the other. All the President seems to have indicated to Davies was that he wanted Hitler and his cohorts dispatched quickly,

and though he had come around to the idea that a trial was
necessary, he thought it could be done perfunctorily before a
military tribunal. It is possible that Mr. Davies used this occasion to advise the President to move cautiously regarding
charges of conspiracy and crimes against humanity because
they were so legally innovative. But the account of this conversation in the ambassador's papers is so covered with Mr.
Davies's postwar rewrites that it is impossible to be sure of
what was actually said.[34]

Two days later, on 12 January, Davies had a meeting with
Rosenman. He so sharply attacked what he considered the
radical and dangerous legal proposals contained in the War
Department plan that Rosenman was compelled to ring up Bernays during the discussion in hopes of acquiring arguments
that would help him beat back the ambassador's criticisms.[35]
On the following day (13 January, the date of the Bernays-
Wechsler redraft), Davies was still not satisfied, and he sent
Rosenman a huge packet of legal documents, many of which
had originated in the UNWCC debates on the criminality of
aggressive war. Along with these papers, the ambassador sent
a murky note that seemed to suggest Hitler and his aides
should be tried and convicted solely for traditional war crimes,
and that the task of rendering aggressive war and genocidal
atrocities criminally punishable should be left to the peace conference or the new United Nations organization.[36]

By discounting the ambassador's linguistic vagaries, one
might assume that he had merely lined up with the legal conservatives who so wished to avoid immediate radical innovation
that they were ready to risk courting public anger when word
got out that the Allied governments felt Hitler could not be
legally punished for attacking neutral countries such as Holland or sending millions to the gas chambers. But it is seldom
easy to determine anything specific regarding the ambassador's
views. This time the main confusion arises from the fact that
in his note to Rosenman, ostensibly espousing legal conservatism, Mr. Davies also seemed to cite with approval a com-

mentary by the Soviet legal authority A. W. Trainin, who went much further even than Bernays or Chanler in recommending legal innovation to strike at Nazi "crimes." Although the Russians had not spelled out their wishes in detail, they definitely wanted a form of broad, tough, war-crimes prosecution that would not be hamstrung by the technicalities of lawyers or prevailing western legal practice.

As on most other occasions, Mr. Davies was prepared to look with great generosity on a position taken by the Soviet Union. This was not because he strongly sympathized with the political left—corporate lawyers tend not to be raging leftists—but primarily because he realized it was the Russians, far more than the Westerners, who had paid the enormous human price required to tear the guts out of the Germany army. He hoped that if he could awaken the American people to some realization of what the Soviets had accomplished in the war, his fellow countrymen would agree that the West owed the Soviet Union an immense debt of gratitude. In an environment of concession and consideration a permanent reconciliation between East and West, Communist and capitalist, would then be possible. Few observers today would deny that Mr. Davies was right when he predicted that a Western failure to adequately recognize the Soviets' wartime achievements and sacrifices would help to poison the postwar atmosphere. But the ambassador's overall picture of Russia and his vision of the way to achieve long-term Allied harmony were an astonishingly naive blend of ignorance and dreamlike illusion.

What made Mr. Davies such a formidable factor in the Washington of 1944–45 was not that he was a conservative lawyer-diplomat with a "leftist" mission, and certainly not that his ideas were realistic, or markedly coherent. His primary significance arose from the exploding energy with which he was able to carry his pet causes right to the desk of Franklin Roosevelt. To the leaders of JAG and other conservative legalists who had been losing on the war-crimes question, he seemed like a valuable ally, if not an avenging angel. They were in no position to examine too critically the vagaries of his views; what they needed was political clout. Mr. Davies looked rather like a legal conservative and definitely like an official with access to the President who was urging caution on war-crimes policy. That was enough for them. They immediately took the ambassador to their bosom and began to supply him with materials that would be useful in attacking the War Department's conspiracy/criminal-organization plan.

The most important document that the JAG officers gave to Davies was a legal opinion on the merits of Bernays's plan; General Weir had elicited it from Edmund M. Morgan, acting dean of the Harvard Law School and a former lieutenant colonel in the judge advocate general's office.[37] General Weir had posed two questions for Dean Morgan; the first asked if it would be legally appropriate to use the conspiracy approach in prosecuting the Nazi leaders for having attempted "to dominate other peoples by acts violative of the laws and customs of war." Dean Morgan replied that in his opinion this was purely an academic question, because if the Germans had prepared such a plan and not implemented it, no one would have thought to prosecute them merely for the act of planning. Therefore the Allies should not concern themselves with prosecuting a conspiratorial plan, which was not generally recognized as a criminal offense under international law; but they should strike at the actual criminal acts that the Nazis had committed.

Turning to General Weir's second question, if prewar persecution of German nationals by the Nazis could be taken as part of a "chain of conspiracy . . . to dominate other peoples by acts violative of the laws and customs of war," Morgan was even more categorically negative. According to the Harvard Law School's acting dean, "no one would dream" of calling such persecutions in themselves "violations of the rules and customs of war." If that fact was combined with a recognition that no such thing "as an international crime of conspiracy to dominate by acts violative of the rules of war" existed, it seemed obvious to Morgan that "a negative answer [to the question] seems imperative." "The conspiracy theory is too thin a veneer," Morgan declared, "to hide the real purpose, namely the creation of a hereto unknown international offense by individuals *ex post facto.*" Having uttered the Latin phrase most likely to cause lawyers' knees to wobble, the acting dean advanced the view that it would be better to abandon the whole conspiracy approach as "not only unwise but unjustifiable." If the Allies pushed ahead they "would violate basic principles of Anglo-American law" and thereby lose the "reasoned approval of civilized communities." [38]

This was a weighty legal argument that gained added force from the prestige and honored position of its author. When it was combined with the fact that the opponents would participate in the next general meeting on war-crimes policy, which was scheduled for Rosenman's office on 16 January, in the company of the assertive Mr. Davies, the supporters of the conspiracy/criminal-organization plan were in for a serious challenge. Bernays did not have a detailed knowledge of what was going on in the opposition camp, and as usual was probably too optimistic, but he did work hard to prepare for what he saw as something "in the nature of a showdown meeting." [39] He tried to make certain that the Navy Department had totally distanced itself from the major war-crimes question, and that there would be no trouble from that quarter. Arrangements were also made through Colonel Cutter to have Secretary Stimson kept informed of developments as the fight over war-crimes policy approached a climax.[40] In addition, together with Mr. Hackworth, Bernays made some specific revisions in the 13 January draft to meet the wishes of Judge Rosenman. These changes, which were made on 15 January, included a provision recommending the creation of a seven-member court—preferably staffed with military personnel—four from the Allied Big Four and three who would serve as representatives of the smaller United Nations. An additional short passage was added explaining that in the proposed system, the Big Four would have exclusive responsibility for establishing the court and or-

ganizing the proceedings. The UNWCC would not be abol-
ished immediately, but its right to consider and debate policy
questions would be eliminated, and henceforth it would serve
merely as an agency to collect and collate information regarding
enemy war criminals.

The last revision made by Hackworth and Bernays touched
on a more significant issue, because Judge Rosenman wished the
memorandum to discuss Soviet and British views on war
crimes. He obviously hoped something might be said to convince doubters that the conspiracy/criminal-organization plan
could be sold to America's allies. Both the JAG leaders and Ambassador Davies had claimed the British and Russians would
never agree to the War Department plan, and Hackworth and
Bernays were given the task of answering them. Regarding the
Soviet Union, they inserted a passage that, in effect, confessed
they knew nothing definite about Soviet war-crimes policy except that the Kremlin seemed to favor the "judicial process." [41]
Actually there was ample information in Washington by this
time demonstrating that Soviet Russia wanted a trial of the
major Nazi leaders, and the statement on this subject that was
included in the revision was much more hesitant than the
available information warranted.

In contrast, the account of the probable British attitude
toward the conspiracy/criminal-organization proposal that Bernays and Hackworth gave was more extensive. But it also
seemed disingenuous, or at least more labored. The British
aide-mémoire of 30 October 1944 (attacking the UNWCC
proposal for the establishment of a treaty court) was obviously
a bad omen for them, and Bernays and Hackworth could only
deal with it effectively by contending that the treaty court described in the 13 January memorandum was significantly different. Their revision therefore cited a number of special liabilities contained in the aide-mémoire, such as the necessity for a
long-term commitment by the powers, and the fact that the
Soviet Union was not a member of the UNWCC. But no mat-

ter how they twisted and turned, Bernays and Hackworth were unable to come up with anything pointing to likely British support for the conspiracy/criminal-organization proposal. The most they could say was that they did "not regard the British objections to the War Crimes Commission's Draft Convention as *nooooooarily* precluding assent to the proposals now advanced." [42] [Italics added]

The revisions made by Hackworth and Bernays thus failed significantly to strengthen the memorandum, and by bringing the issue of British opposition out into the open, they provided the plan's critics with another point of attack. When this problem, inherent in the plan, but now made explicit, was combined with the difficulties Bernays had created by his heavy emphasis on aggressive-war prosecution and a treaty court, there was good reason for even the strongest supporters of the plan to begin to lose heart. In the second week of January, an anonymous critic in Mr. McCloy's office disapprovingly noted the stress on a treaty court and aggressive war contained in the 13 January draft, and he remarked dryly that "possibly Col. Bernays did a little too good a job on this." [43]

On 16 January Cutter sent a note to McCloy indicating that the 13 January draft needed revision; it tipped too strongly in favor of a treaty court and did not make it sufficiently clear that a conspiracy/criminal-organization prosecution could only embrace prewar atrocities and aggressive war if these had been steps in a plan that had "resulted in wartime war crimes." [44] But Cutter's doubts went even further. He suspected that retoning or even substantial redrafting would not, in themselves, resolve such basic problems as the probability of British opposition, and he recommended that a "high level" four-power conference should be held immediately to clear the air. Even at home, Cutter voiced uncertainty: Would rushing into another head-on clash in Rosenman's office, such as the one scheduled for that very day (16 January), bring a satisfactory solution? Perhaps, the colonel mused, it would be a good idea to call off the battle and follow up a suggestion once apparently made by Mr. Stimson that the plan should be turned over to an independent group for further study and recommendation.[45]

But on the home front at least, the counsel for caution had come too late, and the usual group—Hackworth, McCloy, Bernays, and Wechsler—were joined by Ambassador Davies (and perhaps a JAG representative) in Judge Rosenman's office during the afternoon of 16 January. Although we do not have direct testimony on the details of what took place during this session, it is obvious that the supporters of the conspiracy/criminal-organization plan were somewhat on the defensive.[46] By the end of the discussion the group had decided another meeting should be held two days later, with a top officer from JAG and the attorney general himself present. At this time those who objected to the conspiracy/criminal-organization plan would be given an opportunity to present alternate war-crimes trial proposals. This was a clever maneuver, suggesting the deft hand of Judge Rosenman, because it offered a possibility of taking some of the heat off the defenders of the conspiracy/criminal-organization plan by inviting the critics to try their luck at solving the myriad of war-crimes policy problems.

But the scheme almost backfired when, on 17 January, the Treasury Department learned "through the back door" that the War Department proposal might be close to final approval.[47] Morgenthau and his assistants, who had been lackadaisically logging objections to the plan since McCloy had sent them a copy of the 27 November draft a month earlier, were now jolted into feverish activity. During the early afternoon of the seventeenth, they met in order to make a last-minute effort to pull their major criticisms together and prepare a Treasury position paper. Within Morgenthau's department there was unanimous opposition to using a treaty court, primarily because a treaty would run into trouble in the Senate. Treasury officials were also nearly obsessed with making certain that the plan put no obstacles in the way of Allied nations wishing to secure captured Nazis for trial in the former occupied territories.

But even within the Treasury, there was little agreement on anything else. Some Treasury men had come to conclude that summary execution of the top Nazis was unwise, and that a trial was probably the better course after all. So deeply were the top Treasury officials divided that they decided Secretary Morgenthau should stall cabinet approval of the War Department plan to gain a respite during which they could hammer out a comprehensive policy position on war crimes.[48] No sooner had they reached this conclusion and adjourned their conference than Secretary Morgenthau learned, on the late afternoon of 17 January, that the decisive meeting on the war-crimes question was scheduled for Rosenman's office on the following day.

Morgenthau immediately telephoned Rosenman and asked the judge if a Treasury representative would be allowed to attend. Rosenman's response was cool—with the long saga of the battle over the Morgenthau plan still fresh in his memory, it was not a very inviting prospect—but he finally agreed to meet with a Treasury spokesman at 3:30 P.M. on the afternoon of the eighteenth.[49] What the crafty Rosenman did not make clear to Morgenthau was that the war-crimes conference was scheduled for the morning of the eighteenth and that when the Treasury representative arrived, the best he would get would be a postmortem report. By that time, if all went well, the show would be over.

The meeting of 18 January, the highest-level war-crimes conference held by the American government during World War II, was a major milestone on the road to Nuremberg. Therefore, even at the risk of some redundancy, it is important to consider how carefully, and cleverly, it was structured. The burden of proof was on the critics of the conspiracy/criminal-organization plan, General Weir for JAG and Ambassador Davies. With the President due to leave for Yalta within a week, unless the critics came up with a plausible alternative that could be instantly accepted and put into finished form, there was little other choice except to go along with some form of the conspiracy/criminal-organization plan. In this sense the meeting was clearly stacked. It was also very carefully arranged regarding who was in attendance. With the exception of Weir and Davies, everyone in the room—Rosenman, Wechsler, Hackworth, Biddle, and Bernays—supported the War Department proposal. In addition, great pains had been taken not to overemphasize the War Department presence. The only cabinet member in attendance was Francis Biddle, obviously not from the War Department, but a man who was a convert to the proposal and was the top legal officer of the government.

Prior to the meeting Stimson had briefed McCloy on what course should be followed, and McCloy, in turn, had passed on instructions to Bernays; but both the Assistant Secretary and the Secretary of War were careful not to put in an appearance until after the deliberations were complete.[50] In light of all this finesse and subtle contrivance, one cannot help feeling a measure of sympathy for Davies and Weir, who were condemned to struggle and argue and thus gradually demonstrate that they really had no effective solution to the problem. The others present, like patient lions, needed only to wait until their opponents had exhausted themselves, and then they could move in for the kill.

Of the two critics, Ambassador Davies was probably the easiest to dispatch quickly. Even though he had prepared a paper setting out his views, it ignored many of the most serious difficulties facing the war-crimes policy planners. Davies recommended that the war-crimes question be divided into three subproblems.[51] He proposed that the Big Three at Yalta should simply announce that all the Nazi culprits, large and small, would be speedily tried and disposed of in the various military and civil courts of the several United Nations on the basis of existing laws against war crimes. Then, after the conference, as the second step in his program, the governments of the Big Three would make up a list of arch criminals and work out arrangements for the form of their trial or trials. Whether the proceedings occurred before regular military tribunals, occupation courts, or even a United Nations war-crimes court mattered little to Davies, as long as they were held on the basis of existing—not ex post facto—law. As the third and final step in this recommendation, Davies repeated his suggestion that the occasion provided by the drafting of the post-war peace treaties should be used to establish iron-clad rules making the launching of aggressive war or the perpetration of "crimes against humanity" punishable offenses under international law.

If one views Mr. Davies's proposal from the perspective of those who had been wrestling with the war-crimes question for the previous five months, it is easy to see why it was totally unacceptable. Not only did it fail to face many of the practical legal difficulties—difficulties, such as whether a head of state could be prosecuted under prevailing international law, that had led Bernays and his colleagues to take the leap toward legal innovation—it totally ignored the climate of opinion out of which the war-crimes controversy had sprung. The highly emotion-charged issue of German persecution of their own nationals was passed over in silence by Davies. He also paid no attention to the feeling, which had been growing steadily inside the War Department, that a precedent for limiting future aggression and atrocities should be established through Allied war-crimes policy. Stimson and others had seen enough peace conferences filled with empty gestures regarding aggression and persecutions, they wanted to act while there was a hammer in their hands. On this question, whether rightly or wrongly, the bulk of American public sentiment, which always harbored a deep distrust of diplomats and formal international agreements, was surely much closer to the War Department view than it was to Mr. Davies's pious hopes for postwar understanding.

Similarly, when the ambassador failed to accept the plan for prosecuting criminal organizations and did not develop a device more specific and comprehensive than phrases such as prosecuting culprits "great and small," he put himself on the wrong side of another strong trend in prevailing governmental and public opinion in America. By January 1945, American outrage, not only against Nazis, but against all Germans, was in full flood, and any program that set cautious or traditional limits to the punitive policies to be followed in Germany was in for trouble. Mr. Davies's recommendations were doomed to fail because the central question facing the American government was how to shape a war-crimes prosecution program that would not do excessive violence to traditional law while still satisfying the public's desire to force the Germans to see the folly of their ways. Whatever Mr. Davies had done, he had not even addressed himself to these questions.

The second counterproposal to be laid on the table, prepared by JAG, appeared to be a rather more serious proposition, if for no other reason than because it was a complete memorandum, patterned after those Bernays and his colleagues had prepared.[52] Under the JAG plan, the leaders of Nazi Germany and those of Fascist Italy would be placed on trial and charged with preparing "a systematic and planned reign of terror in the occupied countries," resulting in a plethora of outrageous and barbaric violations of the laws of war. In addition, the enemy leaders would be charged with violation of the third Hague Convention of 1907 because they had launched attacks against neutral countries such as Belgium, Holland, and Norway, "without ultimatum or declaration of war." During the trial, any evidence of acts committed by the enemy leaders prior to the war that showed "motive and intent" to subsequently commit war crimes, would be admissible.[53]

Obviously what the JAG plan had done, aside from including Italian leaders along with the Germans, was to narrow sharply the chargeable offenses. The broad conspiracy charge had been jettisoned, as had the specific count aimed at crimes against humanity. The aggressive-war count was severely restricted, and the position that prewar atrocities had occupied among the charges was reduced to a minimum. Since the JAG plan also dumped the *criminal* prosecution of Nazi organizations, it had no further need for a treaty court. The chief of JAG, General Cramer, had been the one who first stressed the importance of a treaty court in a system of organizational prosecution because it would be needed to provide the constitutional basis for transferring a finding from one court to another. But the treaty-court idea had contained so many political difficulties that it had become a serious liability to the conspiracy/criminal-organization plan.

Now, in late January, the JAG leaders tried to build up support for their own limited prosecution system by stressing that their proposal did not require a new constitutional foundation and therefore could forego a treaty court. The JAG plan proposed that the trial of the major Nazi and Fascist leaders be held before an "international military commission or court," and that by proceeding in this way it would be easier to secure the agreement of the British government. Stretching the truth a bit, the JAG paper claimed that while the British had flatly rejected a UNWCC treaty court in their 30 October aide-mémoire, they had "in effect endorsed" the idea of trial by international military tribunals.[54] Actually the British had shown little enthusiasm for any kind of international court, but the JAG plan, with its many conservative features, would probably have seemed "less bad" in London than either the UNWCC or the Bernays proposal.

The JAG leaders took greater liberties with probability when they implied their plan would be readily approved by the leaders of the Soviet Union. They had located an October 1942 Molotov statement on war crimes, which had heretofore eluded the notice of American war-crimes planners, and near the end of it they discovered the Soviet foreign minister had remarked that a "special international tribunal" for dealing with some war-crimes cases would be acceptable to Soviet Russia.[55] The JAG memorandum cited this remark to show that because the JAG proposal utilized a "special international tribunal," it would satisfy the Soviets; and at the same time, since it recommended using a "military commission," not a treaty court, it would find favor with the British.[56] In actuality this was little more than a game of philological sleight of hand. Molotov's statement had declared that although Russia was committed to judicial procedures, it wanted a wide-open innovative attack on Nazi war crimes, and the foreign minister had merely used the phrase "special international tribunal" incidentally, within a long list of possible war-crimes trial procedures that would be welcome to Moscow.

The JAG plan dodged too many fundamental issues to have any basis of support either in Moscow or among the American officials gathered in Rosenman's office. The political realities of the moment called for innovation, but all the JAG plan did was serve up a series of tepid formulas designed to pay a bit of lip service to the public's angry cries for radical action. Like most efforts to straddle a gap, the proposal failed to produce enthusiasm, even among JAG's conservative allies. When General Royall read the JAG draft a few days after the 18 January meeting, he reported to McCloy that though he found it "much sounder" than those inspired by Bernays, he still wanted all vestiges of aggressive-war prosecution—even those restricted to incidents where attacks had been made without a declaration of war—struck from the plan.[57] There was no way to find a simple compromise formula that would satisfy the advocates of the conspiracy/criminal-organization plan and their traditionalist legal critics at this late date. The JAG had merely produced a cautious hodgepodge that did not face up to the basic political problems and could not completely satisfy anyone.

After everything possible had been said and done regarding the recommendations of Ambassador Davies and General Weir, there was still only one proposal with any political plausibility on the table in Judge Rosenman's office on 18 January. This was the conspiracy/criminal-organization plan. If the group gathered in that room was going to place a policy statement on war criminals in the President's hands before he left for Yalta in the next few days, they would have to make something out of that plan, or give up their efforts altogether. They wrangled and struggled against this fate well past the customary Washington lunch hour. But finally they resigned themselves to the fact that a few elements would have to be taken from the JAG proposal and integrated into a form of the conspiracy/criminal-organization plan—a form that emphasized the judicial approach, eliminated the treaty court, and muted the provisions on aggressive war. At the end of the meeting, to clinch the deal, and presumably to help JAG save face, the incongruous team of Bernays and General Weir was chosen to draft a new version of the conspiracy/criminal-organization plan, which would contain every conceivable feature that could bring a touch of joy to the hearts of legal conservatives.

When the meeting broke up, there waiting in the anteroom was Judge Rosenman's luncheon companion, none other than the Secretary of War.[58] Once again, Henry Stimson demonstrated his ability to move ahead prudently while arranging to be in the right place at the right time. On this occasion there was no repair work to be done. The Secretary was able to relax over lunch as the judge recounted how (war-crimes) peace had been restored to the War Department and Rosenman's "group" —to use Stimson's word—had decided on a program based on "a big trial in which we can prove the whole Nazi conspiracy to wage a totalitarian war of aggression violating in its progress all the regular rules which limit needless cruelty and destruction." [59] The conciliatory Rosenman, when speaking to Stimson, probably laid more emphasis on aggressive war than the decisions taken at the meeting warranted, but in reality the Secretary of War's wishes had largely triumphed on 18 January.

The judge was not so subtle when it came to dealing with one of the departments that was a big loser on this day. Immediately after lunch he went back to his office and called the Treasury to say there was no longer any reason to send someone to discuss war-crimes matters, because the meeting was already over, and "everyone" had agreed that there should be a major trial.[60] As a small sop to Morgenthau and his colleagues, Rosenman added that the group had also rejected a treaty court and had decided that if an international authorizing instrument was required, they would use an executive agreement. The judge thereby stole a long march on the Treasury. All he needed was for Bernays and Weir to complete their drafting work rapidly and well, and Morgenthau, along with the rest of the opponents of the conspiracy/criminal-organization plan, would be routed.

Bernays especially understood the need for speed, and together with General Weir, he worked feverishly throughout the afternoon and evening of 18 January, completing a draft memorandum for the Attorney General and the Secretaries of War and State to send to the President by the following morning (19 January).[61] The new memorandum left the major elements of the original conspiracy/criminal-organization plan in place. The Nazi leaders were still to be prosecuted in a great conspiracy trial, and in that trial Nazi organizations would be declared criminal, thus making possible subsequent simplified proceedings against organization members. The memorandum of 19 January was, however, less impassioned, more concise, and more tightly drafted than that of 13 January. It contained all the revisions prepared six days earlier to meet the wishes of Judge Rosenman: a section on the future of the UNWCC, recommendations on the composition of the main court, and a summary of the position Washington thought the British government held regarding war crimes. The new draft also incorporated a number of features contained in the JAG proposal submitted in Judge Rosenman's office the day before. Like the JAG proposal, the memorandum of 19 January underscored the importance of a judicial procedure rather than political action. The section of the JAG draft that hypothesized about Soviet attitudes toward war crimes was also added to this memorandum, as were the passages in which JAG recounted the great problems of "identification and proof" that would confront every postwar effort to sort out the tangled maze of Nazi crimes and atrocities.[62]

Of much greater importance was the fact that, prompted by JAG, this memorandum muted the provisions on prewar persecutions, and totally recast those relating to aggression, so that every reference to the preparation and launching of an aggressive war was eliminated. What remained was a recommendation that the Nazis be charged with having prepared and implemented a criminal plan that included a whole series of outrages going "back at least as far as 1933" and culminated in "the *waging* of an illegal war of aggression with ruthless disregard for international law and the rules of war." [63] [Italics added] Even though this was a highly ambitious proposition, it was far more circumspect than what had gone before. After all the struggle and controversy that had turned on the aggressive-war question during the preceding two months, those who had advocated mounting a full-scale legal attack to prosecute aggression as a crime had been forced to back off. The memorandum of 19 January contained the most tempered assertion of the criminality of aggressive war of any proposal prepared since November 1944. The seeds of the notion remained in the single phrase "waging an illegal war of aggression," and these seeds would soon sprout when nurtured by Justice Jackson; but in late January 1945 they were deeply buried in the soil of a prosecution plan emphasizing traditional war crimes and mass atrocities.

A pair of significant legal complications for the future were also contained in the provisions relating to criminal organizations in the 19 January memorandum. Following the lead of the JAG draft, and bowing to the views of Wechsler, Hackworth, Davies, and McCloy, the memorandum eliminated the provision advocating creation of a treaty court and replaced it with a tribunal established through executive agreement. The oft-repeated objection that a treaty would produce insurmountable difficulties, both in inter-Allied cooperation and Senate ratification, thereby triumphed, but the decision simply to drop the treaty and substitute an executive agreement left the plan hanging in midair. Regarding the contention that without a treaty a finding of organizational criminality by an international tribunal might not be binding in American civil or military courts, the memorandum merely stated that the cases would be tried by "occupation courts." [64] A large hole was thereby left in a scheme designed to facilitate the routine prosecution and punishment of criminal-organization members. Later revisions failed to fill the hole and the Nuremberg court ultimately threw out most of the plan's provisions on organizational criminality, in part because without a treaty, the chief judge from the United States—ironically it was Francis Biddle—doubted whether such procedures were consistent with American legal practice.

The second peculiarity in the criminal-organization provisions of the 19 January memorandum concerned the rights of defendants. The preceding draft (13 January) had conceded that in secondary proceedings before Allied courts, a defendant might claim he had not known of the criminal purposes of the organization he had joined. The 19 January memorandum, however, deleted this clause and thus established a system that, if it had ever been applied, would have allowed an international tribunal's finding of criminality to be binding on American occupation courts (without a constitutional revision), and would have denied a defendant's right to plead ignorance of the criminal purposes of the organization at the time he had enlisted in it. Surely, unless the defendants were also to be denied counsel, such a system would have been torn to shreds either during the secondary proceedings or on appeal.

But it would be a mistake to carp at specific legal shortcomings in this memorandum as if it had been intended to serve as a piece of legislation or a legal charter. The 19 January memorandum was designed to allow the three Secretaries* to put their case on war crimes to the President so that it could not be torpedoed immediately by political opponents such as Morgenthau or Davies. It was a consensus document that had to be prepared very rapidly and satisfy numerous factions and shades of opinion. As such, it succeeded brilliantly, a credit

---

* Technically, the Attorney General is not a cabinet "Secretary," but for simplicity's sake, I will refer to this document as the "three Secretaries' memorandum."

both to the drafting skill of Bernays, and to the ability of the colonel and the general to temper their differences and find solutions acceptable to all.

Once the drafting was completed, Weir and Bernays began moving from office to office, testing opinions, and ultimately gaining approval, from the important officials who had been involved in the formulation of the plan. They began their trek at 9:00 A.M. on the nineteenth and did not gain the last important signature until the morning of the twenty-second. Among all the departments and senior officials, the approval of the War Department and of Secretary Stimson was the easiest to obtain. McCloy's office requested no revisions, and on the morning of 21 January, Henry Stimson signed the memorandum "with great satisfaction." [65] The Secretary of War noted in his diary that "this difficult question" had been dealt with "in a way which is at the same time consistent with our traditional judicial principles and also will be effective in dispensing adequate punishment and also leave a permanent record in the shape of the evidence collected of the evils against which we have fought this war." [66]

The response of the other officials was not quite so enthusiastic, and minor revisions had to be made in the memorandum at the behest of Mr. Hackworth, Judge Rosenman, and Attorney General Biddle. But delays in signing were primarily caused by the perennial necessity to discuss and consult. Biddle would not sign until Wechsler approved the document.[67] Mr. Hackworth had to talk it over with Secretary Stettinius.[68] A final Navy Department clearance was required, and a copy needed to be forwarded to Ambassador Davies. By the early afternoon of the nineteenth, Herbert Wechsler signaled his agreement, and on the afternoon of the twenty-first, the Attorney General had secured a statement by Secretary James Forrestal that the Navy Department "disclaimed any interest in the project." [69] Subsequently Mr. Forrestal would explain he had not intended to disassociate the Navy Department from the project; but in order to avoid "holding proceedings up" by entering into the "discussions at this late stage," he had decided that if the other three Secretaries approved of the memorandum, he would not interfere.[70] The document was therefore limited to the War, State, and Justice Departments. In the course of 21 January Biddle added his signature to Stimson's, and on the morning of 22 January, Stettinius also signed.

The basic policy statement was thereby completed. The technical problem of implementing the plan in the event that the Big Three at Yalta accepted it and were prepared to officially ratify, had also been taken care of. On 19 January Rosenman had relayed through the Attorney General a request that Hackworth and Bernays draft a paper on this subject. The work was begun on the afternoon of the nineteenth and the three-page summary was routinely completed and forwarded to Judge Rosenman by Mr. Hackworth on the morning of the twentieth.[71] Apparently only the two drafters and Rosenman saw the completed "Implementing Instrument" at this time, but it was actually to have an extended, and highly controversial, life. Although not submitted to the Allies at Yalta, this document, much revised and retitled, was the basis for discussions in London during April, at the San Francisco UN conference in May, and at the four-power negotiations in June 1945.

Since the "Implementing Instrument" was intended to stand in lieu of a formal treaty, and proclaimed, among other points, the transferability of a declaration of organizational criminality to "occupation or other appropriate tribunals," where individual defendants would have had virtually no rights, one suspects that if it had been more widely circulated in January 1945, a number of strong voices might have been raised in opposition to it. But because it was simply drafted and handed only to Judge Rosenman, conservative doubters did not see this most vulnerable item. Therefore only two dissenters to the general plan came forward, and their complaints were so shopworn and poorly timed that they lacked any significant effect.

On 19 January the Treasury Department sent a paper to Rosenman over the Secretary's signature. It was apparently not even read either by Rosenman or by the man who had signed it, Henry Morgenthau.[72] Yet the memorandum, while containing some of the Treasury's most popular leitmotifs, such as the need to eliminate any obstacles in the way of extraditing war criminals, did touch on other hardline points that would arise again in future months. The memorandum contended that if there was going to be a trial, it should follow simplified procedures and that traditional rights of defendants would have to be virtually eliminated. In a peculiar echo of the language Chanler and Bernays had used while championing prosecution of wars of aggression, Treasury officials called for the elimination of legal technicalities because "international law must be dynamic not static," and the respect of the people of the world for international law would rise or fall "in direct proportion to its ability to meet their needs." In regard to organizations, the Treasury insisted that the tribunal should not only make a general finding of criminality, but should also establish "as a minimum a certain type of punishment [for all members] with graduations depending upon the position of responsibility held by such individuals in the organization." This proposition, too, received no hearing in January 1945, but later it would be tossed about by Washington policymakers, including some in the War Department, until the final days of the Nuremberg trials.[73]

Mr. Davies had better luck than the men of the Treasury in getting his critical views to the top of the government pyramid, but the impact was also nil. In conformity with the ambassador's request, Judge Rosenman sent a paper containing Mr. Davies's opinions on to the President's secretary,[74] who quietly filed it away. After declaring that he approved the final memorandum of 19–22 January "with some reservations," the ambassador wandered off on a long, redundant discussion of the considerations he had raised previously. Again he contended that the central problem was political, not legal, and that the Big Three at Yalta should declare their determination to punish the major war criminals while leaving "to their Foreign Offices" the monumental task of developing a program that would sustain established legal principles, satisfy public opinion, meet Soviet demands for wholesale punishment of the Nazis, and respect what the ambassador contended was a British reluctance to deviate from due process.[75]

It was probably merciful that Mr. Davies did not explain how all this was to be accomplished. Since the British were the ones advocating political execution while the Soviets were supporting trials—however perfunctory—the ambassador had managed to get the problem backward to begin with. In addition, he had simultaneously approved the plan prepared by the Rosenman group *and* contended that a completely new program would have to be developed after Yalta. In light of all this, it is difficult to believe that any solutions Mr. Davies might have advanced to the problems—real or imaginary— would have thrown much light on the war-crimes controversy in January 1945, and his memorandum was justly banished to a White House file drawer.

So on 22 January 1945, those who had been pushing for cabinet-level approval of a conspiracy/criminal-organization approach to the problem of Nazi war crimes seemed to have swept on to victory. The final memoranda were more circumspect than some of them wished, and the proposals for utilizing a treaty court and prosecuting aggressive war had been sacrificed, at least for the time being. But three of the most powerful members of the cabinet had, by signing the memorandum, given their endorsement to the basic idea and to the conclusion expressed in Judge Rosenman's report to the President, that the plan

would not only result in speedy and effective justice but would establish an essentially fair procedure which would meet the approval of enlightened public opinion not only of today, but of future generations.[76]

But what did this sick and weary President actually think about the war-crimes question on the eve of Yalta? All Judge Rosenman could do was ask Mr. Roosevelt's secretary to place the memorandum signed by the three Secretaries, together with the "Implementing Instrument," into the "appropriate basket" because, as he noted, the president "wants to take it on the ship with him to read on the way over." [77] Whether Franklin Roosevelt actually ever read the memorandum, and if he did, what his impressions were, we do not know. Judging by his evasive reaction following the Morgenthau plan debacle, as well as his subsequent failure to push vigorously for any solution to the war-crimes problem, it seems highly unlikely that the issue ever really penetrated the layers of exhaustion and pain that were gradually enveloping his consciousness.

Only one American official has left a record of a conversation with the President on the subject of war crimes in January 1945. On 19 January, Henry Stimson had a long meeting with Mr. Roosevelt and used the occasion to elaborate once more on the wonders of the final war-crimes plan. As usual, the Secretary of War explained enthusiastically that a trial, in contrast to political execution, would not only uphold American ideals, but would provide a record showing "the full nature of the Nazi conspiracy or evil plan." [78] According to Mr. Stimson's diary entry, the President listened and, in the Secretary's words, "he assented to what I said." But Mr. Stimson added, a bit resignedly, that "in the hurry of the situation I am not sure whether it registered." [79] Thirty-five years later it is still fair to say that although the conspiracy/criminal-organization plan had won a cabinet battle in January 1945, it is still open to question whether or not the nature of the plan, or the fact of the victory, ever really "registered" on the President of the United States.

CHAPTER 5

FROM YALTA

TO LONDON AND

WARM SPRINGS

Lord Moran [Churchill's physician] says there is no doubt which of the three will go first.[1]

Sir Alexander Cadogan
at Yalta

Marshal Stalin, Prime Minister Churchill, and President Roosevelt, accompanied by numerous aides and advisors, conferred at Yalta in the Crimea between 4 and 11 February 1945. It was the second meeting of the wartime Big Three, and it marked the final occasion when Churchill and Stalin saw Roosevelt alive. The agenda for the sessions was weighed down with important issues, including the recognition of the Lublin Polish government, the zoning and control council structure for occupied Germany, the price to be paid for Soviet entrance into the Pacific war, and the structure of the new United Nations organization. Hovering above the specific points and controversies was the larger issue of what would happen to the tenuous Allied coalition once the shooting stopped. Germany was on her last legs; and with the beginning of massive B-29 raids on the home islands in November 1944, the war against Japan had also entered a new, and decisive, stage. The Big Three were face to face with the moment of truth on their promise to create a brave new world, but the circumstances in which they confronted the problem—and each other—at Yalta were hardly conducive to deep confidence or heady optimism.

A heritage of mutual distrust, rivalry, and suspicion had long marked relations between East and West, and to a much lesser degree, between Britain and America. The wartime alliance had been created largely by accident, more through the savagery of Hitler's attacks than by any desire or initiative of the individual Allied powers. Four years of formal, and often strained, cooperation was a poor shield against the divisive forces of decades of history. The immediate circumstances and uncertainties of the military and political situation in Europe during early February compounded the difficulties. Hitler's forces were weak and tattered, but he had just given the Western powers a bad shock in the Bulge, and the Nazi threats to produce a final cataclysm of wonder weapons, *Werwolf* resistance, and general slaughter were hardly reassuring. In the east, Warsaw had just fallen, and the Russians had driven the *Wehrmacht* from the Vistula defense line. In the west, Anglo-American units continued their slow broad-front advance toward the Rhine. But neither the eastern nor western victory offensives, which were intended to decide the war in Europe in the spring of 1945, had been launched at the time of the Yalta conference. No one then knew which military force, Soviet or Anglo-American, would make the most rapid advance, nor could anyone foresee whether Hitler would fight to the finish against all his enemies, or perhaps open one front and thereby produce a decisive advantage for East or West. The configurations of the political/military map which would exist in Europe at the moment hostilities ended were thus hidden from the men of Yalta behind a cloud of doubt and uncertainty.

Thirty years of historical research and controversy suggest
that the three governments had also failed to develop policies
of striking clarity regarding what they wanted in the postwar
world. Behind the sonorous phrases, a craving for security and
perhaps zones of influence were plainly sought, but little
stands out sharply in the way of firm objectives in the policy of
any of the three powers. An examination of the documents now
available reveals that there was great British governmental confusion about means and ends; and when Soviet actions in the
years 1944–46 are exposed to careful scrutiny, they also fail to
reflect the clear Communist blueprint and timetable so beloved
by frightened cold warriors in the late 1940s and early 1950s.[2]
There was an overall tendency toward caution and defensive-
ness in London and a contrasting expansiveness and hypersensi-
tivity in Moscow, but clarity and precision were in rather short
supply in both capitals.

Compared with the lack of set purpose in Washington, however—and that is the central concern of the present inquiry—
the Soviet and British governments appear to have been para-
gons of political determination. The American leaders obviously
wanted to win the war and to have peace in the postwar
world, but after one goes beyond that, and gives a nod to a
craving for national security, anything resembling consensus
or lucidity vanishes. When scanning the American governmental
records, one can find evidence of almost any policy or political
objective imaginable. The Four Freedoms were there, as was
the program of denazification, a devotion to the principles of
the United Nations, and some touches of "Fortress America."
A dread of communism stood shoulder to shoulder with fears of
revived British imperialism, but on occasion there was also talk
of joining with Britain, Russia, France, and possibly even Nationalist China, to create a military force of four (or five)
policemen to patrol the whole planet. On and on they went—
a Carthaginian peace for Germany, the creation of a worldwide
capitalistic free-trade area, a limitation on special zones of Soviet

influence to assist the interests of American export capital—
every possible policy had at least one dedicated champion or
enthusiastic advocate.[3]

As long as no binding policy decisions had to be made, this
foreign-policy anarchy did little harm, because, as noted earlier,
Roosevelt thrived on having a multitude of possibilities run the
political gamut before he decided which way to jump. By the
time of Yalta most of this time cushion had vanished, however,
and Roosevelt's exhaustion and physical disintegration had deprived him of the means to thread his way deftly through the
conflicting policy choices. The seriousness of the situation was
compounded by the nature of the corps of advisors, who were
supposed to assist the American chief executive during the
Yalta deliberations. Although the U.S. staff was of enormous
size—a perennial characteristic of American diplomatic teams
during the Second World War—it did not include many of the
dominant political figures in the American government; nor did
it accurately represent the prevailing constellation of power in
the administration or on Capitol Hill. Not only were no strong
congressional or party leaders present, but the only cabinet
member in attendance was Stettinius, and of the inner White
House circle, no one other than Harry Hopkins. Stettinius was
definitely a political lightweight and Hopkins was so wracked by
illness that he lost twelve pounds the week before the opening
of the conference. The Joint Chiefs of Staff were there, as were
some State Department professionals including Bohlen,
Matthews, Hiss, and a few diplomatic hardliners such as Jimmy
Byrnes and Averell Harriman. But this collection of individuals
could in no way be considered to personify the major versions
of postwar policy that were struggling for dominance in
Washington.

The Joint Chiefs had controlled the decision-making process
through the war years, but their major concern was to pursue
virtually any course that would help end the war quickly and
cheaply. Obviously such a point of view could not throw much

light on what to do once hostilities ended. Conversely, although State Department professionals who had been pushed into the background of policymaking during the era of military supremacy were now eager to dash forward and assert themselves, such a policy revolution would have been difficult to consummate in the middle of any summit conference. With the inept and hesitant Stettinius as the titular head of the department, it was impossible at Yalta. So in session after session, the dying Roosevelt leaned on the ailing Hopkins; the two men tried to sustain a policy of East-West cooperation based on personal trust. It was a valiant and poignant effort that would be largely destroyed within five months, if for no other reason than because most of the principal figures had been eliminated —Roosevelt dead, Churchill out of power, and Hopkins so ill that he did not live out the year of 1945.

It is now a historical cliché that Yalta contributed to the creation of a political vacuum in which Joseph Stalin was soon able to help himself to a large portion of the initiative in world politics. Less obvious is that the peculiarly unrepresentative nature of the American staff at Yalta also contributed to the creation of an immediate foreign-policy vacuum within Washington during the early spring of 1945. The issue of war-crimes policy graphically illustrates the nature of the problem. None of the powerful men who had played roles in the development of the policy up to the completion of the three Secretaries' memorandum of 22 January 1945 accompanied Mr. Roosevelt to the Crimea. Stimson, McCloy, Rosenman, Davies, Biddle, even Morgenthau and Forrestal—all were missing from the president's entourage at Yalta. Yet it would be difficult to find any proposal related to foreign policy which had been advanced during the year prior to the Big Three conference that had not felt the imprint of some of these men or of their immediate associates. Consequently, their absence accentuated the gap between the hard realities of policy formation in Washington and the freewheeling atmosphere that prevailed in the Crimea. The situation was not as haphazard as that in

Quebec, when the performance of Roosevelt and Churchill had left Stimson and Hull, back in Washington, cowering in terror. But the stakes at Yalta were higher, and many of the decisions made there would not be subject to revision.

The organizational amateurism at the Crimean meeting meant not only that many significant policy questions never received formal consideration by the Big Three, but that when the conference was over, it was not always clear what had actually happened or why. Topics were discussed in corridors and at social gatherings; the President made compromise arrangements without telling some of his important aides; [4] and even in the formal sessions, the American officials who made the stenographic records did not always agree on what had been said or finally decided. In addition, some of the agreements concluded, such as granting Russia special privileges in Manchuria without obtaining the prior assent of the Chinese Nationalist government, were so politically explosive that a veil of secrecy was thrown over large portions of the transcript. Important officials in the U.S. government were thereby left in the dark about much that had happened for months after the conference ended. In late March, for example, Stettinius was fussing about how to let the American delegates to the San Francisco UN conference in on the secret of what the State Department called *subject X*—the grant to Russia of two extra votes in the General Assembly—in such a way that related matters would remain "buttoned up" and not be leaked to the press.[5] Similarly, as late as the third week of May, during a discussion of reparations-labor policy, Henry Morgenthau complained that three of the people most concerned with the topic, Justice Jackson, Mr. Clayton of the Treasury, and Morgenthau himself, had never even seen the provisions of the Yalta transcript that covered the subject.[6]

A generous measure of confusion about what the conference had, or had not, done regarding war-crimes policy was thus probably inevitable in the Washington of late February and early March 1945. The official story that circulated through

most government offices immediately after the return of the
American delegation from the Crimea was that the subject had
not even been considered during the deliberations of the Big
Three. But in the first week of March, Washington learned indirectly that the British government was maintaining that the
question had been discussed, apparently during the sixth
plenary session of 9 February, and that the Allied leaders had
given the three foreign ministers the task of developing a
policy for disposing of the major Nazi war criminals.[7]

A great flurry of activity ensued as State Department records
on the sessions were unearthed and examined, but the results
were less than helpful. The notes that had been made by
"Doc" Matthews contained not a word about war crimes, and
"Chip" Bohlen's notes produced additional confusion.[8] According to the latter, the war-crimes question had arisen peripherally
during the sixth plenary session when Bohlen quoted Churchill
as saying, "these men [that is, the Nazi leaders] should be
shot once their identity is established." Bohlen's record then
continued, without identifying the speaker, by quoting another
remark to the effect that "these men should be given a judicial trial." To cap the jumble, the State Department official had
ended his notes with the statement that "Marshal Stalin
replied in the affirmative." [9]

Despite some tugging and hauling, no one in Washington
was able to make much sense out of this. Whether Churchill
had come out for summary execution and then for trial or (and
this was inherently more plausible) the Prime Minister had
advocated political liquidation and someone else had suggested judicial action remained a total mystery. Just as uncertain was the nature of the proposition to which Stalin had allegedly answered "in the affirmative." The only thing of importance that Washington officials could conclude was that no
matter what may have been said, they had no evidence that the
question of the major war criminals had been given over to
the foreign ministers as London claimed. The fact that the offi-

cial British conference records also do not contain any reference to such a decision,[10] and that during the subsequent six months of discussions Soviet authorities never referred to it, suggests that the American conclusion was right and the British were wrong. By all odds, nothing of importance had in fact been decided at Yalta about a policy on war criminals.

This was, nonetheless, essentially a negative conclusion. American war-crimes planners had focused their efforts on developing a position paper that would provide guidance for the President at the Big Three meeting. Instead of a summit decision, all that had resulted was the memorandum signed by the three U.S. Cabinet members and an implementing instrument, which had only been seen by a tiny handful of American officials. Not only had the Big Three not formally adopted the plan, but the President, after his return from Yalta, still failed to indicate whether or not it had his approval.

In this shadow zone, the law of inertia seemed to prevail, and the conspiracy/criminal-organization plan settled into place as something akin to the de facto American policy during the period from mid-Frebruary to early April 1945. State Department officials generally acted throughout these months as if the plan was an established program of the U.S. government.[11] Army directives for occupied Germany also partly reflected this position by calling for wholesale internment of government, police, SS, and Nazi party officials. But the Army's policy declarations were not altogether clear regarding what these wholesale arrests were supposed to accomplish, and there was a marked uncertainty about what to do with some sections of the SS. As late as 26 April 1945, the orders issued to Eisenhower did not direct him to take into custody rank-and-file members of the *Waffen* (Armed) SS, although blanket internment of all members of other branches of the SS was provided for. Self-evidently, if the whole SS was going to be prosecuted for being a criminal organization, the exclusion from automatic arrest of the regular membership of its largest subsection indicates that someone in the highest levels of the American army did not fully understand the conspiracy/criminal-organization plan.[12]

Furthermore, during late January and early February many officials were so busy with other worrisome aspects of the German occupation problem that they had little time to get a clear grip on war-crimes policy. Although Bernays did join with State Department officials in keeping a careful eye on press information that the Soviet Union would probably be sympathetic to an "innovative" trial system,[13] his major concern during these months was the fate of Allied POWs in German hands, and he had little energy left to push actively for his war-crimes proposal. Other War Department legal specialists were just as deeply troubled by the difficulties that might result from an Allied victory so total that no German government would be left to surrender.[14]

The need to prepare for every possible contingency, as well as to develop a broad range of programs to be implemented in postwar Germany, was so all-consuming that even the planners who belonged to the war-crimes opposition were reduced to nearly total silence. Only one Treasury memorandum touching on the question was produced during this period, and it was merely an intradepartmental note, which, while complaining that the memorandum of 22 January to the President "did not go nearly . . . far" enough, still grudgingly admitted that it "was a great improvement over the previous memorandum which we had seen." [15] Nothing at all was heard from Ambassador Davies or the JAG critics during late January and February and it fell to General Royall to try to hoist the banner of opposition in a memorandum of 21 March. The general contended that since nothing had been done at Yalta regarding the conspiracy/criminal-organization plan and that full negotiations to implement it would take very long in any case, it was essential that a military war-crimes division be immediately established for the European theater; and that this division should cooperate with the British and Russians in creating a

UN military commission to conduct trials. Then, Royall blandly added, the commission should prosecute only traditional war crimes and atrocities and not hold a conspiracy trial, or prosecute aggressive war, prewar persecutions, or acts committed against German nationals.[16]

The only consideration that lent any credence to Royall's thinly disguised effort to scuttle the Bernays plan was his point that the Allies were fast running out of planning time. The war in Europe was indeed coming to an end. On 6 March, units of the American First Army had seized a bridge over the Rhine, and the Remagen bridgehead was soon providing a spearhead through which Western military units slashed into south-central Germany. Nazi resistance in the west shuddered and began to disintegrate. If the Nazi threat to wreak vengeance on POWs and concentration camp inmates could be kept at bay, the only immediate political/military uncertainties left unresolved were how far east Anglo-American forces would need to penetrate before they met the Red Army, and how many weeks would be required to complete any final battle of annihilation. The very speed and scope of these changes guaranteed that General Royall would not be the only one who saw that the moment for decision had come.

In a rerun of earlier scenarios, a controversy surrounding the American representation on the UNWCC was what initially prompted the State Department to activate the war-crimes question once again in early March. Long dissatisfied with Mr. Pell's unorthodox ways, the department had finally managed to squeeze him out of office; but there remained serious residues of difficulty regarding future American representation and policy on the commission.[17] To help clear the air, Acting Secretary of State Joseph Grew suggested, and the President agreed, that Judge Rosenman should make use of a planned trip to London to "survey" the work of the commission and advise Washington on the best course to follow. But when Grew relayed this information to Rosenman, the judge pointed out that Roosevelt had already selected Ambassador Davies to make such a "survey" trip in December 1944. Grew then rang up Davies and learned that the ambassador had as yet done nothing in regard to the trip, but he planned to go in the near future.[18]

The matter rested there for four days, and then on 6 March the department received two messages that provided additional impetus for action. John J. McCloy, pointing to the lack of progress on the war-crimes problem at Yalta, wrote to Grew urging that the three Secretaries' memorandum of 22 January be sent on to the President "with a view to getting it finally approved.[19] Also on 6 March, the State Department received an aide-mémoire from the British government inviting Mr. Hackworth, General Weir (of JAG), and any other representatives the Americans might select to come to London on 15 March for "a general discussion of the subject" of war crimes.[20] The invitation had been prompted by Ambassador Halifax,[21] who was aware that serious policy discussions on the subject were going on in Washington, and he had concluded that Hackworth, and perhaps Weir, represented the more conservative faction in the controversy. Apparently, during December 1944 and January 1945, at the same time that he had been helping Bernays shape his "radical" conspiracy/criminal-organization plan, Hackworth had also given Halifax the impression that he still championed a conservative view of war-crimes prosecution.

This incident highlights a rarely noticed factor that made clear communication between London and Washington difficult during the war. By keeping in friendly contact with numerous officials, British representatives in Washington (and reversing direction, American representatives in London) could pick up a stream of "off-the-record" views, wishes, hopes, and dreams. These often seemed to indicate important trends in American (or British) policy, but were in actuality frequently just the personal whims of isolated individuals.[22] The more successful a British representative was in staying close to American conditions and American officials, the more likely he was to pick up a wide range of "confidential" utterances, especially from Anglophiles such as Hackworth, who always wished to make their views seem presentable to His Majesty's Government. The very closeness of Anglo-American policy cooperation, when combined with wartime Washington's often chaotic administrative procedures, exacerbated the situation. Lord Halifax once compared the American administrative process to "a disorderly day's rabbit shooting. Nothing comes out where you expect and you are much discouraged," wrote the ambassador, adding that, "then suddenly, something emerges quite unexpectedly at the far end of the field." [23] Many of these prize little bunnies, in the form of well-intentioned indiscretions by American officials, found their way into Halifax's hands and then into his dispatches. The cumulative effect, however, was to make it extremely difficult for London to grasp what the American government was likely to do on any given occasion.

In this case the Foreign Office had concluded, on the basis of reports emanating from the British embassy in Washington, that America's war-crimes policy was still in flux, and that London might, with a bit of adroit maneuvering, assist "conservative" Washington officials in their struggle against the "radicals." While noting parenthetically that the question of major war criminals had been given over to the three foreign ministers at Yalta—a remark that, as we have already seen, created considerable consternation and confusion in Washington—the British memorandum of 6 March suggested that a meeting in London featuring Hackworth and Weir could still be useful in tackling lesser matters. Among the questions that the British thought might "profitably" be explored were the treaty court "suggested" by the UNWCC, "proposed mixed military tribunals," and a procedure "for dealing with lists of war criminals produced by the [UN War Crimes] Commission." [24] All of these were old, and relatively unimportant, items; but if the British had been able to get representative American officials to deal with them on British terms in London, it might conceivably have helped to tip the American policy scales in a more cautious direction.

To the mind of Acting Secretary Grew, however, when the British memorandum was coupled with the message from John J. McCloy, it seemed like an opportunity to advance final American approval of the conspiracy/criminal-organization plan and to lay the basis for discussions of that plan with the British government. On 8 March, Grew forwarded to the President both the British message of 6 March and the three Secretaries' memorandum of 22 January. The Acting Secretary told the President that "it would greatly facilitate planning by the State Department and the War Department if they could be informed . . . whether the conclusions and recommendations of the memorandum have your approval." [25] In addition Grew asked the President's permission for Weir and Hackworth to go to London, while reminding Mr. Roosevelt that he had previously appointed Davies to make such a trip, and that Judge Rosenman was also waiting in the wings. Grew's staff was careful to inform McCloy of what they had done,[26] especially because the State and War Departments were once again marching shoulder to shoulder, trying to beat back yet another effort by Morgenthau and his aides to prepare harsher American occupation plans for Germany.

In the end, War and State succeeded in including in the latest general occupation policy statement a provision declaring that war criminals would be tried, for among other things, having "participated in planning or carrying out Nazi enterprises involving or resulting in atrocities or war crimes. . . ." [27] When Mr. Roosevelt gave his assent to this statement, the door of presidential acceptance for the conspiracy/criminal-organization plan was left ajar once again. But still not a word came from the White House indicating that the 22 January memorandum of the three Secretaries had final presidential approval.

Mr. Grew's effort to prime the negotiation pump also ran into some other difficulties. On 9 March, Ambassador Davies got wind of the proposed Hackworth-Weir mission, and he forced Grew to withdraw his request that the President authorize it.[28] Eight days later, however, Dean Acheson, who was alternating

with Grew as Acting Secretary in the absence of Stettinius, sent
a new note to Roosevelt recommending that Rosenman, who
was scheduled to be in London in any case, should be provided
with an advisor from the War Department, and that these men
be directed to open negotiations on war-crimes policy with the
British.[29] This time Mr. Davies raised no objection, presumably
because he had fallen so seriously ill that within two weeks his
doctors would declare him unfit for travel.

Another possible obstacle to a London mission was also
eliminated at this time. A memorandum written on 27 March
by General Weir showed that he was prepared to bow to the
inevitable and support the conspiracy/criminal-organization
plan. Granting that "the state of our thinking has pretty well
coalesced," Weir felt that an international conference was
needed to develop solutions to a number of practical problems,
such as the size of the trial court, the manner of presenting
evidence, and so forth.[30] The general had quite definite ideas
about some features that needed to be included in the trial
system to make a successful prosecution easier. He favored a
military rather than a civilian court with three judges from the
smaller United Nations sitting alongside the tribunal members
from the Big Four. Weir also called for the use of simplified
procedures drawn from continental legal models to facilitate
rapid trials and circumvent problems that might arise if the
defendants were granted the protections customarily used in
common-law courts.

In a related recommendation intended to cope with the wide
scope of Nazi atrocities and the mountain of potential evidence, the general suggested that the court be authorized to use
commissioners, or "masters," to gather evidence of Nazi actions throughout Europe. Weir believed that these reports
should then be admissible, rather like materials customarily
given judicial notice, with little or no right of challenge by
the defense.[31] This idea was later warmly embraced by Justice
Robert Jackson after he was designated United States chief
of counsel, and predictably, it produced protracted discussion

and argument during the negotiations of the "Nuremberg" war-crimes charter in London in the summer of 1945.[32]

In the spring of 1945, however, these controversies lay far over the horizon, and the most significant feature of General Weir's war-crimes memorandum was that his support for the conspiracy/criminal-organization plan, which it revealed, made him a suitable member of a mission to London. By 2 April a three-man team of Judge Rosenman, General Weir, and Colonel Cutter was selected to begin talks with the British. (By omitting Mr. Hackworth, the State Department spared him the travail of trying to reconcile his support for the conspiracy/criminal-organization plan with his protestations of legal conservatism.) But the department did not simply leave the delegation to its own devices. A detailed briefing paper was prepared that summarized the basic points that had been accepted during the discussions culminating in the three secretaries' memorandum of late January. Cutter, Weir, and Rosenman were instructed to advance the proposition that there should be a trial of the major Nazi war criminals and that this trial should be based upon the "common enterprise" theory and a prosecution system directed at criminal organizations.[33]

The State Department briefing paper also contained two points that had not been included in the three Secretaries' memorandum. General Weir's recommendation that the court make use of special "masters" and evidentiary summaries was incorporated into it. A more significant addition referred to the "normal punishment" that should be applied to defendants who were found, in secondary hearings, to have belonged to criminal organizations.[34] All earlier formulations of the plan had been studiously vague on the fate that awaited those convicted as criminal organization members, but the State Department paper of 2 April flatly stated that most of them should be sentenced to "involuntary servitude on rehabilitation work." [35] This recommendation coincided with plans, then being discussed between the Allies, to use German forced labor as a major element in the system of postwar reparations. The idea seemed reasonable at first glance, but as subsequent events were to reveal, it contained a number of pitfalls, not the least of which was that if such a provision had been used, the only punishment Allied courts could have meted out to many Germans would have been a term of forced labor in Russia under murderously harsh conditions. Obviously this prospect should have given the planners pause, and the nonchalant manner in which the State Department officials tossed it into the briefing paper is somewhat surprising.

What is even more surprising and disturbing, was the assumption by the State Department officials involved that they had the authority to add points to those which the three secretaries had agreed to on 22 January. In lieu of a presidential mandate, the foundation of American war-crimes policy was that understanding between Biddle, Stettinius, and Stimson. The State Department briefing paper authorizing Rosenman, Cutter, and Weir to go further on the two specific matters of court "masters" and forced-labor punishment was highly questionable. In addition, another clause in the department's paper opened the door to wholesale revision and expansion. The emissaries were told that in the opinion of Mr. Hackworth, the three Secretaries' memorandum should be treated as a "classified" document, which meant that it was not to be shown to foreign officials, nor could it serve as the basis of negotiations.[36]

Rosenman, Weir, and Cutter were thus left with little choice but to fall back on the "Implementing Instrument" that Bernays and Hackworth had prepared in late January, and by revising it, to produce a paper that might be shown to British officials. This instrument, however, had never even been seen by any American cabinet officer, except possibly Stettinius, and, of course, it had not been officially approved by anyone. Three inexperienced negotiators were thus sent off to London charged with the complex and important task of developing an Anglo-American war-crimes program, but without a solid statement of U.S. policy to guide them. Instead, they were encouraged to

conclude from the State Department briefing they received
that as long as they remained within hailing distance of the
principles of the three Secretaries' memorandum, any arrange-
ment they could make with the British would be welcome in
Washington.

This highly irregular, and potentially dangerous, situation
marked the beginning of a new phase in American war-crimes
planning. Up to 22 January the major effort had been aimed
at attaining War Department, cabinet, and then presidential
approval for some form of the conspiracy/criminal-organization
plan. The three Secretaries' memorandum and the "Implementing Instrument" had unintentionally become the culminating
points in that process because of the failure to secure Mr.
Roosevelt's formal concurrence. To get around this obstacle,
the planners were forced to employ unorthodox methods and
follow seldom-trod paths as they sought to advance their proposal. Inevitably, much of the central control over the plan's
content was henceforth lost as it meandered about seeking
support in every quarter. The London mission of Cutter, Weir,
and Rosenman was the first big step toward an increasingly
eclectic and jumbled trial plan as the three Americans tried to
find some basis of compromise on which to build a common
policy with Great Britain.

On the eve of his first meeting with officials in London, Rosenman received a cable from the ailing Ambassador Davies
urging caution. "There now exists specific law" to punish all
the Nazi "outlaws and criminals" whom the United Nations
might wish to punish, Davies contended, and therefore "retro-
active criminal legislation" should be avoided. If the Allies
made use of ex post facto law, Davies believed that

succeeding generations . . . would see in it a violation of the principles for which we fought. The ideals for which our men died
should not be tarnished by even the shadow of a suspicion that we
have stooped to Nazi methods or have tortured legal principle in
order to wreak formalized vengeance rather than to administer
dispassionate justice under law.[37]

But Davies was a lonely voice telegraphing from the transatlantic wilderness. Among the American negotiators in London, there was little inclination toward any form of legal or political prudence. Cutter, Weir, and Rosenman had come to sell the conspiracy/criminal-organization plan to the British, and they were ready to take generous liberties with traditional legal practice, and with the plan itself, in order to reach an agreement.

Even before leaving Washington, Cutter had made minor rewordings in the text of the "Implementing Instrument," and soon after his arrival in London (3 April 1945) he went ahead with a more extensive revision.[38] Along with simple rephrasings, Cutter also made alterations of substance. He added provisions excluding defenses based on sovereign immunity and superior orders, and put in a section, inspired by General Weir, giving the tribunal the right to employ simplified trial procedures. The colonel also tinkered with the makeup of the proposed court, giving the Big Four authority to select whatever judges might be thought appropriate to represent the smaller United Nations. None of these alterations were, in themselves, of earth-shaking importance, nor did they represent radical departures from what the three Secretaries had agreed upon in the memorandum of 22 January. But it is worth noting that Cutter made these revisions after he had arrived in Britain, and without the specific authority of any cabinet member or other high-ranking officer of the United States government. As such, these changes represented another step into the cloud of shifting proposals and vague authority that characterized the American war-crimes mission to London in April 1945.

The British government attempted to deal with the problem posed by the presence of Rosenman and his colleagues by enfolding the Americans in the warm, conservative embrace of a large group of middle-level officials. At the first meeting, held on 4 April in the offices of Sir William Malkin, Senior Foreign Office Legal Officer, the Americans found themselves facing six British officials including Sir Thomas Barnes (the Treasury solicitor), Mr. G. P. Coldstream of the Lord Chancellor's office, and the Right Honourable Lord Justice William Finlay, Britain's representative on the UNWCC.[39] With Sir William Malkin in the chair, the British tried to narrow the points under discussion, but near the end of the meeting Rosenman declared that any inter-Allied war-crimes agreement should deal with:

1. crimes by and against those who never left Germany
2. crimes before 1939
3. atrocities by and against unidentified persons
4. crimes committed by, and criminal liability of, superiors of the persons actually committing the offenses
5. the disposition of the major war criminals

Sir William Malkin tried to cope with Rosenman's statement by acting as if nothing of importance had happened. But the judge would have no truck with genteel sidestepping. He stated that he had come to discuss all aspects of the war-crimes question with British authorities and that he was prepared to pursue the question "on whatever level might be necessary." Rosenman then inquired disarmingly if it would be better to start his conversations with Prime Minister Churchill or with Foreign Secretary Eden. The mention of the two magic names in Britain's war cabinet seems to have jolted Mr. Coldstream into motion, and he hurriedly advised that it would be best if Rosenman first met with his own superior, the Lord Chancellor, Sir John Simon, and that an appointment could be made for the following afternoon (Thursday, 5 April). Rosenman agreed to confer with Simon but emphasized again that "he was charged with negotiating and coming back with a draft executive agreement on war crimes policy." [40]

In the aftermath of this first Anglo-American skirmish of 4 April, each side sought to clarify its own position and gird itself for the second encounter on the following day. Coldstream wrote a memo to Simon describing what had happened, sprinkling it with phrases in quotation marks such as "personal advisor" and "settling the whole question of War Crimes." [41]

Despite these patronizing jabs at the Americans, Coldstream indicated that the situation was serious. The Lord Chancellor had long feared that Britain might not be able to sell its "shoot-on-sight" program to the Americans and had made some preparations in the event that it became necessary to fall back on a compromise position. Coldstream's memo intimated that if Sir John had a via media up his sleeve, it should be ready on 5 April, because the Americans seemed determined to move quickly.

Rosenman, who was indeed eager to expedite matters, was also somewhat confused by the cool reception he had received from Sir William Malkin and his associates. After the meeting the judge immediately fired off cable #3423 to the State Department, describing what had transpired and underscoring that in Sir William's view, the discussions should not cover the whole range of war-crimes matters, especially not the major criminals. Facing a meeting with Simon within twenty-four hours, Rosenman asked for more instructions. "I assume and understand that I am authorized to discuss these matters fully at the highest level necessary and to attempt to formulate a draft agreement for consideration by the four principal governments concerned" Rosenman wrote, adding "request that I be advised by return cable whether my understanding is correct." [42]

Fortunately for the judge, cable #3423 immediately came to the attention of Acting Secretary Acheson and was not delayed in a tangential muddle within the department. Rosenman's cable had again sent officials scurrying to discover what had happened concerning war crimes at Yalta. It also gave Secretary Stettinius another opportunity to demonstrate he had little grasp of the general situation; he did not realize that Rosenman had gone to London to draft an agreement. In his own words, he thought the judge was merely there to do a "general survey of the situation" and that a regular negotiator would be sent over later.[43] The President became so bewildered by all the confusion that on 6 April he asked the

department what it was actually telling Rosenman. Characteristically, it took Stettinius's office six days to prepare an
answer to this question, and by that time the question was
mute because the President had died at Warm Springs! [44]

Acheson's quick reaction to cable #3423 spared Rosenman
the anguish of fretting about all this. The Acting Secretary told
the judge on 5 April that "complete authority is yours to discuss war crimes matters at the highest level." [45] Rosenman
was also advised by Acheson that no matter what the views of
Sir William Malkin, the United States government would like
the major war criminals to be covered in any *"draft* agreements
reached,"* and that "great importance is attached by the Department to prompt conclusion of comprehensive understand-
ings." [46] Armed with this authorization, Rosenman wrote himself out a set of notes for the next meeting, stressing that
four-power talks should begin soon, and that "the comprehensive nature of the war crimes problem" required the Anglo-
Americans to discuss the major criminals and a wide range of
acts, such as prewar persecutions and the actions of the organizations that had participated in the "Nazi criminal
enterprise." [47]

It is a reasonable assumption that Rosenman entered the
meeting of 5 April believing that he would have to assail
another group of cautious, pedantic British officials. There assembled in the Lord Chancellor's office were three men who had
played prominent roles the day before—namely Coldstream,
Barnes, and Malkin, plus the latter's deputy, Patrick Dean,
and the British Attorney General, Sir Donald Somervell. But
the man who made the difference and confronted Rosenman
with a totally new situation was in the chair, the Lord Chancellor, Sir John Simon. Whatever opinion one may hold of Sir
John's discretion or political views (he had been a leading
"appeaser" in the 1930s), Simon was an experienced and
shrewd negotiator who showed a sure touch when dealing with
Rosenman. Instead of hanging back, the Lord Chancellor chose
to run right at the judge and his aides. He opened the meet-

ing by declaring that in addition to secondary matters, attention would be given to the issues closest to the hearts of the Americans, including the major criminals, broad categories of acts to be punished, and what the British notes of the meeting called "ill-treatment of Jews in Germany." [48]

Since we have both British and American notes recording this long session, it is possible to see different shades of meaning in the way the two groups viewed it. Throughout the meeting, acts that the Americans referred to as prewar crimes, or "German offenses against Germans," appeared as "ill-treatment of Jews," or "maltreatment of the Jews," in the British notes.[49] Simon and his associates obviously assumed that Hitler's persecution of Jews was the driving force in the American desire to broaden the range of prosecutable offenses. But Rosenman and his aides were equally determined not to say that Nazi attacks on Jews were the sole reasons for extending the prosecution beyond traditional war crimes.

This was an important, but measured, difference of emphasis between the British and the Americans, one which it was easy to overlook during the fast-paced meeting presided over by the Lord Chancellor. Simon allowed Rosenman to register his opinion that the Russians and the French should be brought into the discussions "very promptly" and then the Lord Chancellor moved quickly through a series of noncontroversial issues, such as the use of mixed military tribunals. Only after this did he confront the serious subject of what was to be done with the major Nazi culprits. While declaring that Britain did not look with favor on a full-scale trial for Hitler and his confederates and was reluctant to move away from what he called the "Napoleonic precedent," which supported political rather than judicial action, Simon was careful not to belabor the point. Instead, he immediately declared that if Britain's allies would not agree to liquidate the Nazi leaders by summary execution, it might be possible to arrange a compromise based on what the Lord Chancellor called an "arraignment" procedure. Simon then summarized a plan whereby Hitler and a small group of his top aides would be arraigned on a series of charges such as "gross breaches" of the laws of war, "maltreatment of the Jews," and "the domination of Europe." [50] It should be noted in passing that Colonel Cutter subsequently queried the British on whether or not Simon had said that Hitler was to be charged with "criminal violation of treaties by Germany involved in waging aggressive war (in disregard of the Kellogg Pact)." [51] No answer to this question was received from the Lord Chancellor's office and, significantly, no one in either delegation again raised the question of whether or not preparing and waging an aggressive war was a crime or a punishable offense.

Simon's arraignment proposal was not overly concerned with such legal niceties. The proposed "document of arraignment" was to be prepared by representatives of the Big Four and laid before an Allied tribunal, which would then quickly decide the truth of the charges. Once the tribunal had declared, as it presumably would, that the allegations made in the "document of arraignment" were in fact correct, the Allied governments (not the tribunal) would decide on the appropriate punishment for Hitler and "six or seven" of the other top Nazis.[52] Simon contended that his plan would provide the advocates of court action with a portion of what they wanted—there would be a hearing of sorts—while the ultimate fate of the Nazi leaders would be settled in conformity with British wishes, by a political decision of the Allied governments. Not only was this a compromise, in Simon's opinion it would have the additional advantage of providing the Allies with a means to strike at the "persecution of Jews" [53] and other Nazi horrors, which might not be war crimes under a traditional reading of international law.

The Lord Chancellor was quite open and honest with the Americans regarding the tentative nature of his proposal. Although not revealing that it was actually another of his private recommendations to the Prime Minister for use if the war-crimes question arose at a conference of Allied leaders—this one had been prepared for Yalta, as the shoot-on-sight plan had been made for Quebec—he did frankly admit that it had not been seen or considered by the cabinet. Rosenman was not put off by Simon's reservations and qualifications. He was obviously intrigued by the proposal, declaring that at the very least much of it was "consistent with U.S. thought," and—if we accept the British record of the meeting at face value—he found it "novel, ingenious and sound in principal."

However, Rosenman apparently added that there were those in Washington who "undoubtedly would prefer a trial," and he promised to "point out later" some modifications that the arraignment proposal needed. Cutter went a step further and declared that in the U.S. view there should be a trial, not just some perfunctory hearing; but his statement, understandably, did not carry much weight.[54] Rosenman was the leader of the American delegation and a man who stood very close to the President. Since he was obviously anxious to please, and eager to find a solution to the war-crimes difficulty acceptable to Washington and London, the British had every right to conclude that his favorable comments regarding the arraignment proposal presaged something approximating American agreement in principle.

Rosenman's willingness to look sympathetically on Simon's arraignment proposal actually constituted a sharp deviation from the American position as embodied in the three secretaries' agreement of 22 January 1945. That document had emphasized the need for a full criminal-conspiracy trial which would include all the Nazi leaders and followers, from Hitler down through the major organizations of the Third Reich. Once Rosenman had acknowledged that the leaders might be dealt with through something less than a regular trial procedure, he faced a situation where he would either have to abandon the conspiracy prosecution plan entirely, or restrict it simply to the members of "criminal organizations." In the middle of the meeting, he abruptly chose the latter course and declared that the war-crimes problem could be subdivided into three parts:

first the major criminals; then, those who had committed specific violations of the rules of war; and finally, "the great number of Germans" who had been involved with Hitler "in a common enterprise, or conspiracy, for evil." Rosenman then summarized the conspiracy prosecution proposal as if it would be applied only to organizations.

In his explanation of this limited conspiracy proposal, Rosenman emphasized that it would make possible the prosecution of prewar Nazi "crimes." Attorney General Somervell objected to this emphasis and urged that the "center of gravity" of the organizational prosecution case should fall on the atrocities the Nazi groups had committed in the occupied territories. But neither Somervell nor any of the other British officials present made serious criticisms of the general idea of a limited conspiracy prosecution, and Lord Simon was taken with the idea of prosecuting the members of the SS and the Gestapo because, as he put it, they had "belonged to a very bad club." [55]

Thus, on one level, the 5 April meeting resulted in each side tacitly agreeing to a modified version of the other's pet project: The Americans had looked with sympathy on Simon's document of arraignment proposal and the British had found the limited-conspiracy prosecution plan generally agreeable. Both sides also recognized that they could not go much farther until they had consulted with their superiors. While reiterating the need to keep the matter secret due to the ever-present fear of German reprisals, Rosenman declared he would cable Washington for additional instructions. Simon stated that although he would not ask the cabinet to make a "definite decision" at this time, he would request "general approval" to proceed "in principle." [56]

However, this mood of mutual compromise disguised the most important long-term consequences of the 5 April Anglo-American meeting. Rosenman had not accurately indicated the determination of powerful leaders in Washington to derail every suggestion of summary execution and to insist on a formal trial. Furthermore, the judge had not presented the conspiracy/criminal-organization plan to Simon and his associates in its complete form. By allowing the Lord Chancellor to propose the arraignment compromise and then letting him elicit sympathetic reactions from the Americans, Rosenman lost the opportunity to lay out the complete American proposal. He was therefore forced to tuck in bits and pieces of the conspiracy/criminal-organization plan around the arraignment idea. In the process he gave the British a totally misleading impression of what the Bernays plan and the three Secretaries' memorandum had been designed to accomplish. The fragment described to them was so mutilated that if the arraignment procedure had been employed, Hitler and the other architects of the alleged grand conspiracy—the principal defendants in the plan developed by Bernays—would not even have stood in the dock during the prosecution of the organizations. What had occurred in the 5 April meeting was the incubation of a strange hybrid compromise in which the chief Nazis were to be examined and disposed of by a modified form of political execution, while the organization members would face a judicial proceeding with only the ghosts of the alleged "principal conspirators" present.

The best will in the world would probably have had little chance to turn this composite plan into an effective Anglo-American war-crimes program; but Simon, Rosenman, and their associates made a valiant effort in its behalf during the week of 5 April. In the process they created not a little additional confusion and misunderstanding. On 6 April, the two delegations exchanged memoranda outlining their respective visions of the compromise plan. The core of the Rosenman paper was a rephrasing of portions of Cutter's 3 April revision of the "Implementing Instrument." It added a handful of new provisions, a few deletions, and left space for some form of the British arraignment procedure. The document cut out every trace of the earlier plans to prosecute aggressive war, and it adopted Sir Donald Somervell's idea, as well as his language, to the effect that the "center of gravity" in the organizational prosecution should be placed on what the Nazis had done during the war in the occupied territories.[57] This memorandum still spoke of one major trial and a series of secondary proceedings in which the "only necessary proof of guilt" would be an individual's "membership in one of those organizations"; but it also declared that "this need not preclude separate trial of particular German leaders if that is deemed desirable." [58]

It is noteworthy that this American memorandum supported a trial and broad application of the conspiracy/criminal-organization approach more strongly than had the statements made by the delegation at the previous day's meeting. A similar stiffening of the American position was noticeable during a discussion that Simon, Malkin, and Coldstream had with Cutter and Weir on 6 April. The absence of Judge Rosenman— who was apparently off for the weekend conferring informally with Churchill and Eden, primarily on economic matters [59]— may have helped to make a harder American line possible. The two American military officers were careful not to overstep the limits of their authority and Cutter remarked that "he did not feel authorized to speak, except informally, for Judge Rosenman." [60] The Lord Chancellor informed Cutter and Weir that the summary of Rosenman's views that Simon was preparing to lay before the cabinet "would be presented" to the Americans "for scrutiny" as soon as it was completed. Even this courtesy, which bordered on an indiscretion, was not enough to pacify Cutter, who told the British that there was "strong War Department opinion in favor of a trial as opposed to summary punishment." Later Cutter reported to the Assistant Secretary of War's office that during the discussion he thought he had made "some progress . . . in convincing the U.K. representatives of the importance of this point of a judicial trial and of the necessity of doing all possible to support the 'arraignment' by a carefully documented case." [61]

The draft memorandum that Simon sent to Rosenman on this day (6 April) gives some credence to Cutter's claim. The

Lord Chancellor acknowledged that to be effective, a war-crimes program would have to secure the agreement of both London and Washington. Simon also said he now realized that Henry Stimson wanted a trial, and that he (Sir John) was "much impressed" by that fact.[62] Nonetheless, he felt that a full-scale judicial proceeding would produce endless debate and open up a Pandora's box of legal and political problems "with a reaction which we can hardly calculate." Therefore, use of a document of arraignment would be the safer course. Simon made plain that the document "would not be limited to traditional war crimes," but would include "broad descriptions" of all the evil the Nazis had done.

As Simon foresaw the procedure, Hitler and a handful of others accused, probably including Himmler, Ribbentrop, Mussolini, Göring, and Goebbels (only two of these, Ribbentrop and Göring, lived to enter the dock at Nuremberg) would be given the document of arraignment and would receive a hearing where they could present written or oral evidence. Then the tribunal hearing the case would determine whether or not the statements alleged were actually true. Simon emphasized that even though the tribunal would surely decide in the affirmative, a case of this kind was too important to leave to the winds of chance. Since the judiciary had to be kept independent in the Anglo-American system, there was no choice but to let the political authorities of the Big Four—not the tribunal—decide on the final sentence.[63]

On 7 April, Rosenman cabled Washington for guidance on how to deal with the British proposal. In accompanying messages, copies of the Simon memorandum, together with the other major papers and meeting notes that the conference had so far generated, were also sent over. Rosenman's two military aides were especially anxious to get these materials into the hands of their superiors quickly because John J. McCloy was due to arrive in London within a week, and they wanted to be sure he was adequately prepared to deal effectively with Simon and the other British officials. They also wished to guarantee that there was no uncertainty about what had transpired. Together with the packet of documents, Cutter enclosed a short note to McCloy in which he reported that Rosenman "generally liked" the British proposal, subject to a handful of reservations and conditions.[64]

Evidently, until the British cabinet acted on the Lord Chancellor's arraignment plan and the American delegation received instructions from Washington, it was impossible to make serious headway in London. Still, between 9 and 12 April, both delegations took all the practical small steps they could to advance the arraignment/criminal-organization compromise. One of the most important of these was another major redrafting of the American "Implementing Instrument," which Cutter completed on 10 April. The colonel glued a version of the British arraignment proposal into the middle of the American plan; in so doing he broke some of the shackles with which legal traditionalism had constricted the range of prosecutable offenses. The charges to be contained in the proposed arraignment, as seen by Cutter, included persecution of minorities, "cruel and ruthless" oppression in the occupied territories, invasions, the "initiation and waging of ruthless wars of aggression," and even the encouragement of disorders in neighboring countries.[65]

The 10 April draft of the arraignment idea was an odd composite, and its impact was also peculiar. Although the draft contained elements more customarily employed in regular court procedings—such as right of counsel—than did Simon's original proposal, it also gave a political body—the Control Council for Germany—a mandate to set aside a finding made by a tribunal. This was just the kind of tampering with judicial integrity that Simon had been trying to avoid. Since the London discussions ended soon after this draft was completed, it was never shown to the British and therefore had no impact on policy considerations in London. But the draft was taken back to Washington and there it served as the working paper for subsequent policy development. Elements of this arraignment scheme appeared in every war-crimes draft prepared in Washington during the next three weeks, and it obviously took American planners a long time to shake off the effects it exerted upon them. As we will see, traces of this draft were even included in the formal memoranda that the Americans laid before the Allied leaders at the San Francisco United Nations conference in early May.

On the same day that Cutter prepared his redraft (10 April), a small group of officials from the Anglo-American delegations met to try to eliminate some of the practical difficulties likely to be associated with the proposed arraignment/criminal-organization compromise. Neither Simon nor Rosenman were present, and both the American group, consisting of Cutter and Weir, as well as the larger British cadre, led by Somervell, Malkin, Barnes, and Dean, understood that this could be little more than an exploratory discussion. Although Anglo-American differences regarding the proposed "common enterprise" prosecution of the organizations were not grave, and the British generally agreed that this part of the problem should be dealt with "more nearly in the form of an ordinary judicial trial," significant divisions quite naturally occurred over the arraignment procedure. After an afternoon of haggling, what emerged most clearly from the 10 April meeting was the number of issues and the size of the chasm that separated the two groups.[66]

Weir and Cutter understood that they were in a very vulnerable position and on 11 April cabled Washington, urgently renewing their request for instructions on what to do about the arraignment proposal. The initial response from the State Department was a Stettinius cable addressed to Rosenman stating that since Stimson was out of town and Biddle would be unable to give his views until the twelfth, the Secretary of State "would prefer not to send you instructions."[67] The only immediate aid that Stettinius would offer was the suggestion that "under necessity," Rosenman should advance "counter proposals"[68] to make the arraignment look more like a trial. On the following day (12 April), in his own cable to Weir and Cutter, the Secretary of War declared that after a "brief study," he thought Simon's proposal might have some "advantages." [69] But Stimson underscored that even if a simplified arraignment was used, he attached "great importance" to "the proceeding being judicial and not political in character." [70]

In effect, the Secretary of War instructed Weir and Cutter to continue trying to turn the British arraignment proposal into a simplified trial system rather than a procedural overture to summary execution. After the dispatch of the Secretary's telegram, planners in the War Department set to work on a paper embodying the main points that Mr. Stimson had made.[71] Simultaneously, over in the Justice Department, other officials had begun pulling together the views of Attorney General Biddle and his staff. The general opinion in Justice seems to have been even more sharply critical of the British proposal than that in the War Department. A preliminary Justice Department paper found the whole arraignment idea too vague and perfunctory and dismissed it as a mere "investigation leading to political action." [72]

If fate had not intervened, it seems probable that after intensive interdepartmental discussions, Rosenman would ultimately have been instructed bluntly to tell the British that the United States insisted on a trial of the Nazi leaders. But on this afternoon of 12 April in Warm Springs, Georgia, Franklin Roosevelt suffered a massive coronary and died almost immediately. The linchpin of the whole American governmental and war-making machine had suddenly been pulled out, and the American people and their leaders were faced with the urgent necessity of turning inward and closing ranks to hold the system together. The unifying ceremony of a presidential funeral would help to unite the nation, if only in a common grief, and in time the new President, Harry S. Truman, would take charge and put his own stamp on the governmental structure. But in the interim it was essential that there be no radical break with existing practice, no sudden changes or outburst of controversy concerning prevailing policies. More important than solving any specific problem in the days immediately following 12 April was the national need to see that the machine continued to function and that the prosecution of the war did not diminish.

Inevitably then, there was no possibility of securing American cabinet-level agreement on the British arraignment proposal. No interdepartmental conferences took place, and no clarifying instructions were sent to the delegation in London. The American war-crimes negotiation effort was stopped cold, and the situation seemed ripe for an aggressive move by the British to push their plan ahead while the U.S. delegation was incapacitated. But in London too, odd timing, if not a touch of fate, intervened and toyed freely with the situation. Three days before (9 April), Sir John Simon had prepared a formal paper setting out his arraignment scheme, and this document had been circulated to members of the war cabinet on the following day.[73]

When the war cabinet considered the matter at 3:30 P.M. London time (a few hours before President Roosevelt's death), it was faced by Simon's dual purpose document. Sir John had used this opportunity both to provide an informational report on the Anglo-American discussion and to recommend that the cabinet give endorsement "in principle" to a number of war-crimes policy proposals, the most important of which was the arraignment/criminal-organization compromise.[74] The Lord Chancellor told the cabinet that Rosenman conceived of the war-crimes problem as composed of three subproblems, with conventional war crimes at the bottom, the major criminals at the top, and a middle group of leaders who would be defendants in a "common enterprise" trial of Nazi organizations. Simon's presentation thereby spread additional confusion about the American proposal. The war cabinet was not presented with any explanation of the full conspiracy/criminal-organization plan, and the lack of a comprehensive American position paper had its most pernicious effects right here. In the absence of such a paper it was reasonable for the British government to conclude that if the Americans saw the issue as a trilogy of subproblems, then it should be possible to deal with them independently and pick and choose among a number of alternatives.

In accordance with the three-point division of the problem, Simon initially recommended that the cabinet approve the idea of dealing with conventional war crimes through mixed military tribunals and that together with the Americans, the British government now finally, and officially, reject the UNWCC plan for a treaty court. Apparently without debate, the cabinet voted down the UNWCC court, but took no action on a possible use of mixed military tribunals.[75] When the Lord Chancellor next raised the subject of what should be done with the "middle level" criminal organizations, he was again surprisingly successful. Simon had explained to the cabinet that in the "Rosenman" plan, the organizations and their leaders would get a regular trial, and that individual organization members would then be dealt with in secondary proceedings.[76] According to Simon, the beauty of the scheme was that by prosecuting a "common enterprise," the technical problem of extending the definition of traditional war crimes could be avoided. This was the same contention that had lain at the root of the Bernays plan and had helped sustain the conspiracy/criminal-organization proposal through all the policy controversies in Washington. In London on this occasion, the idea was just as successful. Perhaps because they were faced with only a fragment of the full American plan, and perhaps because they wished to make some conciliatory gesture to Washington, the members of the war cabinet—with little or no debate—agreed to the following proposal:

That a special procedure should be provided for leaders and active members of the Gestapo or the S.S., by which a mixed military tribunal would be invited to find that members of those organizations had engaged in a criminal conspiracy, as members of a com-

mon enterprise of a criminal character aimed at promoting a German victory by methods of outrage, torture, etc. When this general
judgment has been given, any members of the Gestapo or the S.S.
could be charged with being a member of this criminal conspiracy
and punished accordingly.[77]

This statement did not contain all the provisions of the
American conspiracy/criminal-organization plan. There was no
explanation of how the secondary proceedings would operate;
the number of organizations cited was very small; and the
charges listed did not include prewar persecutions, actions
taken against Axis nationals, or the preparing and launching of
aggressive war. Yet considering that the British government
was strongly disinclined to have any top Nazi leaders stand
trial, the cabinet's ready acceptance of this statement does
raise the possibility that if the American plan had been laid
before it in its entirety, it might have received a fairly sympathetic hearing, even at this early date.

But the full conspiracy/criminal-organization plan was not
seen by the war cabinet on 12 April, nor were the Americans
ever given a complete account of the cabinet's deliberations.
A word needs to be said about the implications of this latter
failure before we proceed to examine the last action taken by
the British cabinet on this occasion. During the night of 12
April the Lord Chancellor "informally" told General Weir that
the war cabinet in effect had looked sympathetically on the
plan for criminal-organization prosecution.[78] Cutter and Weir
thereupon cabled Washington that the cabinet "seems to have
been favorably impressed by [the] proposal on [the] common
enterprise theory substantially as outlined in 22nd January memorandum." [79] As we now know, this was definitely not what
happened during the British cabinet session of 12 April. The
cabinet never saw anything "substantially" approximating the
system laid out in the memorandum of 22 January. That Cutter
and Weir thought it had reveals how different was the mental
picture of the negotiations that the two sides held. The incident also indicates how easy it would be for the authorities

in Washington to conclude that the British officials were practicing deception or merely toying with the American proposals. If, in fact, the British government had "been favorably impressed" with the full American trial plan, then the final action on war crimes that the cabinet took during the session of 12 April would have been incomprehensible or an instance of sharp practice.

That action, naturally, concerned the arraignment proposal. Recognizing that it was a highly controversial matter, the Lord Chancellor had prudently decided to place consideration of it last, both in his memorandum and in the list of motions laid before the cabinet. In the memorandum, Simon declared he had presented the arraignment idea to the Americans because he was convinced "that agreement could not be obtained between the Big Three to shoot them [the top Nazis] out of hand." [80] Rosenman had stressed that Secretary Stimson was "entirely opposed" to summary execution, and Sir John implied Stimson's view would probably prevail in Washington.[81] Considering this situation, Simon thought the arraignment proposal the best means available to head off a large state trial. Hitler would thereby have a hearing without international law being distorted or tortured, and the way would be clear for a political decision to put the leaders of the Third Reich to death.

Even before the cabinet met, the arraignment idea was generating critical comments from British officials. A memorandum of 10 April, apparently sent to the Attorney General by Mr. Coldstream, already observed that the arraignment would appear to be a pseudo-trial, and therefore would satisfy no one.[82] In the cabinet discussions on 12 April, this point was merely expanded and dressed up in more colorful language. The arraignment idea was criticized for so confusing "political and judicial jurisdiction" that the British government would "get the worst of both worlds." [83] It was claimed that under the Simon scheme purists would be able to charge that there had not been "a fair trial." Since the result of the arraignment "would be a foregone conclusion, these proceedings would tend to bring judicial procedure into contempt," yet Hitler would be allowed to speak and still might succeed in wrapping himself in the cloak of martyrdom.[84] So, in the view of most of the cabinet, the Allies stood to lose all around.

Simon apparently made a rather lame defense of the plan, resting his argument less on the virtues of the arraignment idea than on the contention that something innovative had to be done because the United States and the Soviet Union would not accept summary execution. This statement did produce a few sympathetic echoes from a number of Simon's colleagues. Although no one would endorse the arraignment idea, some cabinet members did recommend that efforts be made to compromise with the Americans and the Russians. In addition, Smuts of South Africa repeated what he had said in previous cabinet discussions, that "to shoot men without trial in this way would set a very dangerous precedent," and he urged that some middle way be found. In passing, Churchill remarked that perhaps Parliament could pass a Bill of Attainder (a law which makes criminal the act, or acts, of a specific person) against the Nazi leaders and the government could then use this as the basis for execution. One may easily imagine how Stimson and other American leaders, who had been nurtured on a constitutional/legal tradition in which Bills of Attainder were held to be akin to works of the devil, would have greeted this idea. But it found no support in the British cabinet either, and in any case was completely overshadowed by a suggestion from Sir Stafford Cripps, which may well win the palm for being the most ludicrous proposal made during any British or American war-crimes policy discussion. The Minister for Aircraft Production "pointed out that Hitler, and many of the Nazi leaders, ranked as soldiers, and it might be possible to treat them as such and refuse them quarter." [85] Actually, Hitler and the vast majority of top Nazis were not ranked as soldiers, and in any event, the Hague and Geneva rules imposed more stringent controls regarding the treatment of captured military officers than did rules applicable to civilians.

A cabinet session where such proposals could be considered seriously was obviously no place to solve major war-crimes policy problems. The best it could do was dispose of some of the impediments to solution. As already indicated, while agreeing in principle to a "middle level" criminal-organization prosecution plan, the cabinet had killed the UNWCC treaty-court idea. It concluded its work on 12 April by registering opposition to a large "state trial" and forbade going further with the arraignment idea because of its inherent "grave disadvantages." Simon was instructed to draw up a statement for dispatch to Washington setting forth the British objections to a large war-crimes trial "as developed in this discussion," and also to tell Judge Rosenman that the arraignment compromise plan had been rejected.[86]

On the night of 12 April, with the American delegation sunk in gloom over the news of President Roosevelt's death, Sir John made the rounds delivering his own doomsday messages to Rosenman and General Weir. He informed them that the cabinet "unanimously" favored a "political disposition" of the top Nazis.[87] Although the British government might agree to the preparation of an Allied statement enumerating the Nazi crimes, it would not accept a trial or even a hearing for Hitler and his associates. The arraignment compromise was therefore dead, and all the preparatory memoranda, drafts, and conference minutes were so much scrap paper. The Lord Chancellor attempted to be as agreeable as possible while administering this bitter pill, but bonhomie provided little consolation. Weir cabled the Pentagon that Rosenman was leaving immediately to attend Franklin Roosevelt's funeral and that the remainder of the delegation thought no further progress could be made in London.[88]

By 13 April 1945, the top officials in Washington had received this message loud and clear. Even while uncertainty prevailed regarding the new President's views on war-crimes policy, as well as most other matters, American officials understood that the bilateral talks in London had failed. If the United States government wished to advance the conspiracy/criminal-organization plan, it would need to put its own house in order and begin searching for ways to cut the ground out from under the feet of the British.

CHAPTER 6

SETTING THE
STAGE

What the world needs is not to turn one crowd out of the concentration camps and put another crowd in, but to end the concentration camp idea.[1]

Robert H. Jackson
May 1945

On the morning of 13 April, when Murray Bernays first learned that the British had rejected the arraignment compromise and insisted on summary execution of the Nazi leaders, he immediately wrote to his superiors that America was "pretty well boxed in" unless the Soviets and French could be brought into the discussions "to break the deadlock."[2] Halfway around the world the Assistant Secretary of War, John J. McCloy, was acting on the same assumption and quietly lining up some of the necessary support. While touring American military installations on the European continent, McCloy took the opportunity to discuss various policy matters with American and Allied officials including Charles de Gaulle. In the course of one of his talks with the French leader, McCloy asked whether the Provisional French Republic would be inclined toward a trial or a summary execution for Hitler and his aides. De Gaulle replied that he, and presumably the Republic, would favor a trial.[3] McCloy apparently did not pursue the matter further,

being content to put this ace in his pocket and move on to
London, where he would make one last attempt to bring the
British to their senses.

This time McCloy did not underestimate the seriousness
of the situation. He knew that the top American leaders much
preferred to work in tandem with the British rather than assault
them and that conciliation would be popular in Washington.
But he also understood that the American government, especially his chief, Henry Stimson, would never tamely accept a
summary-execution plan. Therefore, although the chances of
success were slight, McCloy decided to put the case for trial
before the British once more, and to this end he wrote out for
his own use a four-page briefing paper containing the salient
points that were animating him and his colleagues.[4] Many of
the positions advanced in this paper would later be inserted
into various drafts of the conspiracy/criminal-organization plan.
McCloy's memorandum declared that something out of the
ordinary had to be done with the Nazi leaders because "their
depredations have been so great and so violent that international
security cannot exist if they are permitted to continue un-
checked or uncondemned."

In McCloy's view, what the Allies did about Nazi atrocities
might be more important for the future security of the world
than the preparations then being made for a postwar United
Nations organization. Punishment for violations of international law would "certainly induce future government leaders
to think" before they acted in a fashion similar to the Nazis.
Yet to make use of summary execution would be a retrospective
step, a throwback to an era when warring states killed their
opponents out of hand. The Assistant Secretary contended that
holding a trial before punishing had become almost "a necessary concept" in the thinking not only of "Anglo Saxons," but
also—and here McCloy indulged his 1940s ethnic prejudice
in a way that now seems almost enchanting in its directness—
of Latins and "even Slavs." An effective trial procedure might
be difficult to develop, and some of the niceties of common-

law usage might have to be jettisoned to speed up the proceedings and to accommodate the French and the Russians,
but to McCloy these were merely procedural matters, solvable
through competent drafting. If the French, Americans, and Soviets were united in support for a trial, McCloy asked in a
final rhetorical jab at the Lord Chancellor and his colleagues,
"are the English, who are the ones in whom the concept of trial
before punishment is fundamental, to be the only ones to argue
against the procedure of trial?" [5]

All this sounded marvelously effective in McCloy's memorandum, and for a moment it may have inclined the Assistant
Secretary to hope that the British leaders might change their
minds. But a few minutes inside the meeting room with Simon,
Somervell, Barnes, and Coldstream on 16 April should have
disabused him of that notion. The British officials were too
chastened by the 12 April cabinet decisions to advance any
hints of compromise. When the Assistant Secretary of War tried
to summarize for them the state of American thinking, and
especially the views of Henry Stimson, his statements were
put down in the British notes of the meeting as if they were to
be the basis of a comic-satire script on the wartime American
government. The British notes recorded McCloy to the effect
that "he had had conversations with Mr. Stimson on the
subject of war criminals . . ." and "he thought" the criminal-
prosecution idea had "originated in the State Department." [6]
There is no possibility that John J. McCloy ever said anything
remotely approximating this, but he did say that, unlike Rosenman, he did not have powers to negotiate. That may well have
been sufficient to make the British fluff their last opportunity
to avoid a sharp diplomatic rebuff on the matter of war-crimes
policy.

If they had only listened, the British could hardly have
failed to grasp the situation. McCloy laid before them most
of the material supporting a trial that he had included in his
preparatory paper. Repeatedly he stressed that this was the
crucial moment, a chance "to move forward"; that the Amer-

ican government would find summary execution a step in the wrong direction and an affront to a "fundamental conception of justice." [7] The Assistant Secretary indicated that the United States would be willing to consider compromise proposals on the practical questions and procedures, including the location of the trial and the use of charges related to "breach of treaties," but it would not give in on the basic idea of a judicial proceeding. In reply, the British brought forth various objections and tangential suggestions until ultimately McCloy tired of the irrelevancies and bid both the meeting and the United Kingdom farewell. He left firmly resolved to avoid further useless attempts to solve the war-crimes policy difficulties by trying to conciliate the British. Henceforth, rather than sweet words, the Americans would make use of tough politics, and that was a game McCloy knew how to play rather well.

On the day following, 17 April, McCloy advised Secretary Stimson to send President Truman a copy of the 22 January three Secretaries' memorandum together with "a statement of your view that judicial trial rather than political disposal of the Axis leaders is proper." [8] On that same day, Judge Rosenman had decided on a similar step, and after meeting with Mr. Truman, reported to his colleagues that the President "is definitely opposed to political disposition of [the] top criminals." [9] Harry Truman had apparently left some room for maneuvering, indicating that a compromise such as Simon had proposed was not out of the question. But the new President came out strongly in support of some kind of trial and left Rosenman "in charge" of any war-crimes policy discussions that might arise with the British.[10]

In order to solidify his position and provide Mr. Truman with background information, Rosenman sent the President a highly colored description of what had happened in London during early April. The four-page memorandum, dated 19 April, claimed Rosenman and Simon had agreed that the top Nazis "should be given a special trial before a mixed military tribunal," a statement that wildly exaggerated the judicial char-

acter of the arraignment plan. Rosenman further indicated that
Simon had agreed to procedures whereby the Nazis would
have had "an opportunity to be heard in their own defense,"
while the prosecution's record of Nazi crimes would be "so
fully documented that oral evidence would be practically unnecessary." It may go too far to brand these assertions as false,
but they certainly are not borne out by any of the contem-
porary records of the London meetings. Nor was Rosenman's
account of what had happened to the criminal-organization proposal totally accurate. According to what the judge reported to
the President, one would assume that the whole criminal-
organization plan, including provisions to prosecute prewar
atrocities and violation of treaties, had been presented to the
London government and that "the British conferees accepted
the proposal." [11]

Obviously this was a very distorted picture, and Rosenman
probably painted it this way partially to explain his failure
to secure an agreement. He may also have had second thoughts
about the manner in which he had allowed Simon to set the
focus and call the tune. But there was an additional tactical
reason why Rosenman took the line he did. In his description
of the developments, it appeared that after going through the
motions of negotiations with the Americans, the British group,
by a "unanimous" vote of the cabinet, had willfully scuttled
the arraignment compromise together with all the work of the
conference. In the judge's view it was therefore time to settle
accounts with the British, and he had called together a group
of officials concerned with war-crimes policy to meet on the
following day (20 April). The meeting would explore the most
effective ways to force the British to yield on the trial issue,
including the possibility of bringing the Soviets into the discussions at the earliest possible moment.[12]

Rosenman's success in selling the new President on the notion that the British had "done us wrong" in London certainly
helped to open the door for a more assertive war-crimes policy
by the United States. Such an attitude coincided well with

Harry Truman's feisty personality and his Yankee Doodle love-hate feelings toward Great Britain. As a former judge and a man with a near-mystic faith in the Bench, it was virtually inevitable that he would strongly support the use of a trial rather than summary executions as the best means of dealing with Hitler and his ilk. Truman never had doubted where right and justice lay in regard to atrocities, war crimes, or aggression, and he was confident that any tribunal made up of reasonable men would make a correct finding. Furthermore, unlike his predecessor, Truman was accustomed to working through an orderly administrative system in which subordinates were assumed to know their jobs unless proven otherwise.

Mr. Truman had been given a copy of the three Secretaries' memorandum (22 January),[13] and since its signatories were three of the most powerful members of the cabinet, his natural inclination was to go along with it, especially as he wished to make as few changes as possible in what he took to be the basic operations of the Roosevelt Administration. Whether or not Mr. Truman was given the impression that his predecessor had agreed to the conspiracy/criminal-organization plan we do not know. But it is likely that he gave Rosenman virtual carte blanche, chiefly on the basis of the fragmentary and skewed information contained in the judge's memorandum of 19 April. Harry Truman, however, knew his own mind and was surely no fool. Under other circumstances he might have been somewhat more hesitant or qualified in his endorsement, but he would most certainly have gone for a strong pro-trial position in any event. Thus, everything that happened to American war-crimes policy subsequent to 20 April 1945 rested on a legitimate policy decision and authorization to act from the President of the United States.

Understandably, to men who had been struggling for eight months through clouds of Rooseveltian evasion and delay, a full presidential warrant to move ahead was heady wine. When four of those with the most experience on the war-crimes problem—McCloy, Rosenman, Cutter, and Wechsler (together

with Mr. English, a weak stand-in from the State Department)
—came together on 20 April, the atmosphere was charged with
a sense of momentum and a desire to "get the British." Rosenman made a pass at declaring that the arraignment/criminal-
organization compromise had contained some good features
until vetoed by the war cabinet, but Cutter poured cold water
on that notion by declaring he and Weir doubted that it could
ever have been "stiffened up to be really judicial." [14]

The real business of the meeting, however, was to reach an
understanding on the framework in which the advance should
be organized. McCloy told the group he had obtained de
Gaulle's agreement to the proposition that a trial was necessary. Rosenman stated that he had conferred with Eden and
Ambassador Winant while in London, and though the Americans had wanted to include the Soviets in the talks immediately, Eden was adamant that the Russians not participate
until after Anglo-American discussions had occurred. As Rosenman pointedly remarked, since such talks had been attempted
and failed, henceforth "we'll have to be just as final" as the
British.[15] No more separate approaches would be made to
London. The U.S. government would start immediately to
form a war-crimes executive and planning group to carry forth
a prosecution of Nazi leaders on the basis of a conspiracy/
criminal-organization trial. Drafting of a proposal that could
serve as the basis for discussion at a meeting of the Allied Big
Three (or Big Four) would also be begun.

War-crimes policy developments now tumbled forth thick
and fast. On the day following the meeting (21 April), the
first lists of men who might be chosen to head the U.S. prosecution team were circulating through the War Department. In-
terestingly, on the very first of these, along with a half dozen
other names such as those of Justice Roberts and Sidney Alderman (later a senior staff member at Nuremberg), was that
of Supreme Court Justice Robert H. Jackson, the man who
would actually be appointed U.S. chief of counsel eight days
later.[16] Even as the selection process and the organizing work

went forward in the third week of April, so did the effort to produce a comprehensive American war-crimes paper. Those concerned with this problem, above all John J. McCloy, had at their disposal all the old drafts made by the War Department and the three Secretaries' memorandum, the various compromise proposals developed in London, and a new paper that Lord Simon had just prepared at the direction of the British cabinet.

The Simon paper, which presented the case for summary execution, contained no surprises. The central contention of the piece was that the Nazi chiefs would have to be liquidated because many German small fry would be executed through the actions of Allied military courts, and such a process would be patently unfair unless a like penalty was bestowed on the leaders of the Third Reich. But it would not be prudent or realistic to attempt to net Hitler and his colleagues in a trial, according to Simon, because the Führer would have to be charged with the "totality of his offenses against the international standard which civilized countries try to observe." [17] Such a charge would be so grandiose and would rest on such flimsy legal foundations that the proceedings would be endlessly long and would be denounced as "a put-up job." The defense could be expected to have a field day, for the Allies would have to include such matters as Germany's unprovoked attacks on her neighbors; then the door would be open for Goebbels to go trumpeting that other countries had been busy, not so long ago, "acquiring new territory." [18]

Simon's original paper concluded with a paragraph stating it would "be valuable" if, at the moment of capture, Hitler was presented with a paper chronicling his evil deeds, as long as it was understood that there would be no hearing or trial on the basis of this paper.[19] Apparently the Lord Chancellor and other British officials concluded the Americans would probably *not* understand this, and the final paragraph was therefore omitted from the document sent to Washington.[20] Simon's paper defending political execution also did not contain what he and Somervell considered one of the most telling arguments against a trial. In a secret note to the Permanent Under Secretary of the Foreign Office, Sir Alexander Cadogan, Simon declared that he and Somervell despaired of discovering a trial system that would satisfy both the Soviets and the West. "The Russians seem to start their trials with the confession of the accused," Simon wrote to Cadogan, yet "we don't understand their methods and don't know how the result is obtained. . . . can we visualize a joint court which combines methods so different?" [21] A worthy question certainly, although as the Nuremberg trial ultimately showed, not necessarily a moral one. But the timidity of Simon and Somervell, and their unwillingness to risk putting the point directly to the Americans, meant that it could have no impact at all. Cadogan was in effect being asked to find some magic wand that would put the idea into the heads of Henry Stimson and Harry Truman. One can imagine that the salty Cadogan, who once exclaimed he could not take care of everyone's business because "the Foreign Office is not a department store," [22] probably solved the problem by simply filing the paper. But if the magic wand was found, or even a little tearoom chatter was employed, there is no indication that it exerted any influence on American officials.

In light of these weaknesses and omissions in the Simon memorandum, it is highly understandable that when John J. McCloy sat down to draft an American position paper, he aimed primarily at upholding the trial approach and refuting the advocates of summary execution.[23] It is equally obvious why McCloy drew heavily on the notes he had prepared for his earlier talks in London; one of the central issues was the same on both occasions—the need to make the trial idea seem both necessary and practical. What made the choice between trial and summary execution so important, as McCloy saw it, was that the method chosen to punish war criminals should be the kind of deterrent that could raise international standards of conduct. A trial would involve "implicit condemnation of ruthlessness and excessive force," which would be progressive and consistent with the "fundamental morality of the Allied cause." [24] Political execution, on the other hand, would, in McCloy's words, involve a "descent to the methods of the Axis" and would thus negate "democratic principles of justice." Yet even this did not exhaust the important consequences that hung on the choice between the judge and the political executioner. Not only would a "soundly conceived trial system" set the postwar political tone inside Germany, McCloy also believed, as he had said earlier, that it might be a more important deterrent than the United Nations organization itself, because it would "certainly induce future government leaders to think" before they acted as the Nazis had done.[25]

In McCloy's opinion only three principles would be needed to guide the case against the major war criminals. The trial should be basically fair, definitely expeditious, and should adjudicate everything that had transpired since 1933, including prewar atrocities and the launching of an aggressive war. This task might seem overwhelming, and perhaps contradictory, but McCloy thought it could be realized because of the nature of international law, which was capable of developing "to meet the needs of the times, just as common law has grown, not by enunciating new principles, but by adapting old ones." McCloy was confident that by making use of the suppleness and flexibility of international law, Allied planners would be able to solve the problem. The Assistant Secretary of War thus rested the case for a major war-crimes trial squarely on "the ability of Allied legal brains to produce a fair, expeditious and reasonable procedure to meet the novel situation." [26]

The McCloy memorandum, which was completed and circulated through the upper echelons of the War Department on 20 April 1945, may at first glance appear to be of modest importance, just one more link in the long chain that led from the Morgenthau plan to the London Charter. But this seven-page paper embodies much of the spirit that fueled the final American drive to put across the conspiracy/criminal-organiza-

tion trial plan, and as such it is a major harbinger of the
Nuremberg trial. If one places the McCloy paper alongside
the formal memorandum the Americans used to sell the plan
to the U.S.S.R. and Britain during the San Francisco conference in May 1945, the connection is immediately clear.[27]
The formal memorandum, which was mainly authored by Mc-
Cloy's aide, Colonel Cutter, blended together some of the
chief points of the old 22 January three Secretaries' memorandum with material taken from McCloy's 20 April paper. Of
the five broad sections that make up the formal memorandum
to the Allies, all of section four was copied from McCloy, as
were various shorter passages in other sections. Significantly,
it was McCloy's material that gave the formal memorandum
its tone of idealism and high morality.

Most previous writers on the subject have quite reasonably
assumed that this idealistic tone was in the work of the American war-crimes planners from the earliest days. It is of course
true that some appeals to righteousness do appear in the writings of all those who worked on the war-crimes problem,
and that on one occasion—the debate over aggressive-war policy in November–December 1944—they spilled over into various
draft memoranda. But as should now be obvious to the reader,
until the third week of April 1945 the few formal papers on
war-crimes policy produced by the Americans (such as the three
secretaries' memorandum and the "Implementing Instrument") were all characterized by very calm, matter-of-fact
formulations. Little sense of emotion, outrage, or high mission
showed up until the McCloy memorandum on 20 April, and
from that point on, the idealistic and moral current runs broad
and deep.

As long as the policy struggles had focused on the attempts
by the War Department champions of the conspiracy/criminal-
organization plan to confound their opponents in the Treasury
or JAG, it would have been absurd for either side to try to
wrap themselves in the cause of morality or democracy. But as
soon as the main conflict changed to one between American

advocacy of trial and British support for summary execution, the door was open for appeals to various forms of high law. Ironically then, the first strong stimulus that pointed the American war-crimes planners toward the high road of righteousness came not from a desire to pillory Hitler and his minions, but from a need to discredit Churchill and his colleagues in the British cabinet. But this factor was strongly reinforced by a rising fervor among the American people and their leaders to punish the Germans for the truly heinous atrocities. Just at this time the Western armies, having broken out of the Remagen bridgehead, began fanning out over Germany, overrunning POW camps and concentration camps with the notorious names of Belsen and Dachau.

War Department officials were outraged by the first reports of mistreatment from liberated American military personnel, although subsequently many of these reports proved to be exaggerated. Considering Germany's critical economic situation, and the damage and strain produced by military and air operations in the homeland, the Reich government had (with some exceptions) held pretty well to the Geneva rules in its treatment of Anglo-American prisoners.[28] Of course what it had done to its Eastern European captives, especially the Red Army men who fell into German hands in 1941, is a very different, and horrifying, story. But what produced the white anger among many American authorities in April 1945 were the stories that American soldiers had been maltreated, and whether true or not, these contributed significantly to the feeling of passionate self-righteousness taking possession of American officialdom. On 22 April 1945, for example, Under Secretary of War Robert Patterson told Colonel Cutter that the German mistreatment of American prisoners was "his CHIEF concern at the moment." [Block letters in the original] [29] In view of the reports indicating "terrible conditions and atrocities in recent months," Patterson believed the only way the War Department could avoid "a terrific kickback" from American public opinion was to make sure that the Germans were held strictly

accountable "for the shocking treatment of our men." [30] Such
opinions, emanating from the highest echelons of the department, inevitably breathed new fire into the American war-
crimes policy drafts, which were dedicated to the proposition
that German war criminals should be made to pay 'til the
pips squeaked.

Of much greater importance, both for the moral passion of
the American war-crimes prosecution program and for the
whole postwar controversy over atrocities, the holocaust, and
Allied justice, was what the Anglo-American forces found in the
concentration camps. After years of trying to discount atrocity
reports, including those circulated by the Allied press, American
and British soldiers suddenly found themselves walking through
the entrance gates of hell. Their horror and anger exploded
in the form of scattered instances of "summary justice" to
some concentration camp guards; and in a torrent of reports,
letters, and photographs they proclaimed to the world that the
most extreme of the atrocity stories had been true or had
understated the gruesome reality. On the heels of the troops
came a second army of reporters, photographers, generals (including Eisenhower), congressmen, members of Parliament,
and countless groups of influential citizens from the United
States and the United Kingdom. [31] Every newspaper and news-
reel cinema in the world was soon covered with photographs
of mountains of corpses among which wandered tiny bands
of survivors so emaciated that they were doomed to die even
after liberation.

German apologists would later protest in vain that conditions
had not always been so murderously chaotic. It was true that
during the final months of the war, the ferocity of direct combat did combine with crushing war production demands within
the camps to increase the death toll. Himmler and his aides
had also made things much worse with last-minute attempts
to move masses of starving inmates away from the advancing
Allies by marching them deeper into the hinterland of Germany. With food and medical supplies always deficient in the

camps, and decreasing at an alarming rate during 1945, it was therefore inevitable that at the moment when the SS administration broke down, the surviving inmates would be overcome by universal starvation and disease.

Those "sensitive" souls in the SS *Hauptämte* (Central Offices) who would later claim to be professionally offended by the pictures of disorderly mass death that came out of the camps in 1945 may thus have had a *small* measure of truth on their side. Belsen and Dachau had not always exploited, tortured, and killed in such a chaotic way. The murderous force of the camps had less often come from typhus than from their systematic program to destroy the human spirit and from the dictum that the inmates should literally "labor unto death." The Anglo-American sense of outrage, fed by pictures of bulldozers moving heaps of corpses, was thus slightly off the mark because orderly, not chaotic, killing was the true hallmark of the camps. But to the degree that the Western peoples and their leaders saw the final horrors as the inevitable and predictable consequence of the concentration camp system within a total war, they grasped the situation clearly, and judged it correctly.

A second Allied reaction to concentration camps such as Dachau, though understandable and emotionally justifiable, was not, however, as closely attuned to facts and had much more serious consequences for the future. For years Allied leaders had tried to ignore numerous reports and entreaties that Nazi Germany was carrying out genocide and that something had to be done to stop the mass murder of Slavs and Jews in Eastern European death camps. By a series of complex psychological devices, including some obvious ethnic stereotyping, Anglo-American authorities had managed to remove the reality of mass death from these reports and replaced it with a series of abstractions—statistical studies, bureaucratic phrases, and various other forms of administrative mumbo jumbo. By so doing, they kept knowledge of the Nazi killing operations, and the concomitant demand that radical countermeasures be employed, on the periphery of the Allied war-making system.[32] The Anglo-Americans, in particular, stuck to conventional warfare while trying to mollify critics with assurances; the best way to aid those being persecuted in occupied territories was to throw everything into winning a purely military victory as quickly as possible. The debate still rages over whether or not recommendations made in 1943-44 to bomb Auschwitz were militarily feasible and whether or not they offered any real prospects of saving people from the gas chambers.

What is beyond question is that, in their own minds, the Allied leaders reduced the genocidal atrocities to little more than abstract shadows until Nazi Germany crashed to defeat. When Anglo-American troops liberated the concentration camps they presented Western leaders with a situation they could deal with directly, without having to choose between a number of difficult alternatives. The emotional floodgates were then allowed to open and all the pent-up frustration and anger tore through the bureaucratic defenses. Here was living proof of German wickedness and a transcendent demonstration of the justice of the Allied cause. The Germans really had been engaged in a master plan to exterminate those whom they considered inferior or superfluous. Could anyone now doubt the justice and necessity of a broad prosecution of the Nazi master plan and of the organizations through which Hitler and his deputies had sought to put it into operation?

When the concentration camps were liberated in April 1945, they provided the ultimate emotional punch in the American war-crimes crusade. But in their hurry to be moral, the Western governments, especially the United States, did not get the facts quite right. The Anglo-Americans had not liberated the Nazi death factories. Bad as the concentration camps were, they could not hold a candle to the true mass murder camps in occupied Poland, such as Auschwitz and Treblinka. The Western powers never actually came close to seeing the full-scale Nazi death machine in operation. But the Western governments were so eager to expose the dreadful deeds of the

Nazis—partly because they would no longer have to hide behind their shield of bureaucratic abstraction, and partly because the Americans were so anxious to find a Nazi mass murder plan— that they helped create the impression that the concentration camps were extermination factories, complete with massive gas chambers and crematoria. This conclusion, and the general failure of the Allies to unravel how the Nazi racist system related to the regime's instruments of repression and extermination, would cause some difficult moments for the prosecution and the Bench at Nuremberg.

A potentially more serious consequence emerged in the 1960s and 1970s, when a number of rightist writers in various countries seized on the Allied failure to distinguish between extermination and concentration camps in 1945 to maintain that there never had been any extermination program.[33] This effort was not sufficient to float much of a neo-Nazi revival, but it has probably produced a permanent sore spot of doubt and uncertainty about what actually happened during the Second World War. The neo-Nazis will surely come back to this point again and again, for to much of the public, if one cannot count on the equation that the heaps of bodies at Belsen and Dachau equals a genocidal extermination policy, then what can one accept about Nazism or the war without question?

Therefore when this massive charge of emotional and moral enthusiasm was added to the American espousal of the conspiracy/criminal-organization plan in April 1945, it may not have been an unmixed blessing for posterity. But when viewed in the context of the times, it was, nonetheless, probably inevitable. The American leaders needed an outlet to register their abhorrence of Nazi atrocities, and they were quick to see that the public outcry regarding the concentration camps provided such an opportunity. They were equally quick to recognize that it could be used to help convince influential opinion makers of the virtues of the conspiracy/criminal-organization plan. When the congressional delegation assigned to investigate the camps went to Europe in late April, the officer assigned

to brief them was General Weir, who noted with satisfaction
that the congressmen were "very war crimes conscious." [34]
Following the instructions he had received from the Pentagon, Weir told the delegation that the American government
had a comprehensive war-crimes prosecution program already
prepared and stressed that it would be *"judicial"* not *"political."* [35] Ten days later, when the members of the delegation
returned from Germany, they were received by Secretary Stimson, who steered the conversation so that by the end he could
conclude that the Congressmen:

"were unanimously of the opinion that the so-called atrocities had
represented a deliberate and concerted attempt by the government
of Germany to eliminate by murder, starvation and other methods
of death large numbers of Russians, Poles, Jews, and other classes of
people whom they did not wish to survive." [36]

The furor over the capture of the concentration camps had
thus been fitted neatly into the basic tenets of the common
enterprise theory, which War Department officials were working assiduously to turn into an effective program, both for the
United States and for all the United Nations.

In a flurry of activity during the last week of April, the war-
crimes program was given organizational form, centralized direction, and a basic plan of attack. The first important step
was the creation of a special war-crimes planning group in the
War Department, which was charged with the tasks of drafting
the basic documents, preparing the case against the major
Nazi criminals, and assisting a "special counsel," who would
soon be appointed chief planner and eventually would prosecute the case. Although JAG and other organizations protested
against the plan to subordinate this group directly to the Assistant Secretary of War rather than assign it to one of the regular
subunits of the department, their objections were overridden.
On 26 April, Secretary Stimson approved the formation of a
special war-crimes planning group and placed it under the con-

trol of John J. McCloy. Predictably, the first officer assigned to the new unit was Lieutenant Colonel Murray C. Bernays.[37]

Almost simultaneously with the creation of this group came a basic decision regarding where and under whose direction the United States would make its major move to obtain Allied agreement to the conspiracy/criminal-organization plan. Apparently all the major American leaders concerned—Stimson, McCloy, Rosenman, and ultimately President Truman as well —agreed that an initiative should be made quickly and that the San Francisco United Nations conference, which was scheduled to open within a week, provided a nearly perfect opportunity. The only drawback was that Secretary of State Stettinius was scheduled to lead the American delegation, and Stimson, in particular, had little confidence in his ability. The Secretary of War felt that when Stettinius's general weaknesses were added to the fact that he was not a lawyer, he was "likely to be overruled by the English leaders" on a matter such as war-crimes policy.[38]

On 25 April, Stimson saw the President and secured a statement from him that he "strongly supported" the War Department plan for a trial of the major war criminals.[39] Secretary Stimson also apparently advised the President that Judge Rosenman should be sent to San Francisco as a special emissary to negotiate the war-crimes agreement, with John J. McCloy acting as his assistant. Mr. Stimson, confident his advice would be followed, met with McCloy immediately after leaving Mr. Truman's office and told him "to get ready for a big fight" in San Francisco.[40] Two days later, on 27 April, Mr. Truman informed Under Secretary of State Grew that he wanted Rosenman "to carry on this work to its completion and that Judge Rosenman had undertaken to do so." [41]

A mark of confusion crept in here regarding exactly what Rosenman was appointed to do, presumably because the President was loath to say directly that he lacked faith in his Secretary of State. Consequently the State Department may have been temporarily under the misapprehension that Rosenman was being appointed the American delegate on the UNWCC, and Rosenman himself may have entertained the incorrect impression that he was being given overall supervision of the war-crimes program. But if others were unclear about what all this meant, John J. McCloy was not. As he informed one of his subordinates, he and Rosenman were going to San Francisco to drive home the American program because the "President had approved [the] policy of insisting in negotiations on judicial rather than political disposition." [42] Under pressure the Americans might agree to a "possible separate judicial trial before [a] military tribunal for top Hitlerites," but they would not give ground on the absolute indispensability of judicial process or on the principles of the conspiracy/criminal-organization plan.[43]

In the final days of April, an even more important official was appointed to a position of high authority in the American war-crimes program. After weeks of inquiries and probings, many of which had been carried on through Stimson and Rosenman, Supreme Court Justice Robert H. Jackson quietly signaled his willingness to oversee the preparation and prosecution of the case against the major Nazi war criminals. In a confidential letter to the President on 29 April, Jackson agreed to serve as United States chief of counsel, subject to a few qualifications and conditions. He asked the president to issue an executive order defining his duties so that his authority would be limited exclusively to control over the American case. The Justice was suspicious of the Soviets, as he would continue to be throughout the trial, and believed that they would go their own way on war crimes in any event. Jackson told the President that the Russians probably had evidence, "such as confessions, for example" obtained by methods that would make it impossible for him to "vouch" for them.[44]

Jackson preferred to keep clear of Soviet Russia, but he also wanted to develop the American case at top speed. Although he was aware negotiations with the Allies would be going on, and that a draft proposal was being prepared for San Francisco, Jackson contended that nothing, not even the lack of Allied agreement, should deter the American government from pushing ahead with its plans to try the major Nazi war criminals. "We know some kind of military tribunal must be set up" Jackson declared, adding that "time is of the essence" because people had to be discouraged from "taking the law into their own hands." Since the Justice felt that the three Secretaries' memorandum (22 January) was basically sound, although needing "a good deal of maturing in details," highest priority should be given to drawing up a short code of procedure and assembling evidence to try before a tribunal.[45]

On 1 May Secretary Stimson talked with Jackson by phone and concluded that the Justice "sees eye to eye with all we have done here and is strong for a trial as distinguished from political action." [46] The next day (2 May) saw the issuance of the executive order designating Jackson chief of counsel; [47] another big step had thereby been taken in America's war-crimes program. Considering the low priority inter-Allied cooperation held in Jackson's thinking, and the tendency among War Department planners not to yield on basic points in San Francisco, it is hardly surprising that the State Department played no part in the decision to unilaterally select an American chief of counsel and to appoint Jackson to the post. But it is still somewhat disconcerting to realize that on 2 May, State Department officials first learned of Jackson's appointment by reading about it in the newspapers! [48]

As April turned to May, the rather untidy American war-crimes program was divided into two sections; the diplomatic effort aimed at San Francisco was led by Rosenman, and the organizational effort was centered in Washington under the leadership of Justice Jackson. The common organizational thread connecting the two sections lay in McCloy's special war-crimes office. While the Assistant Secretary himself would be acting as Rosenman's strong right arm in San Francisco, Murray Bernays was taking up service as the first member of

Jackson's prosecution planning team in Washington. The two sections were also brought together through the common need to prepare a memorandum, which summarized the major points in the American plan, and a draft agreement, which could be presented to the Allies at the Conference. In this endeavor the top American war-crimes planners pinned their faith on their drafting ability, for as John J. McCloy had stated, the whole argument for a judicial proceeding rested on "the ability of Allied legal brains to produce a fair, expeditious and reasonable procedure." [49]

As indicated above, most of the burden of the early drafting effort fell on the shoulders of Colonel Cutter. On 25 April, Cutter prepared a survey of the U.S. war-crimes position that was circulated to other war-crimes policy planners under the title of "A Memorandum of Proposals for the Prosecution and Punishment of Certain War Criminals and Other Offenders." The document was then put through a major rewrite on 30 April by a team composed of Cutter, Wechsler, Bernays, and Rosenman; in this form it was laid before the Allies in San Francisco and was subsequently presented by Justice Jackson and other American authorities as the first official exposition of the United States trial plan.[50]

The memorandum was a generally straightforward formulation of the common enterprise theory which, as already mentioned, sought to justify a judicial attack on the Nazis for carrying out a "systematic and planned reign of terror" by making generous use of McCloy's arguments in favor of a trial.[51] It did leave a sliver of room for possible compromise with the British by granting that the top Nazis could be prosecuted in a separate trial, rather than within the general conspiracy/criminal-organization proceeding. In addition, it sought to reassure those who had doubts about the common enterprise approach by noting that much the same effect could be attained by proceeding against lesser Nazis as criminal "accomplices." But even this measured attempt to be conciliatory added an element of vagueness regarding secondary proceedings for the members of organizations that had been declared criminal. The memorandum stated that courts in secondary trials should determine the "extent of the individual's participation" in criminal plans and activities, and then should set an appropriate sentence ranging from death to "reparational labor." [52] For a procedure whose major attraction to many Allied leaders was its promise of disposing of hundreds of thousands of Gestapo and SS members in perfunctory hearings, this clause seemed to suggest court proceedings far too extensive at the secondary level.

Nonetheless, Cutter's memorandum slipped past the armies of legal draftsmen with surprising ease, and after the one revision of 30 April, it moved on to San Francisco unmolested. Not so the colonel's effort to produce a draft executive agreement, which would serve as the basis for negotiations between the United States and its major allies. During the London talks Cutter had already made two revisions in Mr. Hackworth's old "Implementing Instrument" of January 1945.[53] Now, on 28 April, he returned to the task and attempted a comprehensive redraft. Inevitably, the document went down a well-trodden path as it surveyed the plan to prosecute the Nazi leaders and organizations for preparing and executing a "systematic and planned reign of terror." [54] Like the memorandum, it too was somewhat muddled about secondary proceedings after an organization had been declared criminal. In fact, the draft executive agreement went even further than the memorandum and gave the secondary tribunals the task of determining the "nature" and "extent" of each organization member's participation in the criminal conspiracy.[55]

This was a point where lack of clarity was critical, but also endemic, and controversy over the follow-up proceedings would plague every draft and every discussion of the subject right to the end of the Nuremberg trial. If this had been the only vulnerable point in Cutter's draft executive agreement, it, like the memorandum, might well have gone through unscathed. But the colonel had decided to retain, and in some instances to

amplify, the provisions in the agreement originally included to
meet British wishes during the London meeting. The executive
agreement also envisioned a very rapid, not to say perfunctory, trial proceeding, but one in which the chiefs of the Third
Reich would be accused of a bewildering array of offenses extending from murder and the launching of aggressive war to
the creation of "disorder" in states bordering on Germany.[56]

The tendency to include wholesale lists of alleged Nazi
offenses had arisen directly from the British arraignment approach. As long as the Americans focused on a formal trial,
they exercised a measure of reserve in relating the alleged
crimes to some statutory or customary catalog of offenses. The
British were initially even more cautious, and one of the major
reasons why Sir John Simon had put forth the arraignment
proposal was to circumvent just this kind of limitation. The
Lord Chancellor reasoned that if one could forgo customary
court procedure and did not employ a formal judicial hearing,
then one would be free to charge the Nazis with any form of
offensive behavior that might strike one's fancy.

Thus Colonel Cutter's inclusion of a long and wide-ranging
list of alleged offenses in his draft executive agreement was
residue from the London talks. It was not this, or any other
specific provision of this type, that made the draft so vulnerable, however, but the cumulative effect of so many odd bits
and pieces. In one of his first acts as the American chief of
counsel, Jackson zeroed in on the draft executive agreement.
After courteously conceding that the document showed "evidence of most careful preparation," the Justice declared that
it nonetheless required serious revision because its tone and
form did not meet the high standards appropriate to a paper
that would become "one of the basic documents of international law." [57] Jackson specifically found the language "too
impassioned," and he thought the general effect was of "a
court organized to convict." The world had heard enough "fiery
words" in the Justice's view, and a "colder toned instrument"
leading to "sure-footed and discriminating action" would be

far more effective. In addition, Jackson believed Cutter had fallen afoul of the temptation to legislate in too great detail. The war-crimes planners were working in a wide-open area, Jackson reminded his colleagues, and if they were to avoid giving the defendants technical grounds for objection, it was wisest not to go "beyond very basic and general" procedural regulations. "From where I sit" the justice wrote, "one becomes impressed, perhaps over impressed, with the dangerous quality of adjectives and unnecessary phrases in legal documents, for it is surprising how much litigation can be hung on a single word of limitation." [58]

Jackson's critical comments produced a flurry of redrafting and revising. Within forty-eight hours the executive agreement was rewritten and then underwent four consecutive revisions.[59] The basic redrafting was done on 1 and 2 May, probably by Cutter and Jackson, with a helping hand apparently extended by Colonel Bernays. Then in the course of 2 to 3 May, four more revisions were done. In light of all this writing and rewriting, the final form of the executive agreement is surprisingly clear and tightly worded, with few of the characteristics proverbially associated with work produced by committees.

One important effect of the revisions was the near elimination of efforts to compromise with the British. In addition, the extensive rewriting provides a valuable opportunity to see which aspects of the plan produced the greatest disagreements among the planners themselves. As might readily be anticipated, one of the most troublesome spots was the section dealing with punishable offenses. The long list of accusations Cutter had taken from the British was pruned away, and all that remained was a list made up of violations of the rules of war, "initiating" and "launching" of invasions in violation of laws and treaties, and "recourse to war as an instrument of national policy"—the latter phrase derived from the Kellogg-Briand Pact.[60] Only indirect references to prewar acts or crimes against humanity remained.

To broaden and strengthen the accusatory grounds of the

prosecution, Jackson and Cutter employed two strikingly new formulations. At the head of the paragraph enumerating offenses to be punished, there was an unusually bald statement in which the Allies "solemnly declare" that the acts listed were in fact crimes.[61] This unilateral "creation" of law was too much for the legalistic timidity of Bernays and Cutter, who in the first revision immediately struck out the phrase "solemnly declare" and replaced it with the more guarded statement that the Allies would prosecute the "criminal acts" enumerated thereafter. Crimes against humanity were still not added to the list, but Cutter and Bernays did insert a phrase stating that the defendants would be subject to "accessorial liability" for participation "in the formulation and execution of a criminal plan." [62]

The second innovative formulation introduced by Jackson and Cutter passed through the three subsequent pre–San Francisco revisions unchallenged. The clause in question asserted the right of the Allies to proceed against any acts that violated international law, the rules and customs of war, or the domestic statutes "*of any of the United Nations* or any Axis power or satellite." [Italics added] This remarkable statement would, among other things, have empowered the prosecutors to rummage through the law codes of some fifty-odd Allied nations in search of offenses that could be charged against the Nazi leaders. Obviously defendants in any international trial would have stood no chance if handfuls of accusations drawn from the statute books of a group of states could have been thrown onto the scales of justice by the prosecution.

The inclusion and retention of this highly innovative and dangerous clause suggests a rising feeling in Washington that with the Third Reich in its death throes—VE Day was less than a week away—some of the legal niceties could be sacrificed, if necessary, to guarantee conviction of the Nazi leaders. Justice Jackson also seems to have brought a somewhat more aggressive and vindictive tone to the American planning. At the same time, it should be noted, the idea of prosecuting the leaders of the

Third Reich for violations of a multitude of *Allied* and Axis laws constituted a significant shift of emphasis away from that employed in the original War Department plan. If such a shotgun accusation system had been used, there would have been less need for the conspiracy theory to guarantee conviction of Nazi leaders. With fifty criminal codes to hurl against the foe, Allied prosecutors would not have required the thread of conspiracy to get convictions for prewar acts or offenses the Nazis had committed against German nationals.

The tendency of the early May redrafts to edge away from the basic features emphasized in the earlier War Department memoranda also shows up in the way the revised executive agreement treated the question of aggressive war. Since the draft of 13 January, the aggressive-war features of the conspiracy/criminal-organization system had been reduced to a thin shadow. Then the 2 May executive agreement drafts restored the "crime" of aggression to its full glory. They even took over the wording of the Kellogg-Briand Pact by asserting that the "recourse to war as an instrument of national policy" was a crime. Significantly, neither Mr. Hackworth nor any other State Department legal specialist had a hand in the preparation of these drafts. Unquestionably, the responsibility for putting renewed emphasis on aggression came not from diplomats, nor the planners who had been toiling with the war-crimes problem for so long, but from Justice Jackson. He was the one who, building on the earlier work of Colonel Chanler, wished to make it the pivot of the whole case. Henceforth he used all his influence and power to give aggressive war the central position in every declaration on war-crimes policy that the Allies produced from May 1945 until the main Nuremberg trial closed in the fall of 1946.[63]

Later we will again touch on the revived emphasis on aggression brought forth by Justice Jackson, but a number of other points in the redrafted executive agreement of 2 May, especially those regarding defendants' rights, also produced significant reverberations in the months ahead. The first of these was the knotty problem of superior orders. The Jackson-Cutter draft (that is, the basic redraft of 2 May), left to the tribunal full discretion as to whether or not it would entertain a plea of superior orders as a covering defense, a mitigating factor, or disregard it altogether.[64] But the fourth, and last, revision, made on the plane journey to San Francisco by Cutter, Wechsler, and Rosenman, altered this passage so it read that superior orders "shall not constitute an absolute defense" but might be considered in mitigation if the tribunal so declared.[65]

The provisions on rights of organizational defendants in secondary proceedings were also repeatedly revised. The first formulation gave secondary courts "absolute discretion" in any use of the "circumstances" of membership or the "nature and extent" of criminal participation during the trial of "criminal organization" members.[66] The second revision (Jackson, Wechsler, Bernays) changed this passage so that in secondary proceedings the "burden of proof" would rest solely on the defendant "to establish any circumstances relating to his membership or participation . . . which are relevant either in defense or in mitigation."[67] This revision also eliminated "reparational labor" from the specified punishments that might be handed down to criminal-organization members. What remained said such defendants might be sentenced to death or "other" appropriate punishment.[68]

An additional curious, but important, section relating to defendant rights appeared in these revisions. Tentative passages on absentia trials in the first two drafts were converted into a formal provision in the second revision made by Jackson, Wechsler, and Bernays. The passage in question read: "The Tribunal shall determine to what extent proceedings against defendants may be taken without their presence."[69] Its retention in a modified form in subsequent drafts led to much serious criticism of the Nuremberg system for making possible the absentia trial, conviction, and death sentence of Martin Bormann. What has not been clear, until the various drafts of the trial plan could be studied in detail, is why the Americans chose to introduce a principle so sharply at variance with Anglo-American legal practice. The answer surely lies merely in the date of these executive agreement drafts. Adolf Hitler and Joseph Goebbels were reported (correctly) to have committed suicide on 30 April 1945, but Allied leaders had no way of ascertaining whether or not these reports were true. So when the executive agreement was redrafted two days later, Cutter and Bernays, seconded by Jackson and Wechsler, seem to have decided it would be wise to stay on the safe side and provide machinery for trying the allegedly deceased Führer, just to make certain that if he later surfaced alive, the Allies would have a legal mandate to execute him. It was merely an ironic footnote that by September 1945, when the indictment was prepared, the Allied authorities had convinced themselves that Hitler and Goebbels were actually dead, and the only major Nazi official for whom there were not then definitive death details was Bormann. Although information currently available makes it nearly certain that the Nazi Party secretary actually died in Berlin in the spring of 1945, he alone was tried in absentia, and that act helped to produce a veritable library of fictional and purportedly nonfictional works chronicling Bormann's after-life in various remote corners of the world.

In summarizing the features of the redrafted and revised executive agreement, one could go on indefinitely indicating various points where disagreements or different shades of meaning appeared. Some of these were rather significant, but the most important consideration regarding the executive agreement, in addition to the controversies over defendants' rights, prosecutable crimes, and the elimination of the arraignment proposal, was the speed and efficiency with which the whole operation was completed. When Cutter, Wechsler, and Rosenman arrived in San Francisco on the morning of 3 May, Secretary of State Stettinius had already asked for, and received, Russian and British agreement to a meeting on war-crimes policy that very afternoon. Jackson and his associates working in Washington had met this challenge by producing a radically redrafted executive agreement, revised it extensively, and still had it ready for presentation to the Soviet and British foreign secretaries in San Francisco within thirty-six hours!

The rapidity with which all this had been accomplished played a significant part in putting Foreign Secretary Anthony Eden and his British colleagues in San Francisco in a very difficult position. When on 2 May Eden received Stettinius's request that a war-crimes meeting be held the next afternoon, the Foreign Secretary frantically cabled London asking that instructions be sent "most immediately." [70] Eden had good cause to worry, for he knew that the British government had made precious little headway on developing a viable war-crimes policy in the three weeks since the London discussions. Although British officials had received repeated warnings from Halifax, Cadogan, and McCloy among others that the American government was deadly serious about a trial, and that this position had the strong backing of Stimson and the President, London failed to respond with a sense of urgency.[71]

In the course of the leisurely British discussions and exchange of minutes associated with war-crimes matters, however, two significant ideas had emerged. They pointed toward a formula that would ultimately allow London to save some face when capitulating to American demands. Although the British were still repeating the official line that the Nazi leaders should be disposed of through political action, Mr. J. G. Ward of the Foreign Office noted in late April that if the Allies took the Nazi chiefs into custody and began to process them, then even if they were eventually killed, such action would hardly be "summary" execution.[72] Ward also joined with officials in the Attorney General's office to recommend that if all other arguments in favor of political disposition failed, the "onus" for developing an effective trial plan should be put on the Americans, because "this might . . . lead to a greater appreciation of the difficulties." [73]

This was the situation when the British cabinet met at 6:00 P.M. (10:00 A.M. San Francisco time) on 3 May to consider what instructions on war-crimes policy should be sent to Eden. The members had before them another paper by the ever-busy Sir John Simon that frankly admitted there was "a fundamental difference of view" between the British "who advocate summary execution on identification, and the Americans and Russians, who insist on some kind of judicial process." [74] After dancing about the problem, however, Sir John could not come up with any suggestion to convert the Allies to their view, and he finally hinted, like Mr. Ward and the officials from the Attorney General's office before him, that perhaps the best thing to do was to "invite Stettinius to get a document drawn up" in the hope that the Americans would break their teeth on the complexity of the problem. In the course of the discussion, the Minister of State, Richard Law, who spoke for the Foreign Office in Eden's absence, observed that "with the death of Hitler, Mussolini and other leaders, circumstances had changed," and the problem of what to do with an enemy sovereign or the head of an enemy government no longer existed. During the debate an unidentified minister remarked that whatever happened, it would be inadvisable for the British to appear in an open meeting as the only ones demanding that surviving second-line Nazis be denied "an opportunity of answering the charges."

It was again Richard Law, however, who opened the way for a definite cabinet recommendation to Eden. The Minister of State observed that if his colleagues would give up their now pointless advocacy of summary execution, it should be possible to insist that the trial be limited to traditional war crimes. At the same time Law casually recommended the possibility of gathering up the surviving Nazi leaders, presumably men like Göring and Himmler, and lumping them together with those to be prosecuted in Rosenman's "middle level" conspiracy/criminal-organization prosecution. Although unaware he was doing so, the Minister of State was actually recommending that the British government resurrect the American plan of integrating the major criminals into a broad conspiracy/criminal-organization prosecution! As the discussion continued, this idea received support from at least one other minister, but the view which apparently obtained the loudest echo was that Britain should agree to the idea of a trial "in principle," while putting on the Americans "the onus of producing a workable procedure before we committed ourselves finally." [75]

At the close of the discussion, the Prime Minister summarized the principle points and put forward a series of propositions that were approved by the cabinet. The ministers gave an "in principle" endorsement to a criminal-organization trial, but they asked for "a detailed statement of the procedure" to be used both in the main trial and in the secondary proceedings. Regarding the major war criminals, the cabinet declared the British government would not oppose a judicial proceeding, but it would "invite" the Allies to "produce a workable procedure before we finally committed ourselves to agreement that these persons should be put on trial." As an effective device for saving face, a statement was put on the record to the effect that the situation had been "materially changed" by the "death of Hitler and Mussolini and other prominent leaders" and by "the probability that still more of them would be killed before the fighting was over." [76]

A paraphrased version of these cabinet declarations, which gave Eden more latitude to determine if the Americans and Russians had finally decided on a trial before he gave up on summary execution, was immediately dispatched to San Francisco.[77] The cable apparently arrived in California shortly after 1:00 P.M., just before Eden was scheduled to meet with his Russian and American counterparts. But any sense of relief or comfort that it may have occasioned among British officials in San Francisco was short-lived.

The Allied war-crimes meeting of 3 May featured a large list of participants. The ten-member American delegation, headed by Stettinius, Rosenman, McCloy, Wechsler, and Ambassador Harriman, was bigger than the Soviet and British groups combined. Molotov and Gromyko headed a five-member Russian group, while the United Kingdom was represented only by Eden, Sir William Malkin, and Sir Alexander Cadogan.[78] As host and titular head of the American diplomatic army Stettinius opened the meeting; he immediately declared that the United States had "established" its war-crimes policy. He also announced that Justice Jackson had been selected to head the American prosecution team. Then, following a brief consideration of whether or not to bring the French delegation directly into this meeting—a course that was quickly recognized as impractical; the French were invited to attend subsequent sessions—Stettinius turned the meeting over to Judge Rosenman.

The judge amplified on Stettinius's opening remarks by declaring that the "U.S. government had reached a decision in regard to the plans for the treatment of war criminals." In addition to returning some Nazis to the scene of their crimes in conformity with the Moscow declaration, and to traditional trials for violation of the rules of war, which would be carried out by each of the Allies, the United States was preparing to prosecute the Nazi leaders and organizations for their part in a "criminal conspiracy to control the world" by means of broken treaties, persecution of minorities, and a plethora of atrocities. Rosenman paused briefly to reassure the cautiously inclined that the United States did not envision sending all Nazis to the gallows, and that a range of punishments could be utilized, including "rehabilitation" work. But a mass trial was necessary, the judge declared, not only because of its "moral" value, but because it would destroy the nucleus of any future Nazi revival in Germany. Speed was therefore urgent, and Rosenman asked the Allied great powers to quickly appoint prosecutors comparable to Justice Jackson so that a four-power executive group could immediately set to work preparing the case.[79]

One may assume that Eden was made somewhat nervous by the unseemly haste with which Rosenman attempted to push the Allied governments into organizing a major trial. While the

judge was speaking, the Foreign Secretary probably thought he
would be able to slow down this runaway bus by following the
cabinet's direction and putting the "onus" for preparing a
workable trial system on the Americans.[80] But then, just before
he sat down, Rosenman handed the assembled delegates copies
of the American memorandum and the executive agreement.
Evidently the United States had already prepared something
akin to a "workable procedure" and Eden was thus deprived of
the only weapon he had held in his tiny diplomatic arsenal!
The Foreign Secretary was given a brief respite while Molotov
declared that the trial question was "important," and Stettinius announced that arrangements would be made with
Bidault to bring French legal experts into the subsequent
great-power war-crimes policy meetings.[81] Then the British Foreign Secretary made his dignified journey to Canossa. After
noting that with the deaths of Hitler and other Nazi leaders
the situation had "greatly" changed, Eden stated that although
the British government retained its objections to a formal trial,
it would bow to the wishes of its American and Soviet allies.
But the British government still wanted to "review" the trial
plans, both as they applied to major war criminals and the
organizations. London continued to feel that the fewer individuals "dealt with by a formal state trial the better." [82]

Despite its qualifications, Eden's statement cleared the way
for the technical work necessary before the American trial plan
could be accepted formally. Each delegation quickly appointed
its representative legal experts—Golunski and Arutyunian for
Russia, Malkin for Britain, and Rosenman and Hackworth for
the United States. The foreign ministers' meeting then broke
up, with assurances by the Americans that French experts also
would be selected and that the four groups of lawyers would
soon carefully examine the proposal, which as Stettinius emphasized again, had the "full support of the American Government." [83] In the immediate aftermath, Rosenman cabled the
President with obvious relief that the British had dropped their
insistence on summary execution and would go along with

the American proposals, if the "Russians join us in favoring [a] trial." [84]

The American intention to meet separately with the technical experts of Britain, France, and Russia in the course of 4 May proved impossible due to the crush of general UN business, and the experts from the four powers therefore first came together on 5 May.[85] Since none of the delegations, except the American, had received formal authority from their home governments to accept the draft executive agreement as a basis of discussion, the talks had a tendency to vacuousness, with much time expended on trivial details. Golunski of the U.S.S.R. raised the questions of who would determine which Nazis were major criminals and who would have first claim if a number of authorities wanted the same man. The Soviet representative was also worried about what could be done regarding the "prevention of propaganda" during the trial and hoped that some of the sessions could be held *in camera*.[86] Rosenman, who was chairman, conceded that a provision outlining jurisdictional procedure would have to be added, but he offered the Russian little hope that his wishes of limiting "propaganda" by using closed court sessions could be satisfied. The most serious criticisms of the executive agreement concerned its imprecision on what was to be done if the tribunal did not agree unanimously on any matter, and the perennial question of whether or not the "crimes" enumerated in paragraph 6 were sufficiently comprehensive, precisely enough worded, and accurately reflected "international legal opinion." But the general tone of the session was more positive than negative. Sir Alexander Cadogan said he thought his government would be willing to sign the agreement "pretty much as it stands," and Rosenman declared that the group should aim at formal acceptance, "if possible" before the delegations left San Francisco.[87]

After the meeting ended, Rosenman cabled Mr. Truman that "we are making progress" and that the Americans were urging upon the others "the necessity of speed." The judge thought that if the Allied technical delegations came to the next meeting, scheduled for 8 May, with expanded authority, they might be able to come close to securing an agreement.[88] But although the British were prepared to proceed on the assumption that London would accept the final result, the French and Soviet legal specialists had still heard nothing from their home governments. So instead of moving on to a consensus, this room full of lawyers began to tear away at the soft spots in the draft agreement, again concentrating on the paragraph 6 characterization of "crime" and on the lack of clarity about what would happen if the tribunal were locked in a tie vote. Rosenman, however, was not prepared to play the game of revision forever just because the French and Russians were slow in receiving instructions; on 10 May he informed the other three delegations that he was leaving for Washington but would return to finish the draft revisions as soon as Paris and Moscow had sent along their authorizations.[89]

In the meantime McCloy, Wechsler, and Cutter were left in San Francisco, where they busied themselves making alternate drafts of the main sections of the agreement that had prompted Allied criticism. It should be remembered when gauging the tone of these criticisms, as well as the mood of the American legal specialists, that on the previous day, General Jodl had signed an unconditional surrender document at SHAEF headquarters. The war in Europe was over, and with its end the last lingering threat of German reprisals against Allied POWs was gone. The need for caution and hesitation was eliminated, and the time for action against the surviving Nazi leaders was at hand. Under these circumstances it is not surprising that the American draftsmen in San Francisco showed a tendency to be tough, to extend the list of prosecutable "crimes," and to create the firmest possible legal foundation for the "innovative" charges, such as those aimed at prewar persecutions and aggressive war.

One draft among the various revisions declared, in a clause adopted in later forms of the plan, that "those who participate in the formulation and execution of a criminal plan involving multiple crimes are liable for each of the offenses committed and responsible for the acts of each other." [90] Another draft reverted to the idea, once edged aside in Washington, of having the Allies simply take the legal bull by the statutory horns and declare certain acts criminal without troubling to cite any legal basis for the assertion. This formulation merely added a heading to the list of offenses in paragraph 6 asserting that the Tribunal "shall be bound" by the principle that the "following acts are criminal."

The planners also tried to find a more effective and respectable form for giving the Allies the right to prosecute the Nazi leaders for violations of the Allies' domestic laws. One formulation restricted such prosecution to the violations of "domestic law of any of the parties" who were signatories of the executive agreement, and another, apparently prepared by John J. McCloy, completely eliminated the clause. But the basic idea of punishing the Nazis for breaking *Allied* laws coincided too well with the tough and assertive mood of May 1945, and it would appear again in memoranda prepared in Washington later in the month.

Despite the fervor and industriousness shown by the American legal specialists, their various redrafts did not succeed in placing secure legal underpinnings beneath the catalog of offenses in paragraph 6. At the end, as at the beginning, a cautious observer might still ask if prewar persecutions or the preparing and launching of aggressive war had in fact been recognized as crimes punishable under international or German law at the time the acts were committed by the Nazis.

The San Francisco revisions were also not very successful in solving other problems raised by the Allied legal critics. A provision was added stating that the tribunal's presiding officer should be chosen by lot. A revised draft of a related passage declared that all decisions should be made by a "majority vote of all the members," but it did not explain what to do if no majority was attainable. An additional section of this revision, in fact, made the situation worse by stating that if the tribunal found itself "in disagreement" regarding the judgment to be rendered on an accused, the individual in question should be made to stand trial before a new tribunal. What was meant by "in disagreement" was not made clear, and without such clarification, it is difficult to see how the court could have functioned at all.

On only two points did the San Francisco revisions produce plausible solutions to difficulties, and in both instances it was by taking the harshest and most punitive position possible. A clause was added specifying that a finding of criminality against an organization by the main tribunal would be binding during all proceedings in occupation courts, and the burden of proof in such cases would fall on the accused member to establish his innocence or produce evidence pointing toward mitigation. Another section declared the control council would arrange to return individuals to the scene of their crimes and that the four powers agreed to turn over "persons" in their custody to "any party to this agreement" who "demanded" them. The state "demanding" the individual would be under no obligation to show cause, and the individuals forceably transferred need not have been Nazis or criminal-organization members or even Germans. One would be hard pressed to find another such wide-open extradition procedure! [91]

On balance, despite all this redrafting activity, the San Francisco meetings produced only one solidly beneficial development for the American war-crimes planners, and that was Britain's "in principle" acceptance of the trial approach. Since the Soviets and French never did receive authorization to negotiate during the UN conference, the talks between the various groups of experts could not pass beyond raising problems. When the last members of the American war-crimes planning delegation returned to Washington in mid-May, no real negotiations had taken place; and all they brought with them was a handful of tentative solutions they had drafted to meet problems raised by Allied representatives. Thus the responsibility for the further development of the war-crimes plan still lay exclusively in the hands of United States officials, and one last act in the pre-Nuremberg drama had to be played out in Washington. Significantly, the final round of redrafting would be based on documents which embodied the harsh provisions engendered by Allied criticism in San Francisco and the general tendency toward forgoing caution and restraint that VE day had produced.

The first two weeks of May also saw other important changes affecting the war-crimes planning staff. Not only was the war in Europe over, but with Justice Jackson in firm control of the organizational machinery and President Truman actively supporting the conspiracy/criminal-organization plan, the new "Office of the Chief of Counsel for the Prosecution of Axis Criminality" could pretty well write its own ticket. For example, when General Clay attempted to put Jackson's prosecution team under the authority of the American section of the control council for Germany, he was slapped down hard by the Pentagon.[92] The Joint Chiefs of Staff also made sure that American military officers in Germany cooperated by holding in custody everyone whom Jackson might possibly desire to use as individual or organizational defendants. A draft directive of 15 May even contemplated ordering the generals at SHAEF to detain every German who was "charged or suspected" of committing acts since 30 January 1933 "which outrage common justice or involve moral turpitude in connection with the persecution of Germans or non-Germans on racial, religious, or political grounds." [93] If this idea had been pursued vigorously, with a generous interpretation of the word "suspected," it seems probable that the majority of the German population would shortly have been behind barbed wire.

The only thing approximating a serious challenge to Jackson's authority came, predictably enough, from Henry Morgenthau and one of his Treasury associates, Edward W. Pauley, the American representative on the Allied Reparations Commission. Morgenthau and Pauley had developed a paper for the commission in late April that authorized use of the forced labor of all Gestapo and SS personnel as a form of reparations payment. Although the Treasury had received a general endorsement of the plan from many important officials in other departments, some, such as Leo Crowley, the Foreign Economic Administrator, opposed any such procedure unless the individuals had at least had a court hearing. Then, on 14 May, the Treasury people learned Justice Jackson also maintained that only those who had "first been adjudged by some court to be guilty" should be required to do forced labor.[94] On receipt of this news, one Treasury official commented that he did not "see why Jackson has anything to say about it." [95]

Stimson leaned on Pauley to make him talk with the justice. At the same time the Secretary of War summarized the whole history of the Morgenthau plan controversy for Mr. Truman, in order to help keep the President committed to the "moderate" occupation program for Germany.[96] With this pressure bearing down upon him, Pauley yielded enough to meet with Jackson on 17 May. In their discussion, the Justice pointed out that to arbitrarily take all the organization members for forced labor "would make it farcical to conduct trials concerning the conspiratorial character of these organizations or the guilt of their members." He also agreed with Averell Harriman that if masses of Germans were merely handed over to the Russians without some protective guarantees, their treatment was bound to be "appalling by American standards." [97]

No sooner had Pauley finished with Jackson than he learned that Judge Rosenman also opposed using the organizations for forced labor without a court ruling. Faced with this broad range of criticism, Pauley telephoned Morgenthau and recommended that another general meeting on reparations policy be held so that Jackson would be able to present his case. When Morgenthau merely grumbled and was slow to take the initiative, Pauley told the Secretary it was time for him to "pitch in" and help or the whole plan to use masses of German reparational labor might be lost.[98] In consequence, a meeting, called for 18 May, featured McCloy and Jackson, as well as Morgenthau,

Pauley, and a large number of other Treasury and State Department officials. Pauley explained to the group that he saw forced reconstruction labor as one of the most important forms of reparation payment that Germany would be able to provide, and that he was aiming at a figure of 5 million such laborers, with a high percentage of them destined for work in Eastern Europe, where much of the war's most serious destruction had occurred. Jackson replied that the criminal-organization trial he was planning would not net anything like the 5 million that Pauley had mentioned, and in any event, the Justice averred, he would not be associated with a pseudo-trial whose only aim was "to get labor for Russia." [99] When a Treasury official cited a Gallup poll indicating that the American public would be happy to see German forced labor go to Russia, Jackson exploded, "I don't give a damn what the Gallup Poll says. I have seen sentiment change over night in this country" the Justice declared, and "if you are going to decide on the basis of the Gallup Poll, you will be out on the worst limb, if I'm any judge." Jackson, who indeed thought of himself as a judge, and a good one too, went on to explain that if the Allies conscripted 4 to 5 million laborers, they would be "hitting at a lot of interests outside of Germany" and "you'll see sentiment change." Just "let [atrocity] stories get out of Russia," Jackson predicted, and public support for the forced-labor program would evaporate.[100]

This outburst of Jackson's, blending together legal sensitivity, realistic political judgment, and a generous admixture of anti-Soviet feeling, actually marked the highest point achieved during the meeting. From there the proceedings degenerated into a carnival of bizarre ideas, reversed roles, and ludicrously exaggerated comments. A Treasury official launched the festivities by suggesting that all SS and Gestapo people should be put to work on forced-labor projects, and while they were so employed, Jackson should try, convict, and sentence them to terms of forced labor. This would presumably have been rather like an on-the-job training project for prospective convicts. Jackson

carefully explained that such a system just would not do under
traditional notions of "appropriate judicial process." Again and
again, the Justice summarized the conspiracy/criminal-organi-
zation plan, noting once that if the other Allies did not move
fast enough, the U.S. government might go ahead with the
project on its own.

Gradually Jackson won a grudging acknowledgment that he
was right about his trial plans from most of those present, but
not from Henry Morgenthau. In a dramatic effort to convince
the Secretary, John J. McCloy—of all people—presented what
must stand as the classically crude portrayal of the Nuremberg
trial idea as a blueprint for a kangaroo court. "After Justice
Jackson puts the Gestapo on the stand," McCloy is quoted as
saying, "and has indicted them like the American Sugar Company or whatever it was, then he says, 'By God, you're guilty,' "
and the courtroom doors would open for masses of Gestapo
men to be marched away as forced laborers. Not to be easily
outdone, Mr. Riddleberger of the State Department chimed
in to say that the SS could be dealt with in the same way because, as he solemnly, and incorrectly, assured those present,
the SS was composed exclusively of volunteers. Thereupon
McCloy remarked that in the search for defendants, and laborers, the German general staff should not be overlooked because
it would be "a very good thing to indict." [101]

In spite of this formidable competition, Morgenthau managed to win the palm for the most surprising opinions uttered
during the meeting. Although prepared to send 5 million Germans into forced labor with hardly a second thought, the Secretary was troubled by the unorthodoxy and doubtful humanity
of the conspiracy/criminal-organization plan. "Can anybody
give me an example in the history of the world where you have
found an organization guilty?" Morgenthau asked rhetorically.
"Has any court ever convicted an organization?" Before those
around him could cite such instances as the antitrust parallels
so beloved by Henry Stimson, Morgenthau swept on to suggest
that the notion of routinely convicting individual organization

members was also highly suspect. "Under civil liberties and everything else," the Secretary noted, "you have to give each man a hearing." [102]

Ultimately Morgenthau was brought up short, however, less by an argument based on rules of procedure or equity than by cold, hard, political facts. Whatever one might feel about the various rights and wrongs involved, Justice Jackson stressed to his critics, the point at issue was one to be determined by the President of the United States. Then, playing his trump card, the justice emphasized that President Truman had already decided that the fate of the Nazi organization members would be settled by a trial. Jackson's declaration was met by expressions of confused disbelief by a number of Treasury officials, who didn't comprehend how the forced-labor reparations policy had been allowed to develop so far unchallenged if Mr. Truman had already given a green light to Justice Jackson. But Henry Morgenthau, wise in the ways of Washington, quietly signaled to one of his assistants and John J. McCloy to join him for a chat in the hall. While the three men were out of the room, Jackson and the lower-level Treasury officials continued to rephrase and rerun their earlier arguments. When Secretary Morgenthau returned, he matter-of-factly stated that "inasmuch as the President of the United States has decided," he withdrew his objections; he agreed that every American agency must insist organization members could only be assigned to forced-labor duties on the basis of a court ruling.[103]

Justice Jackson had clearly triumphed, and any meaningful conflict regarding policy was over. Mr. Paulcy moaned that the American government could no longer offer the shattered states of Europe any prospect of serious assistance through reparations, but the champions of trial would give him no help or mercy. McCloy even declared that before the Western powers handed over any Germans to the Soviet Union for labor, whether POWs, organization members, or volunteers, the West should exact from Moscow a commitment "to observe the Geneva convention." [104] Yet, as with most such bitter political conflicts, there were some after shocks. The Justice was still chafing six years later because Morgenthau's people had implied he was soft on Nazis,[105] and even though Morgenthau had openly admitted the defeat, he still tried a bit of political intrigue to undermine Jackson's position. On the evening of 22 May, the Secretary of the Treasury made a secret call at the French embassy in Washington in an effort to turn the French against the plan to prosecute criminal organizations. Although Morgenthau drove his "point home pretty hard," and French officials made a few reassuring noises, such wild adventures had no chance of reversing the course of events.[106] The Paris government soon came out strongly in favor of the American prosecution proposal, and in any event, Morgenthau's position of power in Washington was crumbling. The Secretary of the Treasury was a Roosevelt man through and through, and it was an open secret that the new President was less than enamored with Morgenthau's ideas and style. After two months of speculation about his future, Morgenthau tendered his resignation on 6 July 1945.

The departure of Henry Morgenthau merely formalized the results of the 18 May meeting; Justice Jackson was in control, and political opposition to the conspiracy/criminal-organization plan was no longer possible in Washington. Jackson's team was free to work its will, assembling evidence, putting together a prosecution organization, and preparing a final proposal to lay before the British, the French, and the Russians. Even prior to the 18 May meeting, Jackson's people had made modest headway on the evidentiary problem. As early as 5 May, tentative arrangements were made for the OSS to aid in providing documentary material to the chief of counsel's office, and one month later (7 June) a formal agreement was concluded between Jackson and William Donovan, the director of the OSS, whereby the latter agreed to give Jackson assistance "in all respects." [107] By 9 May the first steps had been taken to establish a special interrogation team that could garner evidence from captured officials of the Third Reich, such as Schacht, von Papen, and Field Marshal von Rundstedt.[108]

On 13 May, Jackson's staff completed a blueprint of the case, and this planning memorandum was approved by the Justice four days later (17 May). The latter document is especially interesting because it not only reveals the focus Jackson's people wished to give to the prosecution, but it also indicates their major assumptions about what kind of evidence would be necessary to sustain the accusations. According to the planning memorandum, the primary charge against the Nazi leaders would be that "sometime prior to 1 September 1939" they had "entered into a common plan or enterprise" to establish "complete German domination of Europe and eventually the world." [109] All of their acts, including those "which may not have been criminal *per se* but which were used in preparation, furtherance and execution of the criminal plan" would be targets for the prosecution. Since conspiracy to prepare and wage aggressive war thus became the central element of the case, it was essential to relate all, or nearly all, of the Nazis' heinous activities to this basic charge. Not only would foreign-policy measures such as the making of "false treaties," the use of fifth columns, and even "genocide" have to be linked to the primary accusation, but domestic acts such as "dividing the German citizenry on a racial basis" and the carrying out of "unlawful expropriations" would need to be presented as preparatory moves directed toward the fundamental objective of an ever-expanding aggressive war.

A basic approach thus entered the American trial planning that was bound to produce serious difficulties. By making aggressive-war conspiracy the transcendent theme of Nazism, Jackson and his aides found a convenient legal heading under which to collect the various accusations they wished to make against Hitler and his associates. But they also set off on a course that historically was highly suspect. The historical research of the past thirty-five years has established ever more decisively that

Nazism was not a single uniform force, but a complex, confused, and essentially eclectic phenomenon in which the pur-
suit of raw power, as well as racism, expansion, and other elements, played important roles. When Jackson and his aides
tried to turn aggressive-war conspiracy into Nazism's heart and
soul, the inevitable result was that some of the most prominent and atrocious actions of the Third Reich, such as the mass
extermination of Europe's Jews and Gypsies, were made to
appear less important in their own right; and the causal forces
which had produced them were twisted and distorted. Today no
serious historian would maintain that Hitler slaughtered the
Jews and Gypsies of Europe merely as a calculated step in a
fixed plan to conquer first Europe and then the world. But this
was the historically inaccurate focus that the planning memorandum, like McCloy's 20 April memorandum before it, fixed
on the American prosecution planners; and that focus contributed not a little to the ultimate confusion, and the historical
errors, that characterized many of the court sessions at
Nuremberg.[110]

The difficulty was compounded by the misguided belief, held
by the planners in mid-May, that they could whip the case together quickly and comparatively easily. The planning memorandum emphasized that "time is of the essence" and that the
main effort should be centered on obtaining public records,
speeches, decrees, magazine articles, and other documents
"readily" available to substantiate a case that would basically
prove itself.[111] There was little awareness that emphasis on a
Nazi aggressive-war conspiracy might lead to troubles in handling evidence, or that the huge numbers of captured enemy
records falling into Allied hands would, through their sheer
mass and complexity, turn the trial into a far more involved and
intricate enterprise.

The memorandum on trial preparation, which Jackson's staff
completed on 16 May, was somewhat more realistic in regard to
these matters than the planning memorandum of the thirteenth, but essentially it still saw the trial as a simple, straight-

forward operation. While granting that evidence would have to be found to show that there actually had been a Nazi plan to gain "complete domination of Europe and eventually the world," and that organizations "composed of volunteers" really had tried to implement it by "unlawful means," the memorandum on trial preparation assumed such evidence would be found relatively easily.[112] The memorandum did note in an off-hand manner that the papers of "enemy" leaders might be seized and used against them, and it also put forth a plan to net evidence from the interrogation of captured Nazis. Declaring that "the privilege against self-incrimination" would not be extended to the trial defendants, the memorandum stated that those being interrogated "should be warned that any refusals on their part to answer questions" would be "construed" as an admission of guilt.

In this manner the memorandum hoped to make interrogation records readily "admissible in evidence," and thereby shape the Nazis' own statements into a simple yet overpowering force for the prosecution.[113] As with so many other features of the early prosecution preparation, however, this proposal ultimately backfired because the harsh warnings served as an encouragement to those interrogated to give vague and vacuous replies to prosecution questions. In addition, the final charter which served as the statutory basis for the trial, did not deprive defendants of all protection from self-incrimination and the Nuremberg court refused to routinely admit the records of defendant interrogations as evidence. Therefore, despite enormous expenditures of time and energy, the pretrial interrogation of defendants carried out between May and September 1945 exerted only a marginal influence on the actual court proceedings.[114]

The optimistic hopes regarding the gathering of documentary evidence envisioned by the memorandum on trial preparation also turned out to be illusionary. The system outlined in the 16 May memorandum delegated the responsibility for preparing the case and marshaling the necessary evidence to the OSS and JAG. The former was assigned the task of developing and documenting the accusations on crimes against humanity and conspiracy, while the latter undertook a similar duty for the charges relating to aggressive war and traditional war crimes. For a month and a half, the OSS disguised the fact that it was making little or no headway with its share of the case preparation. But in early July, even Colonel Bernays, who had long entertained rosy notions of the value of OSS sources and expertise, was forced to admit that the few scraps the intelligence organization had produced were largely useless as evidence.[115]

Although JAG lawyers had supposedly been researching Nazi war-crimes cases for years prior to Jackson's appointment, the weakness of their efforts and the inapplicability of their approach to the task confronting the chief of counsel became obvious much more quickly. In a report to John J. McCloy on 5 May, the chief of JAG, General Cramer, granted that although the department had restricted its case preparation to traditional war crimes committed against American personnel, only the "spade work" had been done and the results were not very promising.[116] However, a report from a JAG officer charged with investigating war criminals in Germany showed that even this estimate was much too favorable. On 6 May, Lieutenant Colonel Byrne Bowman, who was assigned to war-crimes investigation with the 106th Infantry Division, sent General Weir a summary of his discouraging and largely fruitless activities.[117] The 106th division had the task of guarding nearly 2 million German prisoners of war in a series of improvised camps, one of which had received sixty thousand prisoners in its first nine days of existence. Bowman told General Weir that all the Americans could do was keep the prisoners fed, and try to hold them inside the single strand of barbed wire that marked the outer perimeter of the camps. Prisoners trying to escape were shot every night, and Bowman assumed that those killed constituted only a fraction of the men who succeeded in getting away. Under these circumstances, screening for war criminals was impossible. Many of the prisoners had not even been interviewed, and as Bowman noted, with contraband weapons still circulating among the prisoners, potential prosecution witnesses inside the "enclosures" could easily be liquidated before effective processing took place.

JAG officials in Washington were honest enough to give fairly wide circulation to Bowman's report, and on 21 May, in a meeting between General Weir and the chief of counsel and his staff, the deputy chief of JAG went further toward acknowledging the failure of his office's work on war-crimes preparation. General Weir conceded that JAG did not have a single case ready for trial. His office was not even prepared to prosecute the perpetrators of the "Malmédy massacre" because, as Weir declared, "all were in tanks" and nobody saw them.[118] Left to get whatever consolation he could from the incorrect assertion that "our people subsequently thoroughly took care of all of them anyway," the general admitted that Malmédy was "washed out" as a war-crimes case.[119] Thus even the incident which had served as the catalyst to advance the conspiracy/criminal-organization plan could not be used as evidence of Nazi criminal intent!

In the course of the meeting Weir did mention the possibility of obtaining war-crimes evidence from the Soviet Union; and there were snatches of speculation on using the Nazis' harsh treatment of commandos, and Goebbels's incitement of the population to kill American airmen, as instances of a general conspiracy to commit war crimes. But as Bernays recognized, by concentrating on instances of atrocities against U.S. personnel, JAG had picked up the wrong end of the stick. Jackson and his staff were interested in proving the existence of a broad Nazi war-crimes and aggressive-war conspiracy, but the Nazis had been relatively lenient in their treatment of U.S. servicemen. In Bernays's words, "Americans were treated much better than other nationalities," and therefore nothing of importance "for our purposes" would ever materialize from JAG's preparation activities, even if they did become more efficient.[120]

The obvious conclusion to be drawn from the meeting of 21

May was that much of the "case preparation" being discussed in memoranda prepared by Jackson's staff was little more than airy fantasy. JAG had nothing in hand, had revealed its inefficiency, and was headed in the wrong direction; yet in the memorandum of 16 May, Jackson's people had declared that they were depending on JAG to put together half the case, including sections on aggressive war and traditional war crimes. Furthermore, by 18 May even Justice Jackson had come to the conclusion that despite the brave talk, no one in Washington had any hard material to convince a court that the SS was actually a criminal organization. He even told Henry Morgenthau that JAG had no more evidence against the SS "than we've got here on this table." [121]

In light of these danger signs it may seem difficult to understand why Jackson did not call a temporary halt to the conspiracy/criminal-organization trial preparations in order to ascertain if evidence could be found to make the basic accusations stand up in court. The Justice's deficiencies as an administrative leader were surely among the major reasons why such a bold reexamination decision was not made. Although renowned as a trial lawyer and legal draftsman, and certainly a strong and competent Supreme Court justice, Robert Jackson was not a dazzling administrator. As one of his close assistants during the years 1940–45 recently remarked, Jackson was able to get by in the 1930s and early 1940s as solicitor general and attorney general because he could depend on an existing bureaucratic machine. But when, after years on the Bench, he tried to return to the bureaucratic wars as chief of counsel, and he was faced with the need to build up an organization from scratch, the results were disappointing. Confusion, erratic leadership, and inefficiency plagued the chief of counsel's office from first day to last, and in the words of the same former close associate, the administrative side of Nuremberg "was a disaster." [122]

But not all of the failure to look at the underpinnings of the case should be charged to Justice Jackson's inability to get on top of the situation and control it. None of the officials involved in war-crimes planning were overly concerned with questions of evidence or historical fact. They were lawyers and bureaucratic leaders, not police investigators or historians. Their primary interest, as was revealed repeatedly in the policy controversies of late 1944 and early 1945, focused more on winning the political struggle in Washington than in making sure that they could convict the Nazi leaders for what they had actually done in Europe. They shared the general public view that Hitler and his associates were so evil, their actions so dreadful and notorious, that proving a case against them would be relatively simple once a broad, streamlined trial system had been developed. As John J. McCloy had noted in April, Washington believed the crucial question was not primarily one of evidence or even of legal theory, but of procedure.

Clear, accurate information regarding the Nazi actions was a secondary consideration for McCloy, Bernays, Stimson, and the others as well as for Justice Jackson. Although Jackson and his staff later passed through a period of grave discouragement and depression in July–August 1945, when it momentarily appeared the necessary evidence would not be forthcoming,[123] they were saved by the bureaucratic mania of Nazi officials, which provided enough evidence to send ten of the surviving top officials of the Third Reich to the gallows. Perhaps this result indicates the correctness of the intuition and faith of the men of Washington, but it seems more likely that they succeeded chiefly due to simple good luck. In any event, the documentary abundance, which nearly swamped the prosecution, not to speak of the defense, at Nuremberg, was ironically a very late and peripheral development in a planning process that had put the trial system first and the evidence last.

In mid-May Justice Jackson chose simply to turn his back on the signs of trouble in the evidentiary foundations of the case, and he instead focused the attention of his staff and associates on revising and polishing the draft executive agreement that had been prepared for the San Francisco conference. He

was conforming to the prevailing pattern of American planning
on war-crimes policy. Once again, as had happened so frequently in the past, the planners threw themselves into the task
of reworking the basic trial scheme. However, this time the redrafting went forward on two separate and largely independent
lines, and both redrafting projects sought to word the provisions
concerning the basic charges so that the prosecutors would be
given a very free hand. This approach made it easier for the
prosecutors to circumvent some of the hazards of a trial system that had been developed without a careful apprising of the
available evidence. By drafting the executive agreement so that
it gave the prosecutors carte blanche to lodge virtually any
charge they wished against the Nazis, the particulars of the extant evidence became less important. All that would be necessary to gain convictions under such a system, once it had been
accepted by the four powers, would be for the prosecutors
to scout out what evidence was at hand and frame the accusations to fit whatever they found. This—making the crime fit
the evidence—bore little resemblance to due process, but it
coincided with the main thrust of the American trial planning,
and it would also serve as an insurance policy to guarantee that
the prosecution would win some kind of case.

All of the discussion and rewriting produced in mid-May was
based on the executive agreement that had been developed for
San Francisco, into which Colonel Cutter had incorporated the
suggestions made by the French, British, and Soviet legal experts during the conference (draft 2).[124] Due to the immediate
post-VE Day atmosphere as well as Allied demands, these revisions had contained provisions harshly unfavorable to the defense, a tendency sustained and expanded in the last round of
Washington memoranda drafting. The first of the important
mid-May documents was a long legal and technical critique of
draft 2, which was produced by a group perhaps headed by
Wechsler and Hackworth. This detailed commentary on the
executive agreement, which for the sake of convenience we may

call draft 2A, was soon shelved in favor of drafts 3 and 4, which will be considered shortly. But draft 2A broke important new ground in expanding the charges that could be brought against the Nazi leaders.[125] The first significant feature was a provision similar to one used earlier, which authorized charges against Nazi officials for acts committed against the nationals of "any country," if the acts were violations "of the domestic law of such country." Since the Nazis had invaded at least ten nations and had engaged in combat against many more, such a clause would have made accusation virtually synonymous with conviction, because every German leader had acted in ways that conflicted with the laws of some Allied belligerent state. A second new clause in draft 2A put forth an extremely elastic definition of international law, which would only work to the disadvantage of a German defendant. Claiming to follow the lead of the fourth Hague Convention of 1907, it declared that

International law shall be taken to include the principles of the law of nations as they result from the usages established among civilized people, from the laws of humanity, and the dictates of the public conscience.[126]

Obviously, with international law so defined, no German leader could have had much of a chance before an Allied court in 1945, but it is highly doubtful if this quotation, so used, accurately reflected the intention of those who had drafted it in 1907. The men who prepared Hague Convention IV had been afraid that some new military invention they had not foreseen, and therefore had not covered by their rules, might be employed for murderous purposes. Rather than leave the door open for unrestricted use of such a weapon, they sought to set limits in advance by stating it could only be utilized in conformity with the aforementioned statement. Hague Convention IV did not declare this to be a general definition of international law, and it only sought to use the phrase in cases where a new weapon transcended the bounds of written international agreement. Surely when the American war-crimes policy planners made it into a general, and highly subjective, definition, they went far beyond anything intended in 1907.

The second effort to redraft the executive agreement in mid-May also made use of references and definitions that greatly expanded the offenses the Nazi chiefs could be charged with. Prepared between May 15 and 19, it bore more of the imprint of Jackson's staff. It also enjoyed the distinction of being the final embodiment of the American conspiracy/criminal-organization plan. Although it is not clear who initially prepared the document, at a meeting of 19 May draft 3 was reformed by Jackson, Bernays, Wechsler, and Cutter, as well as three officials in the chief of counsel's new hierarchy, Colonel Kaplan, Mr. Shea, and Mr. Alderman.[127] Through this revision draft 3 became draft 4 and thereby emerged as America's official war-crimes proposal. Draft 4 was the document that was laid before the representatives of Britain, France, and Soviet Russia at the London conference in June 1945 and served as the foundation of the London Charter.

Drafts 3 and 4 were not mere cosmetic changes of earlier forms of the executive agreement. Although they retained the basic principles of the conspiracy/criminal organization plan, these drafts shifted the order of the main provisions, made a number of significant additions and deletions, and rephrased nearly every sentence of the document that had been laid before the Allies in San Francisco. Amid all these changes and innovations, two general features stand out. First, drafts 3 and 4 show a tighter legal hand than earlier forms of the executive agreement. Justice Jackson clearly utilized his great gifts as a draftsman to produce a document to serve the interests of the tribunal that would hear the case. Most of the ambiguities regarding deadlocked votes and similar matters were removed, and the court was granted more leeway in determining how it would handle the case. A fair share of the praise for the subsequent success of the Nuremberg Tribunal in steering its way through complexity and controversy should be credited to the sensible revisions included in drafts 3 and 4.[128]

The second important characteristic of drafts 3 and 4, as already indicated, was a tendency to tip the scales heavily in favor of the prosecution. Draft 4 took over in entirety the elastic definition of international law that draft 2A had appropriated from the fourth Hague Convention. Similarly, the earlier provision that allowed the Nazi leaders to be convicted for violating the domestic laws of any of the Allied states was only somewhat softened. Draft 3 made them liable for violations of the laws of the Allied Big Four "or any Axis power or satellite," and the final form of this clause in draft 4 declared that an individual could also be prosecuted for violations of "the domestic law of the country" in which the act had been committed.[129] Even this, of course, did not mean that the Nazi defendants would thereby be freed from liability under international law, custom, or the principles of conspiracy and common enterprise. Not only was the wide-open definition of international law that had been derived from Hague IV used, but both drafts 3 and 4 listed a whole collection of prosecutable offenses, and specifically instructed the tribunal that it was compelled to hold that they were "criminal." Draft 3 included in the list a series of acts associated with aggressive war, such as violation of treaties and "recourse to war as an instrument of national policy," but draft 4 cut out the reference to treaties and the passage quoted from the Kellogg-Briand Pact, leaving only invasions or initiation of war "in violation of law." Apparently on this point, the caution of Washington officials was strong enough to limit Justice Jackson's eagerness to prosecute aggressive war.

The Justice seems to have returned the favor by adding a note of limitation on another point in the list of punishable offenses. From the earliest days of the conspiracy/criminal-organization plan, every draft memorandum had included a charge declaring that the Nazi leaders would be punished for offenses committed against German nationals on "political, racial or religious grounds." Drafts 3 and 4 cut the word "political" from this list, and it is reasonable to assume that this happened because Justice Jackson, with his increasingly conservative political attitudes, was less than enthusiastic about prosecuting the Nazis for persecuting Communists and other German leftists.[130]

One last point regarding the list of punishable offenses contained in drafts 3 and 4 needs to be made. In a clever piece of drafting, the conspiracy/common-enterprise count was removed from paragraph 12 (paragraph 6 in earlier memoranda), where the other offenses were enumerated. In light of the experience of San Francisco, paragraph 12 was bound to become a center of controversy among the Allies. Since in the new memorandum the conspiracy/common-enterprise provision was placed in a separate paragraph (13), a casual reader steeped in continental law would come across no immediate reference to conspiracy and would now be less troubled by the list of offenses in 12. Tucked away in paragraph 13, the conspiracy/common-enterprise charge seemed more akin to a principle of procedure than the offense that the Americans were determined to make the central accusation of the whole indictment. Conspiracy à la paragraph 13 stood a better chance of avoiding the heavy guns of French and Soviet criticism.

However these points would be received by America's Allies, there was precious little comfort in drafts 3 and 4 for prospective defendants. The only thing contained in them that might be considered a bright spot for the defense was a clause that, while banning appeals to superior orders as a covering defense, did allow the tribunal to consider them in "defense or mitigation . . . if justice so requires." But from beginning to end, drafts 3 and 4 were primarily battle plans for a Carthaginian trial. Both drafts granted the tribunal the right to try Nazi leaders in absentia, providing only (in the words of draft 4) that the court determined "for what reasons" the proceedings against defendants were "taken without their presence." Even the members of organizations declared criminal by the main trial did not elude the scrutiny and the sharp phrasing of these drafts. Draft 4 stated that a finding of organizational criminality "shall be conclusive" in any hearing held to determine the fate of organization members, and that in such a hearing the burden of proof to produce evidence, either of innocence or mitigating circumstances, would fall completely on the individual defendant.[131]

Thus it is fair to conclude that drafts 3 and 4, like the summary draft made in San Francisco (draft 2), went further in deviating from a number of customary Anglo-American legal principles, such as the presumption of innocence and the ban on ex post facto punishment, than had earlier drafts of the conspiracy/criminal-organization plan. They reflected the increasingly vindictive tone prevailing since Justice Jackson's involvement and the arrival of VE Day. Furthermore, draft 4 was not a very clever diplomatic move. Until early June the British, French, and Soviet governments presumed that the draft the Americans had presented to the other powers in San Francisco would be the basis of discussion at the four-power conference in London. Consequently, there was more than a little confusion and resentment when the United States dropped this totally new memorandum on the table just before the conference convened.[132]

Yet viewed in the context of American war-crimes policy planning, draft 4 was in many ways an appropriate climax to the planning that had begun in August 1944. Not only did it represent the peak of precision and clarity in drafting, it also embodied many of the important points championed by powerful individuals who had been involved in various phases of the preparatory process. Secretary of War Stimson and President Truman had obtained a plan for the international trial that was dear to their hearts. Assistant Secretary of War McCloy, Colonel Bernays, and Colonel Cutter could be content that the fundamental principles of the conspiracy/criminal-organization plan had been preserved intact. Mr. Hackworth and Assistant

Attorney General Wechsler, as well as Justice Jackson, all of whom had been anxious to avoid slipshod legal work, were surely gratified by the technical excellence of the final product, although it was probably somewhat too innovative for Mr. Hackworth's tastes. Even Colonel Chanler, along with Secretary Stimson, Justice Jackson, and Colonel Bernays, had special grounds for satisfaction, because under draft 4 the issue of aggressive war could finally be made the subject of an international trial.

When in early June 1945 draft 4 was transmitted to the representatives of Britain, France, and Soviet Russia, the exclusively American road to Nuremberg came to an end. From that point onward the United States government would be unable to determine war-crimes policies and procedures solely, or perhaps even chiefly, on the basis of Washington power politics. The time when a handful of Americans could meet in a Pentagon office and shape and revise the fate awaiting the leaders of an enemy state was over, and henceforth Jackson and his aides would have to take their chances in the give and take of great powers' cooperation. But draft 4 served as the battlefield on which this diplomatic-legal struggle would be decided; and though each of America's allies succeeded in making revisions and rephrasings in the U.S. plan, the final documents closely resembled the original American proposal. When the dust finally settled in September 1945, there stood the London Charter and the indictment with most of the basic points of the U.S. proposal still in place. Jackson, Stimson, McCloy, Bernays, and their associates had won the Allied struggle over war-crimes policy, and the Nazi leaders would therefore meet their end as Washington had wished.

CHAPTER 7

CONCLUSION

Are all thy conquests, glories, triumphs, spoils,
Shrunk to this little measure?

Julius Caesar
Act III

If the net is cast too widely when appraising the significance and impact of the American war-crimes planning that led to the Nuremberg trial, the central issues may be lost in a welter of moralizing and loose speculation. As those who presided over the proceedings at Nuremberg learned to their sorrow, the case touched on so many issues of modern history and so many dark and threatening aspects of human nature that it was extremely difficult to keep the trial within manageable limits. Consequently, the bulk of this discussion will be restricted to two major themes, how the American planning helped shape the immediate impact of the trial and the importance of that planning in the trial's longer-range effects. Only after this has been done will there be a bit of hypothesizing about possible connections between the war crimes policy planning in 1944–45 and some general tendencies that American administrations seem to manifest in their relations with the twentieth-century world.

Regarding the immediate effects of the trial, one of the most important, as I have argued elsewhere,[1] was its role in preventing a general bloodbath. In the angry and violent atmosphere of 1945 there was a very real possibility that thousands of Germans, innocent and guilty alike, could become the victims of lynch justice. Among the American planners, at least Justice Jackson realized this danger,[2] and it was one of the reasons why he contended that a comprehensive trial program needed to be developed quickly. To the degree that the four-power trial system regularized what was to happen to the Nazi leaders, and encouraged the development of procedures to deal with other offenders, it allowed time for tempers to cool, and thereby probably saved many lives. In a very real sense this result, which might be called the immediate humanitarian impact of Nuremberg, was an outgrowth of the American trial plan; if the Allies had made no preparations for dealing with the Nazi leaders, or if they had utilized the British recommendation of summary execution, it is difficult to see how the mood of vengeful anarchy could have been controlled.

Having given the trial, and the American plan that lay behind it, due credit for shielding some innocent people, it must also be acknowledged that it indirectly helped other individuals with black marks on their records to elude punishment. Not only did the complex court proceedings provide wily defendants such as Papen and Schacht with opportunities to wriggle free, but the duration of the case gave culprits such as Eichmann time to avoid capture; it also produced second thoughts among some of the Allied powers. The monolithic image of all Nazis as beasts, lacking every human dimension, gradually became clouded in the courtroom. A picture of the Third Reich took shape there in which Hitler's Germany appeared to be a complex and constantly changing phenomenon, displaying at least a few shades of gray. At the same time, Western officials were coming down from the summit of their wartime enthusiasm and moral euphoria, while across the whole world cold-war tensions were rising. Consequently, by the fall of 1946, when Nuremberg's judgment day finally came, the fate of a man like Albert Speer was decided in an atmosphere where Western political leaders and judges were more willing to look with sympathy on a clean-cut and apparently repentant professional man with strong anti-Soviet tendencies.

But the responsibility of the Nuremberg trial system for the Allies' failure to deal effectively with Nazi criminality goes deeper still. As we have seen, the conspiracy/criminal-organization proposal was created as an alternative to the Morgenthau plan. It was developed by a government leery of long-term, expensive commitments in postwar Europe, and therefore it sought to purge Nazi Germany through a judicial operation that would move swiftly through the Third Reich from top to bottom. Sensitive to any criticism implying the plan deviated from due process, the fathers of the Nuremberg system were nonetheless anxious to make the prosecution so comprehensive that all malefactors would be punished and Germany would be made safe for democracy. Since they lacked hard, accurate information on how Hitler's system actually operated, they stretched the bounds of legal propriety so that the prosecution would be able to advance any charges against the Nazi leaders and organizations that the evidence might ultimately warrant. The plan was thereby spread over the horns of a very serious dilemma.

For the system to work as intended, the prosecution had to convince a court, which was trying to appear legally respectable, that it should overlook shaky evidence, as well as its scruples, and condemn millions of organization members on the basis of collective guilt. In order to achieve this result, the prosecution had, at the very least, to establish that the members of the six organizations (SS, SA, Gestapo-SD, the Reich Cabinet, the High Command of the Armed Forces, and the Leadership Corps of the Nazi Party) ultimately charged as criminal were all volunteers who should have known that the organizations had criminal purposes. To prove such an accusation exceeded the facts, the evidence, and the ability of the Nuremberg prosecutors. In consequence, the tribunal quashed the criminality charges against three organizations; and in regard to the

Gestapo, the SS, and the Leadership Corps of the Nazi Party, which were declared criminal, such stringent qualifications were added that simplified secondary proceedings against individual members were made impossible.[3]

The Nuremberg Tribunal decreed that in any secondary hearing the prosecution would be required to show that the individual was a voluntary member who had known of the criminal purposes of the organization at the time he joined. The great dream of sweeping thousands, perhaps millions, of hard-core Nazis to the gallows or into labor or internment camps through administrative hearings was thereby rendered impossible. If the Western governments were going to unravel the whole ugly tapestry of Nazism, they would be forced to carry out a complete investigation of German (and Axis satellite) society. Then they would have to bring the culprits to justice before thousands of Allied courts. The British and Americans had not wished to assume the responsibility or cost for any such enterprise during the war, and they were even less inclined to do so after the Nuremberg Tribunal rendered its verdict in the fall of 1946. So twelve top Nazis were sentenced to death, and seven others were sent to prison by the main Nuremberg Tribunal. A few hundred more were imprisoned and a handful put to death by special French, British, and American occupation and military courts. The courts of some occupied countries, especially Poland, imprisoned and executed more, and German courts, then and since, have jailed additional culprits.

But a systematic campaign to identify and apportion blame and punishment to all those responsible for the evils of Nazism was never carried out. Such an enterprise may never have been a practical possibility in any case. Certainly with a clear retrospective eye, we can see that it could not have been done through the conspiracy/criminal-organization plan. Therefore, if Nuremberg failed to deliver on its inflated promise to settle humanity's score with Nazism, the root of that failure lay in the conspiracy/criminal-organization plan itself.

However, the trial system that the Americans had convinced

their Allies to use at Nuremberg was not created simply to punish the Germans. It had also sought to provide the victorious peoples with a feeling that their cause had been just and their prodigious sacrifices worthwhile, giving "meaning to the war against Germany," in Telford Taylor's phrase.[4] This motive had been discussed in the first formulation of the conspiracy/ criminal-organization plan made by Colonel Bernays in September 1944, and it was periodically reiterated in many of the subsequent conferences and redrafts. On some occasions, the broad goal of providing Allied populations with a sense of achievement was narrowed somewhat, and focused on a desire to show that the policies and diplomatic actions of Allied governments prior to hostilities had been proper and necessary. The trials succeeded quite well in fixing in the public mind that the sole responsibility for the war lay with Hitler. It has only been in the last few years that historians have begun seriously to wrestle with the question of whether or not the war was a simple matter of "Nazi black" and "Allied white." Even now the various forms of apology and revision, ranging from A. J. P. Taylor to David Irving, have not been able to move the public consciousness very far from the Nuremberg contention that this indeed was "Hitler's war."

The United States government was not so fortunate in convincing the whole American public that it had been forced into aiding the Allies in the months before Pearl Harbor because of a systematic Nazi attack on American neutral rights. Although those assembling documents for the prosecution in the summer of 1945 were alerted to watch for any evidence substantiating President Roosevelt's claim—that the American merchant ship *Robin Moor* had been torpedoed by a U-boat in 1941 as part of a deliberate plan to injure, or threaten, the security of the United States—nothing regarding this or similar incidents was ever found.[5] Washington was therefore unable to exploit the trial to confirm the specific reasons President Roosevelt had employed when justifying his assertively pro-Allied policy in 1941. But the American government, like other Allied governments, did emerge from the proceedings strengthened by the nearly universal conviction that the Nazis were so horrible that virtue had indeed lain with everyone who opposed Hitler.

Perhaps this unprecedented worldwide consensus would have formed without the Nuremberg trial, and possibly the Allied peoples would have had a similar exhilarating sense of triumphant righteousness even if the conspiracy/criminal-organization plan had not been used. But it seems unlikely. Because the Nuremberg proceedings produced such a comprehensive record of the Nazi infamy, every authority in postwar Europe and America could point to it and show not only that the war had been necessary, but that no matter how unpleasant things might look at the moment, they would have been infinitely worse if Hitler had triumphed.

In a Western Europe wasted and impoverished, desperately seeking some focal point around which to rally, Nuremberg helped to provide a moral foundation on which to build anew. Further east, in the Soviet Union and the territory of her newly acquired satellites, there were few bright spots or sources of pride and confidence except that of having decisively defeated the armies and extermination squads of the Third Reich. Little wonder that Moscow never tired of pointing to the Nuremberg record, while stressing the pivotal role that the Soviet government and the Russian people had played in the destruction of Hitler's Germany. Even in the United States, where not everyone was overly enthusiastic about the new responsibilities that America faced as a superpower, Nuremberg helped to smooth the way in the postwar world. The trial record, with its detailed coverage of Nazi aggression and expansion, seemed to be reminding Americans that they really had had no choice; isolationism had failed, and in order to stop the nightmare of Hitlerism, the United States had been forced to become a superpower. Nuremberg helped America to see itself as a reluctant giant, and this sense of inevitability, in turn, made the mission of establishing a *pax Americana* easier to bear.

While the conspiracy/criminal-organization plan, as well as

the trial itself, produced a mixed bag of immediate results, only a portion of which matched the intentions of the American planners, the long-term consequences bore even less resemblance to the hopes and dreams of men such as Henry Stimson, Murray Bernays, and Robert Jackson. After thirty-five years, it seems safe to conclude that Nuremberg did not produce a world in which aggression and atrocities ceased to exist, or one where they were controlled through a system of international courts. Perhaps such a world will come about some day, but Nuremberg was not a powerful enough influence to produce it. What the trial did do, however, was to implant certain concepts, including aggressive war and crimes against humanity, into the public mind with such force that they became integral elements in the thinking of late twentieth-century man. Every international crisis, from Cambodia to the Soviet occupation of Afghanistan, has produced renewed talk of "war-crimes trials," of "genocide," and of the need to punish the perpetrators of aggression.

On one level, such talk merely adds additional confusion to situations that are already confused enough. Without an international court system that has the authority to intervene in important crises, and the power to try cases and enforce decisions, characterizing aggression as "an international crime," analogous to murder or larceny, is at best a verbal whimsy. It may actually make the resolution of foreign-policy crises more difficult because it blurs the line between moral condemnation and possible legal redress. Driven on by an aroused public, which believes it has "law" on its side, a government may push beyond the point where a cold calculation of the power situation would have taken it. Since at the final crossroads of any mortal diplomatic crisis there will be no court, but only armed force, the dangers of loose talk about law and trials should be obvious.

Yet it is still possible that just this imbalance, between the harsh realities of power politics and the popular idea that international relations should be regulated by judicial processes, may ultimately lead to a major change in the way sovereign states deal with one another.[6] If the popular belief in international court action should become so powerful and so universal that it swamps the major states' dependence on armed force as the basis of international security, it would constitute a true diplomatic revolution. On this crucial point, however, it is still too early to render much of a judgment. Nuremberg did not in itself produce an era of court-enforced law in international relations, and it may actually have contributed to the dangers of our present situation; but if mankind should succeed in grasping the nettle, then Nuremberg will have been a major turning point in human history.

In light of the trial's varied, indirect, and clouded consequences, it is fair to say that the architects of the conspiracy/criminal-organization plan were lacking in foresight. But that does not necessarily mean the process by which the Nuremberg trial plan took shape is of any less importance. One glance at the men involved should convince an observer that the failure to accurately foresee the results of the policy was not due to deficiencies of ability among those who made the decisions. It would have been virtually impossible to have amassed a more knowledgeable and able body of lawyer-politicians in 1944 America than Stimson, McCloy, Wechsler, Hackworth, Biddle, Rosenman, Bernays, Chanler, and Jackson. Nor is it realistic to contend that if this group had been faced with a tougher and more gifted opposition, they would have been compelled to see straighter. The advocates of the conspiracy/criminal-organization plan went up against formidable American competition in the form of JAG lawyers, Henry Morgenthau, Jr., and a reluctant President Roosevelt; they also had to meet, and master, a strong British counterforce led by Sir John Simon and Winston Churchill. Thus the failure of Stimson, Bernays, and their associates to accurately chart the future can hardly be attributed to the shortcomings of these particular individuals.

The fathers of Nuremberg also cannot be fairly accused of failing to master the course of subsequent events because they did not use the regular government planning system effectively.

Tactical miscalculations did occur, and President Roosevelt's administrative system was unorthodox, but the foregoing narrative testifies to the care and thoroughness that went into the development of the plan. Every point, every clause, was repeatedly discussed, revised, and redrafted. At certain junctures outside events such as the Malmédy massacre did save the plan from likely defeat, but even these developments failed to still the critics, whose objections repeatedly forced the plan's authors to make additional alterations and revisions. Since the chief participants were all lawyers, they gave this problem a special measure of serious attention, as the numerous drafts and redrafts clearly show. Allowing for errors of judgment and a few instances of negligence, one suspects that few important decisions made by a major power in recent years have enjoyed such a lavish expenditure of time, thought, and reconsideration as did the conspiracy/criminal-organization plan of 1944–45.

One might object that the Nuremberg preparations were flawed by an unusual degree of tunnel vision, since little attention was paid to the conditions actually prevailing in Nazi Germany. This defect certainly contributed to the trial's difficulties as well as to its uneven effects, but the failure to look much beyond the confines of Washington was not a feature peculiar to planning on war-crimes policy. It is a truism among politicians and political scientists that governmental decisions are not only made in the centers of power, they are shaped almost exclusively by the forces that can converge at such points of decision. Groups unable to get their demands or desires heard at these times, whether they are minorities or defeated enemies, will play little or no part in policymaking. Nor is it reasonable to expect that the conditions or circumstances prevailing among such voiceless groups will somehow manifest themselves in the counsels of those with power. Perhaps as Faulkner said of art, political power "takes care of its own," but it certainly does not "share its bread." [7]

Adding all of these considerations together, a plausible conclusion is that the American development and application of the conspiracy/criminal-organization plan in 1944–45 was a valid and natural result of the customary system of government decision making. To discover why its results were relatively disappointing, it would seem reasonable to look deeper. Before beginning our examination, however, the reader should be reminded that a researcher and writer who has labored long on any topic is inclined to extend to the object of that labor a special, transcendent significance. When one has pursued a matter sufficiently to acquire the stooped shoulders and squint that Erasmus long ago saw as the scholar's real hallmark, the result is unlikely to be a declaration that the subject has only marginal importance. We are all too easily persuaded that our labors have uncovered a new Rosetta stone. Having armed ourselves with this note of caution, it is worth exploring the possibility that the troubles which accompanied the Nuremberg trial plan may provide clues to the causes of other American problems with the rest of the world.

The first and most obvious reason why those who made the decisions in 1944–45 failed to hit the mark lay in the range and complexity of the problems they faced. Men such as McCloy, Stimson, and Morgenthau were forced to cope with a bewildering array of problems whose scale and numbers tended to swamp the capacity of anyone to keep matters in perspective. As McCloy later remarked regarding his postwar career as high commissioner for Germany, it was heady stuff to be able to turn to one's secretary and say, "take a law," [8] but this did not mean the officials were actually in control of the situation. The traditionally small and weak federal government had drastically expanded its domestic powers in America during the great depression of the 1930s. Then by relaxing its grip at home, Washington managed to radically extend its diplomatic and military activities during the wartime era of 1940–45.

The approaching end of hostilities in 1944–45 forced the U.S. government to take a commanding lead, both at home and in the economic, military, and diplomatic structure of the postwar world. Few governments accustomed to a relaxed care-taker role have ever been called upon to expand their powers and functions so rapidly. Washington certainly did not completely botch the job, but there were evident signs of strain within the system of executive authority in 1944–45, quite apart from the decline in Franklin Roosevelt's power and the inexperience of Harry Truman. When leafing through the papers of officials such as Stimson and Hopkins, one sees that in those years they were forced to make hourly hops between subjects as serious and diverse as the atomic bomb, military strategy, inflation, postwar rationing, occupation policies, and universal military service. These officials seemed increasingly like men who, fearing they were about to drown, took to slapping at the water in all directions. When on 12 April 1945, Mr. Truman remarked he was saddened by Eleanor Roosevelt's loss, she declared that she felt even sorrier for him because of the burden he was about to assume. The lady knew of what she spoke.

Yet the sheer size and complexity of the issues involved is only one side of the crisis. The way the decisions were made— that is, the decision-making system itself—also contributed to the severity of the problem. Because no one knew when the Third Reich would collapse, it seemed wise to begin the planning as early as possible. Since there were few precedents for guidance and the problem had ramifications that concerned many departments, large numbers of officials were drawn into the process of planning and decision making. Work on the issue tended to crest on various occasions, such as the preparation of Bernays's memorandum, the formulation of the first War Department draft, the completion of the three secretaries' memorandum, and so on. Outside events, including the Malmédy massacre, the London mission of April 1945, and the death of President Roosevelt, prompted a number of these important reformulations. On each of these occasions there was some consensus among those who participated in preparing an interim formulation of the plan. None of these formulations was conclusive, but so much labor and compromise had gone into them that it became unthinkable simply to jettison them later on. The importance attached to particular elements might subsequently increase or decrease, but once points had found their way into the basic plan, they were seldom completely eliminated again.

The stress on prewar persecutions is a good example of this preservative tendency. The emphasis on prewar persecutions made sense in August–September 1944, when the War Department was trying to gather the support of officials worried by protests from the War Refugee Board and the American Jewish Conference. Since a number of government advisors had themselves been victims of Nazi repression in the 1930s, it was only natural that they would favor righting those wrongs. But as Morgenthau's power waned and information on the far greater atrocities the Nazis had perpetrated during the war flooded into Washington, the retention of this stress made little sense. Yet those who had been involved in these early decisions never seem to have considered permanently altering this element of the plan. After a momentary eclipse in the San Francisco drafts, prewar persecutions resumed their position in the final American executive agreement and the London Charter. This had little to do with political acumen or, as the eternally suspicious might suppose, philo-Semitism. Hitler's killings, especially the extermination of Jews, had mainly been carried out during the war, and wartime acts would have been the easiest to prosecute under prevailing international law. Prewar atrocities continued to be central to the conspiracy/criminal-organization scheme, primarily because the planning process had a life of its own, which prevented the removal of this or any other basic feature—such as listing the whole SS as a criminal organization after Malmédy—once it had found a place in a major formulation of the plan.

The source of this difficulty was indecisiveness and protracted planning. Because President Roosevelt did not indicate clearly if he favored the conspiracy/criminal-organization proposal, the planning and reformulations went on and on with ever more elaborate embroidery. Yet when the idea of a conspiracy/ criminal-organization prosecution was finally approved by President Truman, the extended planning had not helped to make the system more effective in dealing with the situation the Allies actually faced in Germany in 1945. Long-term planning had backfired. The plan had become its own reality, and it would have been applied no matter what conditions had prevailed in Europe at war's end.

That Washington officials had too much to do in 1944–45, and that the war-crimes policy planning was flawed by being too protracted and elaborate, does not necessarily mean there was something peculiarly deficient in the American system. Governments have long been hobbled by excessive obligations and too much planning. As Montaigne said four hundred years ago, "great and distant enterprises" tend to "perish from the very magnitude of the preparation made to ensure their success." [9] Yet there has been a special quality of excess in American foreign relations in the postwar years that, when combined with an inclination toward overmoralizing, has often produced serious difficulties. Since the war-crimes policy planning of 1944–45 also showed these tendencies in rich and variegated forms, a final moment of reflection on such matters seems appropriate.

As European critics of the United States are especially eager to note, Americans love to preach to the world. Certainly the United States war-crimes policy planners believed that their country and its allies not only were justified in judging and condemning the Nazis, but that they had a moral right to cleanse and purify German society. Simultaneously these same men held that their allies, especially the British, were lacking in moral awareness when they took a different tack on war-crimes policy than the Americans. In consequence, the first torrent of moralizing that went into the planning papers was not intended to produce contrition among the Germans, but to shame the British into abandoning their opposition to a trial.

Beneath the surface of policymaking there bubbled another moral consideration—atonement. The United States had backed out of its international commitments at the end of World War I, and many Washington officials felt this isolationist folly had contributed to the instability of the world and the subsequent rise of the authoritarian and aggressive Axis governments. The fervor with which Washington, and the country at large, embraced the idea of creating a postwar United Nations organization to act as a super League of Nations betokened not only a desire for world peace and security, but a need to confess past sins and pledge that they would not be repeated. In regard to war-crimes policy too, the spirit of atonement was rife, for it had become a truism in Washington that the failure to carry out a rigorous program of occupation and punishment in Germany in 1918–19 had laid the seed bed for Hitler's growth. Since the United States had led the flight from this responsibility in 1919, it was up to Washington to lead the way to a better solution in 1945. That the purging of Germany, through the routine disposal of thousands of "criminal-organization" members without a full trial, might not be compatible with the new era of peace and understanding associated with the United Nations seems not to have occurred to anyone. For repentent sinners and those attempting to rectify the errors of the past, current conditions are usually less important than their own sensitivities.

The use of public policy and governmental power to attain a sense of moral contentment stretches and twists the realm of political activity to such a degree that it, in itself, is an instance of something akin to what the Greeks called hubris. But the whole of the war-crimes policy planning was shot through with excess and a failure to accept reasonable limits. The idea that the gigantic atrocity of Nazism and the Second World War could have been moved before a court, examined, and judged is at least very odd. The belief that it could have been done quickly and accurately, without excessive violence to customary principles of law, is breathtaking. Here is excess with a vengeance, and when one realizes that this was to be done as a program of "purge and run," * because the United States government and the American people were still unwilling to assume the burdens of a long period of occupation, the dangers and paradoxes of the situation are painfully self-evident. Americans do have a tendency to believe that they can do anything, and do it quickly. Their refusal to recognize limits or obstacles is also one of the sources of the restless energy that gives Americans strength and an inordinate capacity to get things done. After carping at American planning—filling the hallways with snide remarks—even most British officials ultimately admitted that American energy and determination had beaten the odds and turned Nuremberg into a more successful enterprise than they had thought possible.[10]

Yet everything is not always attainable and energy is not always enough. If there is a broad lesson to be learned from the Nuremberg planning (which avoids the pitfalls of penance), it may be that Americans must somehow discover a sense of precision and limit in foreign relations, without losing the sources of strength contained in their eagerness and optimism. Only thus will the country be able to avoid the dilemma that Herodotus lamented after the great conflict of his age:

> Of all man's miseries the
> bitterest is this:
> To know so much and have
> control over nothing.[11]

---

* Some historians have characterized Nazi occupation policies in the phrase "grab and run," while officials in the War Department in 1944 spoke of the Morgenthau plan as a policy of "smash and run."

GUIDE TO FREQUENTLY
CITED SOURCES

Asst. Sect.—RG (Record Group) 107, Assistant Secretary of War, 000.5, War Crimes, Modern Military Branch, National Archives, Washington, D.C.

Bernays Papers—Murray C. Bernays Collection, University of Wyoming.

CAB 21—War Cabinet Committee on War Crimes, Public Record Office, London.

CAB 65—W. M. (45) Conclusions (War Cabinet Minutes), CAB 65, Public Record Office, London.

CAB 66—W. P. (45) (War Cabinet Papers), CAB 66, Public Record Office, London.

Cadogan—David Dilks, ed., *The Diaries of Sir Alexander Cadogan, 1938–1945* (London, 1971).

Davies Papers—Joseph E. Davies Papers, Library of Congress, Washington, D.C.

FO—British Foreign Office General Correspondence Records, FO 371, Public Record Office, London.

FRUS, 1944—*Foreign Relations of the United States, 1944*, vol. I (Washington, D.C., 1966).

FRUS, Malta and Yalta—*Foreign Relations of the United States, The Conferences at Malta and Yalta, 1945* (Washington, D.C., 1955).

FRUS, 1945—*Foreign Relations of the United States, 1945*, vol. III (Washington, D.C., 1968).

Illegal and Inhumane Warfare—Illegal and Inhumane Warfare, 740.00116-EW, Diplomatic Branch, National Archives, Washington, D.C.

Jackson Report—*Report of Robert H. Jackson, United States Representative to the International Conference on Military Trials, London, 1945* (Washington, D.C., 1949).

JAG—RG 153, Judge Advocate General, Federal Records Center, Suitland, Maryland.

LCO 2—Lord Chancellor's Office, LCO 2/2981/x/j. 7320, Public Record Office, London.

Morgenthau Diary—*The Morgenthau Diary (Germany)*, 2 vols. (Washington, D.C., 1967).

Reaching Judgment—Bradley F. Smith, *Reaching Judgment at Nuremberg* (New York, 1977).

RG 165 Personnel—RG 165, Personnel G-1, 000.5, Federal Record Center, Suitland, Maryland.

Rosenman Papers, War Crimes—Papers of Samuel I. Rosenman, Box 7, War Crimes File, Harry S. Truman Library, Independence, Missouri.

Rosenman Papers, S.F. Conference—Papers of Samuel I. Rosenman, San Francisco Conference File, Box 3, Harry S. Truman Library, Independence, Missouri.

Stimson Diary—Diary of Henry L. Stimson, Roll 9, Yale University, New Haven, Connecticut.

740.00116EW—740.00116EW, General European War File, Diplomatic Branch, National Archives, Washington, D.C.

NOTES

Preface

1. Quoted in *The New York Review of Books*, 20 January 1977, pp. 16.
2. For a comprehensive current bibliography of published works on the subject, see John R. Lewis, *Uncertain Judgment: A Bibliography of War Crimes Trials* (Santa Barbara, 1979).
3. Diary of Henry L. Stimson, Vol. 48f, Roll 9, Yale University, *passim* (hereinafter cited as Stimson Diary); Papers of Henry L. Stimson, Roll 110, Yale University, *passim*.
4. See especially Henry L. Feingold, *The Politics of Rescue* (New Brunswick, N.J., 1970), and John Morton Blum, *V was for Victory* (New York, 1976), p. 167f.
5. *Stimson Diary*, Vol. 48, 23 August 1944, p. 18.

Chapter 1

1. See especially John Gimbel, *The American Occupation of Germany* (Stanford, Calif., 1968).
2. *Complete Presidential Press Conferences of Franklin D. Roosevelt*, vol. 24, no. 962, 29 July 1944 (New York, 1972), pp. 32–34.
3. See Bradley F. Smith and Elena Agarossi, *Operation Sunrise, The Secret Surrender* (New York, 1979).
4. *Interim Directive for Military Government of Germany* (21 August 1944) and *Handbook of Military Government for Germany* (1 September 1944), Walter Bedell Smith Collection of World War II Documents, boxes 28 and 35, Dwight D. Eisenhower Library, Abilene, Kansas.
5. *Handbook on German Military Forces* (TM-30-450), Washington, D.C., December 1941).
6. Ibid.
7. *Interim Directive* and *Handbook*.
8. British aide-mémoire, 19 August 1944, *Foreign Relations of the United States, 1944*, vol. I (Washington, D.C., 1966), pp. 1351–53. (Hereinafter cited as *FRUS*.) One may speculate on the political motives, such as a fear of political change, a desire to cover up some questionable acts of its own, and so on, behind London's opposition to innovation in the punishment of war crimes. But as early as 22 June 1942, the issues of holding a trial of major Nazi leaders and of prosecuting a broad range of atrocities was placed before the law officers of the crown, who strongly advised against such action on legal grounds. This set the tone for all subsequent British policy dis-

cussions. "Treatment of War Criminals," W. P. (42) 264, 22 June 1942, CAB 21 (War Cabinet Committee on War Crimes), 1509, Public Records Office, London, (hereinafter cited as *CAB 21*).

9.   Memorandum for the Files, 24 May 1944, RG 153, "Conference with Mr. Hackworth," *JAG*, Box 1606, Folder 103–24, Federal Records Center, Suitland, Maryland. (Hereinafter cited as *JAG*.); State Department Policy Committee Recommendations, 20 May 1944, RG 59, "Records of Harley A. Notter, 1939–1945," Policy Committee Documents, Box 14, Diplomatic Branch, National Archives, Washington, D.C.

10.   Roosevelt to Pell, 10 March 1944, RG 59, "Records of Harley A. Notter, 1939–1945," Policy Committee Documents, Box 14, Diplomatic Branch, National Archives, Washington, D.C.

11.   Cabinet minutes note by Robert A. Lovett, 18 August 1944, Papers of Henry L. Stimson, Roll 110, Yale University, New Haven, Connecticut.

12.   *The Morgenthau Diary (Germany)*, vol. I (Washington, D.C., 1967), p. 462. (Hereinafter cited as *Morgenthau Diary*.) This is a memorandum by Harry Dexter White. Significantly, the report itself is also in the Hopkins Papers, RG 24, "Treatment of Germany," Box 333, Franklin D. Roosevelt Library, Hyde Park, New York; see also, Warren F. Kimball, *Swords or Plough Shares* (Philadelphia/New York, 1976).

13.   *Morgenthau Diary*, vol. I, pp. 7 and 450. It is unlikely that Morgenthau actually obtained the *Handbook* in Britain as was later claimed.

14.   White to Hilldring, *ibid.*, p. 424.

15.   "Morgenthau's Inside Story," *The New York Post*, 24 November 1945, p. 2.

16.   Dwight D. Eisenhower, *Crusade in Europe* (Garden City, New York, 1949), p. 287; Dwight D. Eisenhower to Cadet Robert Paul Leary, 8 May 1950, General of the Army Files, Box 61, Dwight D. Eisenhower Library, Abilene, Kansas.

17.   See John Morton Blum ed., *From the Morgenthau Diaries*, vol. III, *Years of War, 1941–1945* (Boston, 1967) and Henry L. Feingold, *The Politics of Rescue* (New Brunswick, New Jersey, 1970).

18.   Morgenthau notes, 18 August 1944, *Morgenthau Diary*, vol. I, p. 416.

19.   *Stimson Diary*, vol. 48, 21 August 1944, p. 11.

20.   White notes on talk with Hilldring, *Morgenthau Diary*, vol. I, p. 424.

21.   Morgenthau notes, *ibid.*, pp. 426–27.

22.   Ibid.

23.   *Stimson Diary*, vol. 48, 23 August 1944, p. 19. Since Roosevelt's health and capacity is a question from this point on, it may be useful to note that one of the best features of a recent popular book on FDR is that it puts the health issue in context. See Jim Bishop, *FDR's Last Year* (New York, 1974).

24.   *Stimson Diary*, vol. 48, 23 August 1944, p. 19.

25.   Morgenthau notes, *Morgenthau Diary*, vol. I, pp. 426–427.

26.   Ibid.

27.   *Stimson Diary*, vol. 48, 24 August 1944, p. 22.

28.   Morgenthau notes, *Morgenthau Diary*, vol. I, pp. 439–440.

29.   Ibid.

30.   *Stimson Diary*, vol. 48, 25 August 1944, pp. 27–28. It is especially obvious in this entry that Stimson dictated the passage long after the event, and it should be a warning not to put too much stock in the literalness of Stimson's quotations, either in the diary or the published "memoirs" based

on it. Henry L. Stimson and McGeorge Bundy, *On Active Service in Peace and War* (New York, 1947).

31. Morgenthau notes, *Morgenthau Diary*, vol. I, p. 447; *Stimson Diary*, vol. 48, 25 August 1944, pp. 27–28.

32. Ibid.

33. Ibid. The context is not altogether clear and the remark may have been made in the cabinet.

34. Presidential memorandum, 26 August 1944, *Morgenthau Diary*, vol. II, pp. 443, 444.

35. Ibid.

36. Memorandum, Morgenthau to the president, 25 August 1944, *Morgenthau Diary*, vol. I, p. 443f. But the president did have a copy of the *Handbook.* See President's Secretary's File, Box 104, Franklin D. Roosevelt Library, Hyde Park, New York.

37. Morgenthau to White, *Morgenthau Diary*, vol. I, p. 448.

38. Ibid.

39. Treasury conference minutes, ibid., pp. 503–509.

40. Ibid., p. 466f.

41. Henry L. Stimson and McGeorge Bundy, *On Active Service in Peace and War*, (New York, 1947).

42. See especially Forrest C. Pogue, *George C. Marshall*, 3 vols. (New York, 1963–73).

43. *Stimson Diary*, vol. 48, 13 September and 3 October 1944, pp. 73 and 117–118.

44. Ibid., 3 October 1944, pp. 117–118.

45. Ibid., 4 September 1944, pp. 33–34.

46. Record of Stimson-Cramer conversation, JAG, Box 1603, File No. 103, Bk. 2–51.

47. Treasury meeting notes, 4 September 1944, *Morgenthau Diary*, vol. I, p. 485f.

48. Ibid.

49. *Stimson Diary*, vol. 48, 4 September 1944, pp. 33–34.

50. Notes of Meeting, 4 September 1944, *Morgenthau Diary*, vol. I, p. 503.

51. *Stimson Diary*, vol. 48, 4 September 1944, pp. 33–34.

52. In a notorious incident at the Moscow conference of 22 October 1943, Hull said he would take out the top Axis leaders and have "a drumhead court-martial" one day, and "at sunrise on the following day there would occur a historic incident." *Foreign Relations of the United States, 1943*, vol. 3, (Washington, D.C., 1963), p. 612. (Hereinafter cited as *FRUS, 1943.*)

53. *Stimson Diary*, vol. 48, 5 September 1944, pp. 35–36.

54. In addition to the documents cited here, for Roosevelt's foreign-policy views, see especially Robert Dallek, *Franklin D. Roosevelt and American Foreign Policy, 1932–1945* (New York, 1979), p. 472f.

55. Statement on war criminals, Illegal and Inhumane Warfare, 740.00116 EW/10-2744, Diplomatic Branch, National Archives, Washington, D.C. (Hereinafter cited as *Illegal and Inhumane Warfare.*)

56. Memorandum for Mr. Stettinius, 28 August 1944. RG 107, Assistant Secretary of War, 000.5, War Crimes, Box 16, Working File, Modern Military Branch, National Archives, Washington, D.C. (Hereinafter cited as *Asst. Sect.*)

57. Memorandum for the cabinet committee on Germany, 5 September 1944, *Foreign Relations of the United States, The Conference of Quebec 1944.* (Washington, D.C., 1972), p. 96. (Hereinafter cited as *FRUS, Quebec.*)

58. *Stimson Diary*, vol. 48, 5 September 1944, p. 35.

59. Ibid.

60. Ibid., p. 36.

61. Ibid.

62. Hopkins to the president, 5 September 1944, President's Secretary's File, Box 44, Germany, 1944–45, Franklin D. Roosevelt Library, Hyde Park, New York. The harshness of Hopkins's views on Germany at this period may be seen in his margin comments on a copy of the postsurrender directive, which McCloy sent him on 6 September (Box 333, Hopkins Papers, RG 24, Franklin D. Roosevelt Library, Hyde Park, New York). But it is possible that he tried to make them seem as "tough" as possible because there are hints that he was interested in obtaining the post of American occupation administrator in Germany. Notes of lunch talk with Hopkins by Henry Morgenthau, 4 September 1944, *Morgenthau Diary*, vol. I.

63. Henry Morgenthau to the president, 5 September, 1944, *Morgenthau Diary*, vol. II, pp. 105–108.

64. Henry L. Stimson to Henry Morgenthau, 5 September 1944, Papers of Henry L. Stimson, Roll 110, Yale University, New Haven, Connecticut.

65. Ibid.

66. *Stimson Diary*, vol. 48, 6 September 1944, p. 45f.

67. FDR to Hull, 3 September 1944, shows that Murphy was rejected because he was not "sufficiently tough." Cordell Hull Papers, Box 54, File 170, Library of Congress, Washington, D.C. For what happened in the cabinet regarding Hopkins and Byrnes, see *Morgenthau Diary*, vol. I. While this section of the book in hand was being written, the chancellor of West Germany was in South Carolina paying tribute to the memory of James Byrnes's support for West Germany. History does have its ironies!

68. *Stimson Diary*, vol. 48, 6 September 1944, p. 45.

69. Recording of telephone conversation, Morgenthau to Hopkins, 5 September 1944, *Morgenthau Diary*, vol. I, pp. 521–524.

70. Record of Treasury meeting, 6 September 1944, *Morgenthau Diary*, vol. I.

71. *Stimson Diary*, vol. 48, 5 September 1944, p. 36.

72. Ibid., p. 37.

73. For a more extended discussion of this question see Bradley F. Smith and Elena Agarossi, *Operation Sunrise, The Secret Surrender* (New York, 1979).

74. *Morgenthau Diary*, vol. I, pp. 558–570.

75. Treasury notes, 8 September 1944, *Morgenthau Diary*, vol. I, p. 588.

76. *Stimson Diary*, vol. 48, 5 September 1944, p. 35.

77. Treasury notes, 8 September 1944, *Morgenthau Diary*, vol. I, p. 589.

78. *Stimson Diary*, vol. 48, 7 September 1944, p. 49f.

79. Ibid.

80. Ibid.

81. Ibid., 8 September 1944, p. 53.

82. Ibid., 13 September 1944, p. 73.

83. Ibid., 7 September 1944, p. 49.

84. Ibid., 9 September 1944, p. 57; Treasury meeting record, *Morgenthau Diary*, vol. I, pp. 609–611.
85. Ibid.
86. *Stimson Diary*, vol. 48, 9 September 1944, p. 59f.
87. The document was sent to the War Department on 8 September.
88. Stimson to Hull, 11 September 1944, RG 107, Secretary of War, German War Crimes Subfile, 000.5, Modern Military Branch, National Archives, Washington, D.C.
89. *Stimson Diary*, vol. 48, 6 September 1944, p. 45f.
90. Ibid., 12 September 1944, p. 68.
91. *Morgenthau Diary*, Book 771, p. 140, Franklin D. Roosevelt Library, Hyde Park, New York.
92. *Stimson Diary*, vol. 48, 14 September 1944, p. 73.
93. *Stimson Diary*, vol. 48, 13 September 1944, p. 73.
94. Ibid. Bishop has the facts wrong but the mood right. Jim Bishop, *FDR's Last Year* (New York, 1974), p. 140.
95. Ibid.
96. Ibid., 15 September 1944, pp. 83–86.
97. Treasury conferences, examples, *Morgenthau Diary*, vol. I, pp. 591–604.
98. Ibid., especially pp. 591–596 and 601–602.
99. Treasury conference of 20 September 1944, *Morgenthau Diary*, vol. I, p. 627.
100. 18 October 1944 discussion between White and Morgenthau, *Morgenthau Diary*, vol. I, pp. 718–719. It is White who was nearly always on the Secretary's side, who gets him to grant that the Morgenthau plan and lend-lease were discussed together, though the agenda showed that the former came first.
101. Treasury conference, 20 September 1944, *Morgenthau Diary*, vol. I, p. 627.
102. Ibid., and Winston S. Churchill, *Triumph and Tragedy*. (Boston, 1953), p. 156.
103. This whole question still needs a thorough study since it is highly complicated. An indication of the sources from which it might be constructed can be found in Bradley F. Smith, *Reaching Judgment at Nuremberg*, (New York, 1977), p. 29f and related footnotes. (Hereinafter cited as *Reaching Judgment*.)
104. Memorandum, "Major War Criminals," 4 September 1944, *FRUS, Quebec* (Washington, D.C., 1972), pp. 91–93.
105. *Reaching Judgment*, p. 30.
106. *Stimson Diary*, vol. 48, 16–17 September 1944, p. 82.
107. Ibid., 20 September 1944, p. 92.
108. *FRUS, Quebec* (Washington, D.C., 1972), p. 467.

Chapter 2

1. 11 November memorandum, Papers of Samuel I. Rosenman, Box 7, War Crimes File, Harry S. Truman Library, Independence, Missouri. (Hereinafter cited as *Rosenman Papers, War Crimes*.)

2. *Stimson Diary*, vol. 48, 20 September 1944, p. 92.
3. Ibid., 16–17 September 1944, p. 82.
4. Ibid.
5. *Morgenthau Diary*, vol. I, pp. 627–28.
6. Memorandum, 19 September 1944, Papers of Henry L. Stimson, Reel 110.
7. *Stimson Diary*, vol. 48, 20 September 1944, p. 92.
8. Appendix of Stimson to Stettinius, 27 October 1944, 740.00116 EW/10-2744, Diplomatic Branch, National Archives, Washington, D.C. (Hereinafter cited as 740.00116 EW), *Stimson Diary*, vol. 48.
9. Ibid.
10. The approval and related materials are filed under the date of 15 September 1944, RG 165, Personnel, G-1, 000.5, Box 313, Federal Records Center, Suitland, Maryland. (Hereinafter cited as *RG 165, Personnel*.)
11. Appendix of Stimson to Stettinius, 27 October 1944, 740.00116 EW/10-2744.
12. Notes of the meeting transmitted from Bernays to Berry, 23 September 1944, *RG 165, Personnel*, Box 313.
13. Ibid.
14. Memorandum, President to the Secretary of State, 29 September 1944, President's Secretary's File, Box 44, Germany, 1944–45, Franklin D. Roosevelt Library, Hyde Park, New York.
15. *Stimson Diary*, vol. 48, 3 October 1944, pp. 117–118. Stimson talks about the press leaks in his diary (p. 104f.), including Hull's worries and Stimson's conviction that the leaks began with a Treasury source giving material to Drew Pearson.
16. White notes of a talk with Robert Murphy (who referred to the President's remark). *Morgenthau Diary*, vol. I, p. 776.
17. The President's reply to the Secretary of State, 20 October 1944, Papers of Edward Stettinius, Box 218, Folder "S-Secretary," July 1944, University of Virginia.
8. *Foreign Relations of the United States, Conferences at Malta and Yalta, 1945*, (Washington, 1955), pp. 145–149 (Hereinafter cited as *FRUS Malta and Yalta.*)
19. Cramer to McCloy, 27 September 1944, *Asst. Sect.*, Box 15, Jan. 1943–Dec. 1944 File.
20. Ibid.
21. Noted in JAG paper on European war-crimes transmitted from Cutter to Bernays on 22 November 1944. Murray C. Bernays Collection, Box 4, Trial and Punishment File, University of Wyoming (Hereinafter cited as *Bernays Papers*).
22. 1 October 1944, *Asst. Sect.*, Box 15, Jan. 1943–Dec. 1944 File.
23. Bernays to Henry, 14 October 1944 (*Bernays Papers*, Box 1), shows his tendency to keep up the pressure. See also Cutter to McCloy, 5 October 1944, on papers supplied to Bernays. *Asst. Sect.* Box 15, Jan. 1943–Dec. 1944 File.
24. The correct date is supplied by the document of 5 October 1944 cited in the previous note. Bernays describes the incident in two "memoir" statements, and although he puts it too early by a month, by stating that it took place during the Dumbarton Oaks Conference he tends to confirm the early October date. Bernays to Mrs. Bernays, 10 June 1945, and Bernays to R. A. Winnacker, 18 August 1949, *Bernays Papers*, Box 1.

25. 4 October transmission, Cramer to Cutter, *JAG*, Box 1606, Folder 103-24.
26. Report, Berry to Henry, 2 November 1944, *RG* 165, *Personnel*, Box 313.
27. Donovan to McCloy, 6 October 1944, Transmitting Research and Analysis report no. 2577, *Asst. Sect.*, Box 16, Working File. It was a bad week for OSS reports. When Roosevelt sent Morgenthau one which indicated the importance of German farm-machinery production to all of Europe, Morgenthau replied on 9 October, "in the words of your son Johnny, 'so what?'" President's Secretary's Files, Box 169, Franklin D. Roosevelt Library, Hyde Park, New York.
28. Cramer and Cutter to McCloy, 9 October 1944, *Asst. Sect.*, Box 15, Jan. 1943–Dec. 1944 File.
29. Bernays to Berry, 20 October 1944, *Bernays Papers*, Box 4, Trial and Punishment File.
30. See Bernays's comment in the document cited in note 29.
31. *Stimson Diary*, vol. 48, 9 October 1944.
32. Copy of Halifax letter as attachment, Draft, Stimson to Halifax, *Illegal and Inhumane Warfare*, 740.00116 EW/11-744.
33. Stimson to McCloy, 10 October 1944, *Asst. Sect.*, Box 15, Jan. 1943–Dec. 1944 File.
34. Draft, Stimson to Halifax, 18–19 October 1944, *Asst Sect.* Box 15, Jan. 1943–Dec. 1944 File.
35. Ibid., penciled note attached. Halifax did mention a conversation with Stimson, and asked for guidance on British policy—which apparently was not forthcoming—but there is no indication that he passed Stimson's views on to London. Halifax to Foreign Office, 19 October 1944, British Foreign Office General Correspondence Records FO 371/39005/8199 Public Record Office, London. (Hereinafter cited as *FO*.)
36. *Stimson Diary*, vol. 48, 23 October 1944, p. 177.
37. Ibid., 24 October 1944, p. 180.
38. Bernays to Mrs. Bernays, 10 June 1945, *Bernays Papers*, Box 1.
39. Ibid.
40. *Stimson Diary*, vol. 48, 24 October 1944, p. 180.
41. Ibid., 24 October 1944, p. 181.
42. Ibid., 24 October 1944, p. 182.
43. Ibid., 25 October 1944, p. 183.
44. Ibid., 27 October 1944, p. 188.
45. This incident has produced a flood of subsequent statements, mainly occasioned by Elliott Roosevelt's account (*As he Saw It*, [New York, 1946], p. 188f.). It has been especially popular to use as an indication of Soviet brutality and British dedication to the rule of law because of Churchill's angry reaction to Stalin's remarks. However, not only is it not clear whether Stalin was jesting or making a serious proposal, but the significant point is that even in this discussion Churchill seems to have opposed war-crimes trials based on what he saw as *ex post facto* law. (See William D. Leahy, *I Was There*. [New York, 1950], pp. 205–6). Therefore the end result was that whether Stalin wanted to get rid of one or fifty thousand Nazis, he wanted to use his kind of trial. Churchill, with his doubts about whether or not a real trial of the Nazi leaders could be held, preferred to have no trial, and just shoot them on the basis of a "political" decision. So we end up with a paradoxical result: The man horrified by the idea of perverting

trials, or the horror of mass killings, came out in favor of summary execution of Hitler and his aides.

46. Memo of Pasvolsky-Sobolev conversation, 28 September 1944, RG 24, Hopkins Papers, Box 333, Franklin D. Roosevelt Library, Hyde Park, New York.

47. Morgenthau-White discussion on the latter's talk with Gromyko, 5 October 1944, *Morgenthau Diary*, vol. I, p. 701.

48. Churchill to Roosevelt, 22 October 1944, *FRUS, Malta Yalta*, p. 400, See also *Churchill, Taken from the Diaries of Lord Moran: The Struggle for Survival, 1940–1945* (Boston, 1966), p. 208.

49. Ibid.

50. War Cabinet Minutes, 131st Conclusions, 4 October 1944, CAB 21/1509/7970.

51. Churchill to Eden, 24 October 1944, FO 371/39005/8199.

52. Stimson to Stettinius, 27 October 1944, 740.00116 EW/10-2744.

53. Ibid.

54. Ibid.

55. Bernays to Henry, 27 October 1944, *Bernays Papers*, Box 4, Trial and Punishment File. Bernays did receive serious praise for his work; see McCloy to G-1, 26 October 1944, in *Bernays Papers*, Box 1.

56. Cutter to Weir, 2 November 1944, *JAG*, Box 1605, Folder 103-19A.

57. British aide-mémoire, 30 October 1944, *FRUS 1944*, vol. I, pp. 1389–91.

58. Ibid.

59. Cutter to Bernays, 4 November 1944, *Asst. Sect.*, Box 15, Jan. 1943–Dec. 1944 File.

60. Agenda, 9 November 1944, *Asst. Sect.*, Box 16, Working File. The handwritten note on the document seems to be Cutter's, and the material in this box tends to have been prepared by him.

61. Ibid.

62. Minutes of the meeting of 9 November 1944. *Asst. Sect.*, Box 16, Working File.

63. Ibid.

64. Ibid.

65. Ibid.

66. Ibid.

67. 11 November memorandum, *Rosenman Papers, War Crimes*.

Chapter 3

1. David Dilks, ed., *The Diaries of Sir Alexander Cadogan, 1938–1945* (London, 1971), p. 565. (Hereinafter cited as *Cadogan*.)

2. See Henry L. Stimson and McGeorge Bundy, *On Active Service in Peace and War* (New York, 1947), p. 10f.

3. *Stimson Diary*, vol. 49, 19 November 1944, pp. 34–35.

4. Ibid., 21 November 1944, p. 39.

5. Ibid., 19 November 1944, pp. 34–35.

6. Ibid.

7. Ibid., 21 November 1944, p. 39.

8. Ibid., vol. 48, 6 September 1944, p. 45f and 13 September 1944, p. 73f. See also below, Chapter 2, pp. 24–25.

9. *Stimson Diary*, vol. 49, 21 November 1944, p. 39.

10. Memorandum of Roosevelt-Stettinius conversation, 15 November 1944, Memorandum of conversations, Edward Stettinius Papers, Box 724, University of Virginia.

11. See below, Chapter 1, pp. 17–18.

12. The many standard biographies of Franklin Roosevelt contain long and usually laudatory passages on his gifts as a juggler of political views, ideologies, and politicians, but less attention has been paid to the effect of his last illness on this style of governing. For the best recent coverage of the foreign-policy aspects of the question, see Robert Dallek, *Franklin D. Roosevelt and American Foreign Policy, 1932–1945*, (New York, 1979).

13. Memorandum by McCloy, 18 November 1944 and McCloy to CAD, 7 December 1944, *Asst. Sect.*, Box 16, Working File.

14. See Mr. Kane to War Department, c. 16 November 1944, *Rosenman Papers*, *War Crimes* and *Asst. Sect.*, Box 15, Working File.

15. Ibid.

16. Hackworth to McCloy, 16 November 1944, *Rosenman Papers*, *War Crimes*.

17. Ibid., and 11 November 1944 memorandum, *Rosenman Papers*, *War Crimes*.

18. Ibid.

19. Cramer to McCloy, 22 November 1944, *Bernays Papers*, Box 4, Trial and Punishment File.

20. Ibid.

21. Memorandum, 23 November 1944, *Asst. Sect.*, Box 16, Working File; Memorandum 27–29 November 1944, *Rosenman Papers*, *War Crimes*.

22. Ibid.

23. Ibid.

24. Ibid.

25. The three cover letters from McCloy are in *Rosenman Papers*, *War Crimes*.

26. See Samuel I. Rosenman, *Working With Roosevelt* (New York, 1952).

27. The Davies Papers are in the Library of Congress.

28. Journal, Joseph E. Davies Papers, Container 15, Sept.–Dec. 1944, Library of Congress, Washington, D.C. (Hereinafter cited as *Davies Papers*.)

29. The jumble, containing some originals, some rewrites, and some illuminating instances where both the original and the rewrites have survived, is in the *Davies Papers*.

30. Stettinius to the President, 21 November 1944, memos to the President, Edward Stettinius Papers, Box 734, University of Virginia.

31. Ibid.

32. Stettinius to Davies, 11 December 1944, Edward R. Stettinius Papers, Box 721, Joe Davies File, University of Virginia.

33. *Morgenthau Diary*, vol. II, p. 875.

34. McCloy to Stimson and enclosures, 24 November 1944, *Asst. Sect.*, Box 16, Jan.–April 1945 File.

35. Ibid., and G-1 to McCloy, 24 November 1944, *Bernays Papers*, Box 4, Trial and Punishment File; Stimson to the Secretary of State, 27 November 1944, 740.00116EW/11-2744.

36.   Ibid.
37.   See for example Stimson's cover note to McCloy, 28 November 1944, *Asst. Sect.*, Box 16, Working File.
38.   Chanler to McCloy, 1 December 1944, *Asst. Sect.*, Box 15, Jan. 1943–Dec. 1944 File.
39.   McCloy to Chanler, 5 December 1944 and Bernays to McCloy 6 December 1944, *Asst. Sect.*, Box 15, Jan. 1943–Dec. 1944 File.
40.   McCloy to Chanler, 5 December 1944, *Asst. Sect.*, Box 15, Jan. 1943–Dec. 1944 File.
41.   Chanler to McCloy, 7 December 1944, *Asst. Sect.*, Box 15, Jan. 1943–Dec. 1944 File.
42.   Memorandum, 28–30 November, *Asst. Sect.*, Box 16, Working File. The document was slightly revised on the thirtieth, prior to circulation. See also *Stimson Diary*, vol. 49, 28 November 1944, p. 57.
43.   Memorandum, 28–30 November, *Asst. Sect.*, Box 16, Working File.
44.   Ibid.
45.   Report on conference with JAG, and so on, 22 November 1944, *Asst. Sect.*, Box 15, Jan. 1943–Dec. 1944 File.
46.   Ibid.
47.   McCloy to Stimson, 29 November 1944, *Asst. Sect.*, Box 15, Jan. 1943–Dec. 1944 File.
48.   Dorr to McCloy, 9 December 1944, *Asst. Sect.*, Box 15, Jan. 1943–Dec. 1944 File.
49.   Ibid.
50.   General Royall to McCloy, 14 December 1944, *Asst. Sect.*, Box 15, Jan. 1943–Dec. 1944 File. Bernays comments are in a memorandum to General Berry, 27 December 1944, *RG 165-Personnel*, Box 313.
51.   Ibid. (Royall Memorandum).
52.   JAG memo (pre-18 December 1944), *Asst. Sect.*, Box 16, Working File.
53.   Ibid.
54.   Ibid.
55.   Bernays to Berry, 18 December 1944, *Bernays Papers*, Box 4, Trial and Punishment File.
56.   Ibid.
57.   Chanler to Bernays, 20 December 1944, *Asst. Sect.*, Box 16, Working File.
58.   Chanler did succeed in extracting a comment from Sheldon Gluck. He went a long way toward agreeing with the colonel that the Kellogg-Briand Pact might have made an aggressive attack criminally prosecutable. See Chanler to Weir, 27 December 1944, *Asst. Sect.*, Box 16, Working File.
59.   Chanler to McCloy, 27 December 1944, ibid., Box 15, Jan. 1943–Dec. 1944.
60.   Ibid.
61.   Ibid and Chanler to Dorr, 29 December 1944, *Asst. Sect.*, Box 15, Jan. 1943–Dec. 1944 File.
62.   Chanler to McCloy, 27 December 1944, ibid.
63.   Bernays to Berry, 15 December 1944, *Bernays Papers*, Box 4, Trial and Punishment File.
64.   Stettinius to Hackworth, 20 December 1944, 740.00116 EW/2044, *Illegal and Inhumane Warfare.*

65. Hackworth to Stettinius, 22 December 1944, Edward Stettinius Papers, Stimson-Forrestal Folder, Box 732, University of Virginia.
66. Ibid.
67. Agenda for committee of three, 27 December 1944, Edward Stettinius Papers, Stimson-Forrestal Folder, Box 732, University of Virginia.
68. Morgenthau to McCloy, 30 December 1944, *Asst. Sect.*, Box 15, Jan. 1943–Dec. 1944 File.
69. Memorandum for the Attorney General, 29 December 1944, ibid., Box 16, Working File.
70. Ibid.
71. Memorandum, 5 January 1945, Justice Department, War Crimes File.
72. Ibid.
73. Bernays chronology, 27 December 1944, RG 165 *Personnel*, Box 313.

Chapter 4

1. *Morgenthau Diary*, vol. II, p. 874.
2. See James J. Weingartner, *Crossroads of Death* (Berkeley and Los Angeles, 1979).
3. Ibid., p. 65.
4. Ibid., p. 1.
5. *Stimson Diary*, vol. 49, 15 December 1944, p. 96.
6. Ibid., 26 December 1944, p. 120.
7. Ibid., 30 December 1944, p. 139.
8. Ibid., 31 December 1944, p. 144.
9. Bernays to Cutter, 2 January 1945, *Asst. Sect.*, Box 16, Working File.
10. Francis Biddle, *In Brief Authority* (New York, 1962), p. 470.
11. See James J. Weingartner, *Crossroads of Death* (Berkeley and Los Angeles, 1979).
12. See below, Chapter 3, p. 120.
13. 23 November 1944 memorandum, *Asst. Sect.*, Box 16, Working File.
14. This is an argument by elimination, but Rosenman seems to be the only likely candidate for the role of presidential prompter; and even he, who was always inclined to give Franklin Roosevelt credit for a dominant policy role, is strikingly vague on the President's war-crimes views. See Samuel I. Rosenman, *Working with Roosevelt* (New York, 1952), pp. 518–519.
15. President to Secretary of State, 3 January 1945, *FRUS, Malta and Yalta*, p. 401.
16. The Pell papers are in the Franklin D. Roosevelt Library, Hyde Park, New York.
17. Hackworth to Pell, 12 December 1944, *FRUS, 1944*, vol. I, p. 1400.
18. President to Secretary of State, 3 January 1945, *FRUS, Malta and Yalta*, p. 401; Stettinius to the President, 27 December 1944, Box 734 and Pell to the President, 5 March 1945, Box 726, Edward Stettinius Papers, University of Virginia.
19. President to the Secretary of State, Edward Stettinius Papers, Box 734, University of Virginia.

20. See note at end of Bernays to Berry, 4 January 1945, *RG 165-Personnel*, Box 313.

21. Ibid.

22. Ibid.

23. Bernays-Brown memorandum on aggressive war, 4 January 1945, *Rosenman Papers, War Crimes*.

24. Ibid.

25. The Lauterpacht and Trainin materials had been sent to personnel by Katherine Fite of the State Department on 30 December 1944. (The State Department was studying Trainin as early as 18 December—Hackworth to Wechsler, 740.00116 EW/ 12-1844.) One should not infer that the argument favoring prosecution of aggressive war was dependent on either of these two sources, which appeared only as buttressing support more than a month after Chanler had advanced the basic case. There are enough rightist and anti-Semitic writers who attribute Allied war-crimes policy to Communists and Jews without adding to the confusion.

26. Bernays-Brown memorandum on aggressive war, 4 January 1945, *Rosenman Papers, War Crimes*.

27. Bernays to Berry, 4 January 1945, *RG 165 Personnel*, Box 313.

28. I have inferred this from the tone of the 13 January redraft, which Herbert Wechsler helped to prepare and to which Hackworth and Rosenman failed to raise serious objection. Also, please note that Bernays's immediate superiors continued to strongly support his position, even the most extreme views on aggressive war. Henry to McCloy, 5 January 1945, *Asst. Sect.*, Box 16, Jan.–April 1945 File.

29. A note on the back of one copy reads "Draft worked out by Colonel Bernays and Mr. Wechsler, 12–13 January 1945," *Asst. Sect.*, Box 16, Jan.–April 1945 File.

30. Ibid.

31. Ibid.

32. Ibid.

33. Bernays to Rosenman, 13 January 1945, *Rosenman Papers, War Crimes*.

34. 10 January 1945, Journal Entry, *Davies Papers*, Container 16.

35. Bernays memorandum for Davies, 13 January 1945, *Rosenman Papers, War Crimes*.

36. Davies to Rosenman, 13 January 1945, *Rosenman Papers, War Crimes*.

37. Morgan to Weir (and to Davies on 12 January), *Davies Papers*, Container 93.

38. Ibid.

39. Bernays to Cutter, 15 January 1945, *Asst. Sect.*, Box 16, Jan.–April 1945.

40. Ibid.

41. Enclosure, Bernays to Cutter, 16 January 1945, *Asst. Sect.*, Box 16, Working File.

42. Ibid.

43. Notes are attached to 27 November 1944 draft, but they apply to 13 January 1945 memorandum, *Asst. Sect.*, Box 16, Working File.

44. Cutter to McCloy, 16 January 1945, *Asst. Sect.*, Box 16, Working File.

45. Ibid. Either Stimson or Cutter thought that Supreme Court Justice

Robert Jackson would be a suitable member of such a group. This seems to be the first documentary reference to the future U.S. chief prosecutor at Nuremberg in the Washington war-crimes policy papers.

46. This is simply an inference, since the "showdown" meeting was inconclusive.

47. *Morgenthau Diary*, vol. II, p. 872f.

48. Ibid.

49. Ibid., pp. 878–879.

50. *Stimson Diary*, vol. 50, January 1945, pp. 53–54.

51. "Immediate Recommendation to the President," 18 January 1945, *Davies Papers*, Container 16.

52. Memorandum for the President, JAG draft, 18 January 1945, *Asst. Sect.*, Box 16, Working File.

53. Ibid.

54. Ibid.

55. Ibid. The Molotov statement is published in *Report of Robert H. Jackson, United States Representative to the International Conference on Military Trials, London, 1945* (Washington, D.C., 1949), pp. 13–17. (Hereinafter cited as *Jackson Report*.)

56. Memorandum for the President, JAG draft, 18 January 1945, *Davies Papers*, Container 16.

57. Royall to McCloy, 18 January 1945, *Asst. Sect.*, Box 16, Working File.

58. *Stimson Diary*, vol. 50, 18 January 1945, pp. 53–54.

59. Ibid.

60. *Morgenthau Diary*, vol. II, pp. 890–891.

61. Draft of 19 January and Bernays's memo for record of 20 January are both in *Asst. Sect.*, Box 16, Working File.

62. Draft of 19 January, *Asst. Sect.*, Box 16, Working File.

63. Ibid.

64. Ibid.

65. *Stimson Diary*, vol. 50, 21 January 1945, p. 62.

66. Ibid.

67. Bernays's memos for record, 20 and 21 January 1945, *Asst. Sect.*, Box 16, Working File.

68. Ibid.

69. Ibid.

70. Mr. Kane to Admiral Davidson, 25 January 1945, *RG 165 Personnel*, Box 313.

71. See Bernays's memo for record, 20 January 1945, *Asst. Sect.*, Box 16, Working File. The "Implementing Instrument" and Hackworth's explanations are published in *FRUS, Malta and Yalta*, p. 402f.

72. *Morgenthau Diary*, vol. II, p. 890f; Treasury memorandum, 19 January 1945, *Rosenman Papers*, War Crimes.

73. Treasury memorandum, 19 January 1945, *Rosenman Papers*, War Crimes.

74. Davies to Rosenman, 22 January 1945, *Rosenman Papers*, War Crimes.

75. Ibid.

76. Rosenman to the President, 20–22 January 1945, *Rosenman Papers*, War Crimes.

77. Ibid.

78. *Stimson Diary*, vol. 50, 19 January 1945, pp. 57–58.
79. Ibid.

Chapter 5

1. *Cadogan*, p. 709.
2. See for example Adam B. Ulam, *The Rivals* (New York, 1971) and Vojtech Mastny, *Russia's Road to the Cold War* (New York, 1979).
3. My main quarrel with the 1960s "revisionists" is their inclination to elevate some position papers to the status of general policy statements.
4. For the official American side of Yalta see *FRUS, Malta and Yalta*. The main British records are located in the Public Records Office (Kew) in PREM 3, the FO 371 series and Lord Avon's papers in the FO series.
5. Stettinius to Grew, 22 March 1945, Joseph Grew Papers, MSAM 1687.3, V.7. (2), Harvard University, Cambridge, Massachusetts.
6. Conference record, 17–18 May, 1945, *Morgenthau Diary*, vol. II, pp. 1487–1489.
7. Memorandum, no. 105, 6 March 1945, *Rosenman Papers, War Crimes*.
8. *FRUS, Malta and Yalta*, pp. 850 and 854.
9. Ibid.
10. The British records (in PREM 3, Public Records Office) of the plenary session contain no reference to war-crimes policy.
11. See for example the draft instructions to Ambassador Winant, 1 March 1945, *Illegal and Inhumane Warfare*, 740.00116 EW/4-445.
12. JCS (Joint Chiefs of Staff) 1067/6. A handy collection of the directives to SHAEF and related papers may be found in the W. B. Smith Collection, Box 37, Dwight D. Eisenhower Library, Abilene, Kansas.
13. Copy of an article from *Pravda*, plus circulation list, *Asst. Sect.*, Box 16.
14. Charles Fahy Papers, RG 59, Box 31, Franklin D. Roosevelt Library, Hyde Park, New York.
15. Dubois to Morgenthau, 29 January 1945, *Morgenthau Diary*, vol. II.
16. Royall to McCloy, 21 March 1945, *Asst. Sect.*, Box 16, Working File.
17. Grew to FDR, 2 March 1945, 500.CC/3-245, Diplomatic Branch, National Archives, Washington, D.C.
18. Ibid.
19. McCloy to Dunn, 6 March 1945, *Illegal and Inhumane Warfare*, 740.00116 EW/3-645.
20. Memorandum no. 105, 6 March 1945, *Rosenman Papers, War Crimes*.
21. Halifax to Foreign Office, no. 24, 3 January 1945, CAB 122/1353/8032, Public Records Office, London.
22. The records of the British mission to Washington (CAB 122) are filled with such reports.
23. As quoted by the editor, David Dilks, *Cadogan*, p. 401.
24. Memorandum no. 105, 6 March 1945, *Rosenman Papers, War Crimes*.

25. Grew to FDR, 8 March 1945 (filed as part of State to McCloy, 9 March), *Rosenman Papers, War Crimes.*

26. Ibid.

27. *Foreign Relations of the United States, 1945,* vol. III, (Washington, 1968), pp. 471–73. (Hereinafter cited as *FRUS, 1945.*)

28. Grew-Davies memorandum hassle, 9 March 1945, *Davies Papers,* Container 16. This information suggests that Grew did not send the papers to FDR on 8 March or that he only sent a portion of them.

29. Correspondence signed by Acheson, 17 March 1945, Edward Stettinius Papers, Box 227, "Correspondence Signed" Folder, 11–17 March 1945, University of Virginia.

30. *Asst. Sect.,* Box 16, Jan.–April 1945 File.

31. Ibid.

32. *Jackson Report,* p. 338f.

33. *Rosenman Papers, War Crimes.*

34. Ibid.

35. Ibid. For later developments on this question, see below, p. 236f.

36. 2 April, State Department briefing paper, *Rosenman Papers, War Crimes.*

37. 4 April, *Davies Papers,* Container 16.

38. Draft of an agreement on punishment of war criminals, stamped 26 March 1945, *Rosenman Papers, War Crimes.*

39. Record of 4 April 1945 meeting, *Illegal and Inhumane Warfare,* 740.00116 EW/4-1045.

40. Ibid.

41. Coldstream to Lord Chancellor, 4 April 1945, Lord Chancellor's Office, LCO 2/2981/x/j 7320, Public Record Office, London. (Hereinafter cited as *LCO 2.*)

42. Rosenman to Hackworth, 4 April 1945, no. 3423, *Illegal and Inhumane Warfare,* 740.00116EW/4-445.

43. Stettinius to FDR, 7 April 1945, *Illegal and Inhumane Warfare,* 740.00116 EW/4-745.

44. FDR memo, 6 April 1945, attached to Acheson to Rosenman, 5 April 1945, no. 2625, 740.00116 EW/4-645.

45. Acheson to Rosenman, 5 April 1945, no. 2625, 740.00116 EW/4-645.

46. Ibid.

47. Rosenman notes, 5 April 1945, *Asst. Sect.,* Box 15, Alphabetical File.

48. The two sets of notes are *Illegal and Inhumane Warfare,* 740.00116 EW/4-1045 (American), and *Asst. Sect.,* Box 15, Alphabetical File (British).

49. Ibid.

50. Ibid.

51. Cutter to Coldstream, 9 April 1945, *Asst. Sect.,* Box 15, Alphabetical File.

52. Cutter to Sommers and Enclosures, 7 April 1945, *Asst. Sect.,* Box 15, Alphabetical File.

53. Ibid.

54. Ibid.

55. Ibid.

56. Ibid.

57. Rosenman memorandum, 6 April 1945. *Asst. Sect.*, Box 15, Alphabetical File.

58. Ibid.

59. Notes included in *Illegal and Inhumane Warfare*, 740.00116 EW/4-1045; Rosenman to President Truman, 19 April 1945, *Rosenman Papers, War Crimes*, makes clear that he was at Checkers one weekend, and this seems the most likely choice.

60. Notes of 6 April meeting, *Rosenman Papers, War Crimes*.

61. Ibid.

62. *FRUS, 1945*, pp. 1158–1161.

63. Ibid.

64. Cutter to Sommers, and so on, 7 April 1945, *Asst. Sect.*, Box 15, Alphabetical File.

65. Draft "Implementing Instrument," 10 April 1945, *Asst. Sect.*, Box 15, Alphabetical File.

66. Record of 10 April talks, *Rosenman Papers, War Crimes*. Two British documents on the 10 April meeting are also extant, a Coldstream memorandum of 11 April and undated Somervell minutes. Both are in *LCO* 2.

67. Weir and Cutter to War Department and a Cutter letter to Sommers, both 11 April, as well as Stettinius to Rosenman, 11 April, *Asst. Sect.*, no. 5747, Box 15, Alphabetical File.

68. Ibid.

69. Stimson to Cutter, 12 April 1945, *Illegal and Inhumane Warfare*, no. 67164, 740.00116, EW 4-1045.

70. Ibid.

71. Undated draft, *Asst. Sect.*, Box 16, Working File.

72. Under the cover of Cutter to Rosenman, 22 April 1945, *Rosenman Papers, War Crimes*.

73. W. P. (45) 225, 9 April 1945 (War Cabinet Papers), CAB 66/64, Public Record Office, London; W. M. (45), 29th Conclusions, 12 April 1945 (War Cabinet Minutes), CAB 65/50, Public Record Office, London. (Hereinafter cited as *CAB 65* and *CAB 66*.)

74. W. P. (45) 225, 9 April 1945, *CAB 66/64*.

75. W. M. (45), 29th Conclusions, 12 April 1945, *CAB 65/50*.

76. W. P. (45) 225, 9 April 1945, *CAB 66/64*.

77. W. M. (45), 29th Conclusions, 12 April 1945, *CAB 65/50*.

78. Weir and Cutter to Sommer, 13 April 1945, *Rosenman Papers, War Crimes* no. UKX 33596.

79. Ibid.

80. W. P. (45) 225, 9 April 1945, *CAB 66/64*.

81. Ibid.

82. Anonymous to Somervell, 11 April 1945, *LCO* 2.

83. W. M. (45), 29th Conclusions, 12 April 1945, *CAB 65/50*.

84. Ibid.

85. Ibid.

86. Ibid.

87. Weir and Cutter to Sommers, 13 April 1945, *Rosenman Papers, War Crimes*, no. UKX 33596; and Rosenman to President Truman, 19 April 1945, *Rosenman Papers, War Crimes*.

88. Ibid.

Chapter 6

1. Jackson note in Pauley to Stimson, 17 May 1945, *Asst. Sect.*, Box 16, May thru 1945 File.
2. Bernays to Berry, 13 April 1945, RG 319, Records of the Army Staff, Personnel Subject File, 1943–1947, Trial of the European War Criminals, Sec. 65, Modern Military Branch, National Archives, Washington, D.C.
3. Two sets of notes of 20 April 1945 so indicate. Notes by Colonel Cutter, *Asst. Sect.*, Box 15, S.F. File; and B. M. English to Acting Secretary Grew, 21 April 1945, Joseph Grew Papers, MS AM 1687.3 V.7 (2), Harvard University, Cambridge, Massachusetts.
4. Notes for meeting with Lord Simon, 16 April, *Asst. Sect.*, Box 15, Alphabetical File.
5. Ibid.
6. Notes of meeting, 16 April 1945, Lord Chancellor's rooms, *LCO* 2.
7. Ibid.
8. McCloy to Stimson, 17 April, *Asst. Sect.*, Box 16, Jan.–April 1945 File.
9. Sommers to Weir and Cutter, 17 April 1945, *Asst. Sect.*, no. 4964, Box 16, Jan.–April 1945 File.
10. Ibid.
11. Rosenman to President Truman, 19 April 1945, *Rosenman Papers, War Crimes*.
12. Ibid.
13. Ibid., enclosure.
14. Notes by Colonel Cutter, *Asst. Sect.*, Box 15, S.F. File; and B. M. English to Acting Secretary Grew, 21 April 1945, Joseph Grew Papers, MS AM 1687.3 V.7 (2), Harvard University, Cambridge, Mass.
15. Ibid.
16. Bernays to McCloy and McCloy to Rosenman, 21 April 1945, *Asst. Sect.*, Box 16, Jan.–April 1945 File.
17. "The Argument for Summary Process Against Hitler and Co.," 16 April enclosure, W. P. (45) 281, 3 May 1945, *CAB* 66/64.
18. Ibid.
19. Ibid.
20. Simon to Cadogan, 16 April, *LCO* 2.
21. Ibid.
22. *Cadogan*, p. 683.
23. McCloy to Rosenman, 23 April 1945, *Asst. Sect.*, Box 16, Jan.–April 1945 File, contains the 20 April draft. Rosenman to McCloy, of 23 April 1945, ibid., says that the British had given him the edited version of Simon's paper on 21 April. Since McCloy's draft seems so directly keyed to refuting Simon's arguments, I have concluded he had seen a copy of Simon's paper when he wrote his own memorandum. Obviously this is only an assumption that may be wrong.
24. 20 April draft in McCloy to Rosenman, *Asst. Sect.*, Box 16, Jan.–April 1945 File.
25. Ibid.
26. Ibid.
27. Ibid., and the memorandum of 25 April revised up to 30 April, and

so published by Justice Jackson, *Asst. Sect.*, Box 15, Alphabetical File; and *Jackson Report*, p. 28f.

28. Even Bernays admitted this as early as the third week of May. See below, p. 266.

29. Memo of conference with Under Secretary of War Patterson, 22 April 1945, *RG 165 Personnel*, Box 313.

30. Ibid.

31. Although a significant factor in a number of postwar developments, Anglo-American governmental and press reaction to the liberation of the concentration camps needs systematic study. References to the subject abound in both the British and American records.

32. Holocaust conferences have given considerable attention to questions such as the Allied failure to bomb Auschwitz, but little interest has been shown in trying to understand this failure within the context of the Allied war-making system. This, too, is a subject that cries out for careful study of the psychological processes involved.

33. This includes the work of a professor at Northwestern University, who has already received more publicity than he or the rest of his ilk deserve.

34. Weir to McCloy and McCloy to Weir, 28 April 1945, *Asst. Sect.*, Box 16, Jan.–April 1945 File.

35. Ibid.

36. *Stimson Diary*, vol. 51, 9 May 1945, p. 109.

37. Cutter to McCloy, 24 April 1945; Stimson to McCloy, 26 April 1945; McCloy to deputy chief of staff, 27 April 1945, *Asst. Sect.*, Box 16, Jan.–April 1945 File.

38. *Stimson Diary*, vol. 51, 27–29 April 1945, p. 79.

39. Ibid., 25 April 1945.

40. Ibid.

41. Grew memorandum on conversation with the President, 27 May 1945, 740.00116 EW/4-1045.

42. McCloy to Weir, 28 April 1945, *Asst. Sect.*, Box 16, Jan.–April 1945 File.

43. Ibid.

44. Eugene C. Gerhart, *America's Advocate, Robert H. Jackson* (Indianapolis, Indiana and New York, 1958), pp. 308–310.

45. Ibid.

46. *Stimson Diary*, vol. 51, 1 May 1945, p. 86.

47. *Jackson Report*, p. 21.

48. MacLeish-Grew conversation, 3 May 1945, Joseph Grew Papers, MS Am 1687.3, V.7 (7), Harvard University, Cambridge, Mass.

49. 20 April 1945 draft, *Asst. Sect.*, Box 16, Jan.–April 1945 File.

50. Memorandum, 25 April 1945, *Rosenman Papers, War Crimes*; and memorandum revised up to 30 April, *Asst. Sect.*, Box 15, Alphabetical File.

51. Memorandum, 25 April 1945, *Rosenman Papers, War Crimes*.

52. Ibid.

53. See Chapter 5, p. 185f.

54. Cutter made some additional changes after 10 April, but the major redraft was that of 28 April 1945, *Asst. Sect.*, Box 15, S.F. File.

55. Ibid.

56. Ibid.

57. Jackson's comments on 28 April draft, 1 May 1945, *Asst. Sect.*, Box 15, S.F. File.

58. Ibid.

59. The following three documents, since they contain handwritten re-revisions, show the redrafts and revisions (all dated 2 May): *Bernays Papers*, Box 4, Trial and Punishment File 2, (2 documents, drafts 1 and 2); Papers of Samuel I. Rosenman, San Francisco Conference File, Box 3, Harry S. Truman Library, Independence, Missouri. (Hereinafter cited as *Rosenman Papers, S.F. Conference.*) (One document with handwritten revisions shows drafts 3 and 4.)

60. 2 May draft (1), *Bernays Papers*, Box 4, Trial and Punishment File 2.

61. Ibid.

62. Ibid., draft 2.

63. See Bernays to R. A. Winnacker, 18 August 1949, *Bernays Papers*, Box 1.

64. 2 May draft (1), *Bernays Papers*, Box 4, Trial and Punishment File 2.

65. 2 May draft (4), *Rosenman Papers, S.F. Conference.*

66. 2 May draft (1), *Bernays Papers*, Box 4, Trial and Punishment File 2.

67. 2 May draft (3), *Rosenman Papers, S.F. Conference.*

68. Ibid.

69. 2 May draft (2), *Bernays Papers*, Box 4, Trial and Punishment File 2.

70. Eden to Foreign Office, 2 May 1945, no. 101, attached to W. P. 45/281/3, May 1945, *CAB 66/64.*

71. Cadogan to Foreign Office, 22 April 1945, no. 2794, attached to W. P. 45/28/3, May 1945, *CAB 66*; Halifax to Foreign Office, 24 April Public Record Office, London; and War criminals memorandum, 27 April 1945, no. 2854, *CAB 122/1353/8032* (British Mission, Washington, D.C.), 1945, *LCO 2.*

72. Comment on minutes by Patrick Dean, et al., 27 April 1945, *FO 371/51019/U3319.*

73. Ibid., and war-crimes memorandum, 27 April 1945, *LCO 2.*

74. W. P. 45/281/3, May 1945, *CAB 66.*

75. Ibid.

76. Ibid.

77. Foreign Office to U.K. delegation at San Francisco, 3 May, *FO 371/51019/U3450.*

78. *FRUS*, 1945, pp. 1161–1164.

79. Ibid.

80. W. P. (45) 281, Conclusions annexed, 3 May 1945, *CAB 66.*

81. *FRUS*, 1945, pp. 1161–1164.

82. Ibid.

83. Ibid.

84. Rosenman to President Truman, 3 May 1945, *Rosenman Papers, War Crimes.*

85. Cutter to War Department, 4 May 1945, *Asst. Sect.*, Box 15, S.F. File.

86. Meeting minutes, 5 May 1945, *Asst. Sect.*, Box 15, S.F. File.

87. Ibid.

88. Rosenman to President Truman, 6 May 1945, *Rosenman Papers, S.F. Conference.*

89. Malkin recommendations and Cutter notes of 8 May 1945, *Asst.*

Sect., Box 15, S.F. File; Rosenman letters to Malkin, Golunsky, and Basde-vant, 10 May 1945, *Rosenman Papers*, *War Crimes*.

90. Revisions of 8 May executive agreement, *Rosenman Papers*, *War Crimes*.

91. Ibid. There are actually a half dozen redrafts in this file, but the important changes quoted in the text originate in two drafts.

92. McCloy-Clay cable exchanges, 9–14 May 1945, *Rosenman Papers*, *War Crimes*.

93. JCS 332, 15 May 1945 draft, *Illegal and Inhumane Warfare*, 740.00116 EW/4-445.

94. Treasury meeting, 14 May 1945, *Morgenthau Diary*, vol. II, p. 1485.

95. Ibid.

96. Stimson summary, 16 May 1945, Henry L. Stimson Papers, Box 148, Yale University, New Haven, Connecticut.

97. Jackson note in Pauley to Stimson, 17 May 1945, *Asst. Sect.*, Box 16, May thru 1945 File.

98. Ibid.; and Pauley-Morgenthau, 17–18 May 1945, *Morgenthau Diary*, vol. II, pp. 1487–89.

99. Jackson-Treasury conference, 18 May 1945, *Morgenthau Diary*, vol. II, pp. 1493–1513.

100. Ibid.

101. Ibid.

102. Ibid.

103. Ibid.

104. Ibid.

105. Jackson's introduction to Whitney R. Harris, *Tyranny on Trial* (Dallas, 1954), p. xxxxiii.

106. Memorandum on "mission," 22 May 1945, *Morgenthau Diary*, vol. II, pp. 1518–19. (The memorandum does not specifically say the "mission" was performed by Morgenthau himself, but the tone and language of the document indicate this.)

107. Bernays to Donovan, 5 May 1945, *Asst. Sect.*, Box 16, May thru 1945 File; Jackson to Donovan, 7 June 1945 (re IPOG 10), RG 218, CCS 000.5, War Crimes, Sec. 4, Box 3, Modern Military Branch, National Ar-chives, Washington, D.C.

108. Bernays memorandum for chief of counsel, 9 May 1945, *Asst. Sect.*, Box 16, May thru 1945 File.

109. Planning memorandum draft, 13 May 1945, *Asst. Sect.*, Box 16, May thru 1945 File; final version, 17 May 1945, RG 238, Office of the Chief of Counsel for the Prosecution of Axis Criminality, Modern Military Branch, National Archives, Washington, D.C.

110. Ibid.

111. Ibid.

112. Memorandum on trial preparation, 16 May 1945, RG 238, Office of the Chief of Counsel for the Prosecution of Axis Criminality, Box 33, Modern Military Branch, National Archives, Washington, D.C.

113. Ibid.

114. *Reaching Judgment*, p. 84.

115. Ibid., p. 53.

116. Cramer to McCloy, c. 5 May, *Asst. Sect.*, Box 16, May thru 1945 File.

117. Lieutenant Colonel Byrne A. Bowman, JAG to General Weir, 6 May 1945, *Asst. Sect.*, Box 16, May thru 1945 File.

118. Two sets of notes on this meeting are extant: 30 May memo by Lieutenant John R. Clagett (JAG), *JAG*, Box 1603, File 103-1, Bk. 4; and memo by unidentified author, 21 May 1945, *JAG*, Box 1602, File 103-1, Bk. 1.

119. Ibid.

120. Ibid.

121. Jackson-Treasury conference, 18 May 1945, *Morgenthau Diary*, vol. II, pp. 1493–1513.

122. In a spring 1975 interview with the author, a close associate of Justice Jackson during the trial planning made this comment, but he asked not to be identified. Another associate, who worked with the Justice through the whole trial, made a similar remark in an interview of the same period. Even discounting the personal note of bitterness, the same tendency appears in the *Bernays Papers*.

123. *Reaching Judgment*, p. 53.

124. Draft 2, 16 May 1945, *Asst. Sect.*, Box 15, S.F. File.

125. Comments on draft 2, 19 May 1945, *Asst. Sect.*, Box 15, S.F. File.

126. Ibid.

127. Draft 3, *Rosenman Papers*, *S.F. Conference*; draft 4, showing the changes from 3 to 4 in Bernays's hand (*Bernays Papers*, Box 4, Trial and Punishment File 2) is paralleled by one showing them in Cutter's hand (presumably), *Asst. Sect.*, Box 15, S.F. File. A Cutter note to Rosenman, 24 May 1945, *Rosenman Papers*, *War Crimes*, attached to a third copy of draft 4, explains who did the revision.

128. *Reaching Judgment*, p. 303.

129. See materials cited in note 127.

130. Ibid.

131. Ibid.

132. *Reaching Judgment*, p. 44f.

Chapter 7

1. *Reaching Judgment*, p. 302.

2. Jackson to the President, printed in Eugene C. Gerhart, *America's Advocate, Robert H. Jackson* (Indianapolis, Indiana and New York, 1958), pp. 308–10.

3. *Reaching Judgment*, p. 156f.

4. Telford Taylor memorandum, *RG 165 Personnel*, Box 314.

5. Alderman to Jackson, 11 July 1945, *Bernays Papers*, Box 2, Preparation of Evidence File.

6. The revival of interest in the distinction between just and unjust wars seems to point in this direction. See Michael Walzer, *Just and Unjust Wars* (New York, 1977) and Inis L. Claude, Jr., "Just Wars: Doctrines and Institutions," *Political Science Quarterly*, vol. XCV, no. 1 (Spring 1980), pp. 83–96.

7. J. Blotner, ed., *Selected Letters of William Faulkner* (New York, 1977), p. 186.

8.   This is, quite frankly, a fluffed note. I can see the quote, and perhaps hear it, which makes me feel it was part of a symposium. But I can't *find* it.

9.   I am indebted to Professor Charles Burdick for pointing out this remark of Montaigne's.

10.   Comments to this effect begin to show up in November 1945. See, for example, Major Elwyn Jones's comments on the first American briefs, 16 November 1945, *FO* 371/50993/U8874. Lord Shawcross later generalized this view in a letter to the author (1975) and in "Robert H. Jackson's Contributions During the Nuremberg Trial," *The Record of the Association of the Bar of the City of New York*, vol. XXIII, no. 6 (June 1968), p. 398.

11.   As quoted in Alistar Horne, *The Price of Glory* (London, 1964).

BIBLIOGRAPHY

The following bibliography is limited to works cited in the text. For a comprehensive recent bibliography of published works see John R. Lewis, *Uncertain Judgment, A Bibliography of War Crimes Trials* (Santa Barbara, Calif., 1979).

Archives and Manuscript Collections

UNITED STATES

A. National Archives, Washington, D.C.
    1. Diplomatic Branch
        740.00116 EW (General European War Files)
        740.00116 Illegal and Inhumane Warfare
        500.CC/ (Control Council)
        RG 59, Records of Harley A. Notter
    2. Modern Military Branch
        RG 107, Secretary of War, 000.5, War Crimes
        RG 107, Assistant Secretary of War, 000.5, War Crimes
        RG 218, Records of the Combined Chiefs of Staff
        RG 238, Office of the Chief of Counsel for the Prosecution of Axis Criminality
        RG 319, Records of the Army Staff, Personnel Subject File
B. Federal Record Center, Suitland, Maryland
        RG 153, JAG (Judge Advocate General)
        RG 165, Personnel G-1
C. Dwight D. Eisenhower Library, Abilene, Kansas
        General of the Army Files
        Walter Bedell Smith Collection of World War II Documents
D. Franklin D. Roosevelt Library, Hyde Park, New York
        RG 24, Harry Hopkins Papers
        RG 59, Charles Fahy Papers
        Diaries of Henry Morgenthau, Jr.
        President's Secretary's File
E. Harry S. Truman Library, Independence, Missouri
        Papers of Samuel I. Rosenman
F. Library of Congress, Washington, D.C.
        Joseph E. Davies Papers
        Cordell Hull Papers
G. United States Justice Department, Washington, D.C.
        War Crimes Files
H. Harvard University, Cambridge, Massachusetts
        Joseph Grew Papers

I. University of Virginia
        Papers of Edward Stettinius
J. University of Wyoming
        Papers of Murray C. Bernays
K. Yale University
        Diary of Henry L. Stimson, Roll 9
        Papers of Henry L. Stimson, Rolls 110–111

GREAT BRITAIN

A. Public Record Office, London
        FO 371, Foreign Office General Correspondence
        CAB 21, War Cabinet Committee on War Crimes
        CAB 65, W. M. (War Cabinet Minutes)
        CAB 66, W. P. (War Cabinet Papers)
        CAB 122, British Mission, Washington, D.C.
        LCO 2/2981/x/j 7320 (Lord Chancellor's Office)
        PREM 3, (Prime Minister Files)

Letter

Lord Shawcross to the author, 1 April 1975

Interviews

William Chanler, May 1975
Judge A. Cutter, May 1975
Sir Patrick Dean, March 1975
James Rowe, May 1975
Francis Shea, May 1975
Telford Taylor, May 1975
Herbert Wechsler, May 1975

Published Documents

Blum, John Morton, ed. *From the Morgenthau Diaries*, 3 vols. Boston, 1967.
Complete Presidential Press Conferences of Franklin D. Roosevelt, vol. XXIV. New York, 1972.
Dilks, David, ed. *The Diaries of Sir Alexander Cadogan, 1938–1945.* London, 1971.
Foreign Relations of the United States, 1943, vol. III. Washington, D.C., 1963.
Foreign Relations of the United States, 1944, vol. I. Washington, D.C., 1966.

Foreign Relations of the United States, The Conference at Quebec, 1944. Washington, D.C., 1972.
Foreign Relations of the United States, 1945, vol. III. Washington, D.C., 1968.
Foreign Relations of the United States, Conferences at Malta and Yalta, 1945. Washington, D.C., 1955.
Handbook on German Military Forces (TM-30-450). Washington, D.C., 1941.
The Morgenthau Diary (Germany), 2 vols. Washington, D.C., 1967.
Nazi Conspiracy and Aggression, 12 vols. Washington, D.C., 1946–47.
Report of Robert H. Jackson, United States Representative to the International Conference on Military Trials, London 1945. Washington, D.C., 1949.
Trial of the Major War Criminals Before the International Military Tribunal, 42 vols. Nuremberg, Germany, 1947.

Books

Biddle, Francis. *In Brief Authority.* New York, 1962.
Bishop, Jim. *FDR's Last Year.* New York, 1974.
Blum, John Morton. *V was for Victory.* New York, 1976.
Churchill, Winston S. *Triumph and Tragedy.* Boston, 1953.
Dallek, Robert. *Franklin D. Roosevelt and American Foreign Policy, 1932–1945.* New York, 1979.
Eisenhower, Dwight D. *Crusade in Europe.* Garden City, New York, 1949.
Feingold, Henry L. *The Politics of Rescue.* New Brunswick, New Jersey, 1970.
Gerhart, Eugene C. *America's Advocate, Robert H. Jackson.* Indianapolis, Indiana and New York, 1958.
Gimbel, John. *The American Occupation of Germany.* Stanford, Calif., 1968.
Harris, R. Whitney. *Tyranny on Trial.* Dallas, 1954.
Kimball, Warren F. *Swords or Plough Shares.* Philadelphia/New York, 1976.
Leahy, William D. *I Was There.* New York, 1950.
Lewis, John R. *Uncertain Judgment, A Bibliography of War Crimes Trials.* Santa Barbara, Calif., 1979.
Maser, Werner. *Nürnberg, Tribunal der Sieger.* Düsseldorf, 1977.
Mastny, Vojtech. *Russia's Road to the Cold War.* New York, 1979.
Moran, Lord. *Churchill, Taken from the Diaries of Lord Moran: The Struggle for Survival.* Boston, 1966.
Pogue, Forrest C. *George C. Marshall,* 3 vols. New York, 1963–73.
Roosevelt, Elliot. *As He Saw It.* New York, 1946.
Rosenman, Samuel I. *Working with Roosevelt.* New York, 1952.
Smith, Bradley F. *Reaching Judgment at Nuremberg.* New York, 1977.
Smith, Bradley F., and Agarossi, Elena. *Operation Sunrise: The Secret Surrender.* New York, 1979.
Stimson, Henry L., and Bundy, McGeorge. *On Active Service in Peace and War.* New York, 1947.
Ulam, Adam B. *The Rivals.* New York, 1971.
Walzer, Michael. *Just and Unjust Wars.* New York, 1977.
Weingartner, James J. *Crossroads of Death.* Berkeley, Calif., and Los Angeles, 1979.

Periodicals

Inis, L. Claude, Jr. "Just Wars: Doctrines and Institutions." *Political Science Quarterly*, vol. XCV, no. 1 (Spring 1980), pp. 83–96.
Lord Shawcross. "Robert H. Jackson's Contributions During the Nuremberg Trial." *The Record of the Association of the Bar of the City of New York*, vol. XXIII, no. 6 (June 1968), p. 398.

Newspaper

The New York Post

INDEX

Acheson, Dean, 20, 164–65, 171–72
Afghanistan: Soviet occupation of, 253
Alderman, Sidney, 196, 242
Allied powers: conflicts among, 9–10, 34, 49, 61, 63–64, 67, 68, 110, 152–53, 157–59, 162–89, 193–95, 213, 229, 230, 244, 245, 259; postwar planning, 13, 22–23, 152–53; war crimes policy, 9, 10, 134; in World War II, 7–19, 54, 152–53; see also individual countries and leaders
Allied Reparations Commission, 227
American Jewish Conference, 9, 35, 43, 57, 64–65, 72, 258
American Rules of Land Warfare, 58
anti-Semitism, 31, 41, 77, 276n25; see also Jews; Nazi party; SS
Ardennes, 116, 118; see also Malmédy massacre
Armstrong, Hamilton Fish, 41
Arnhem, 54
Arutyunian, A. A., 222
atomic bomb, 115, 121n, 257
Auschwitz, 41, 115, 204, 282n32
Axis powers, see Germany; Italy; Japan

Barnes, Thomas, 169–70, 172, 181, 192
Battle of the Bulge, 114, 115, 116, 153
Belgium, 27, 140; see also specific battles

Belsen, 201, 203, 205
Bernays, Murray C., 50–51, 61–62, 99–100, 106, 108, 131, 138, 142, 167, 190, 207, 209–10, 213, 236, 239, 246, 253, 254, 257, 270n23, 270n24, 272n55; on aggressive war, 84, 98, 123, 125, 128, 129, 135, 143, 144–45, 174, 177, 276-n28; conspiracy/criminal-organization plan, 51–53, 56–57, 59–60, 61–62, 65, 67, 69–70, 71, 73, 79, 81, 84, 94, 108, 113, 116, 117, 118, 119, 120, 121, 122, 125, 126–27, 132, 136, 142–43, 145, 159–61, 162, 165, 166, 168, 169, 170, 175, 184–85, 195, 196, 199–200, 210, 227, 230, 238, 243–44, 245, 249, 250, 251, 252, 255–56, 258–59, 276n28; legal position papers, 51–53, 56–57, 59–60, 61, 65, 72–85, 86, 98, 123–28, 132; personality, 65–66, 70, 99–100, 105, 107, 112, 128–29, 133, 147; secondary trials plan, 83, 84, 85, 210–11; treaty court issue, 72, 85, 86, 122, 128–29, 135, 143, 145; see also "three Secretaries' memorandum"
Bernstein, Bernard, 21
Berry, R. W., 68, 69
Bidault, Georges, 222
Biddle, Francis, 86, 109, 110, 111–12, 117, 126, 136, 138, 144, 181, 182, 254; "three Secretaries' memorandum," 146, 146n, 147, 148, 150, 151, 156, 159, 162, 164, 167, 168, 169, 175, 193, 195, 197, 200, 209, 257

Big Four, *see* Allied powers; France; Great Britain; Soviet Union; United States

Big Three, *see* Allied powers; Great Britain; Soviet Union; United States

Bill of Attainder proposal, 187

Birkenau, 53

blacks: radical Right perception of, 77

Bohlen, Charles P. "Chip," 155, 158

Borchard, Edwin, 106

Bormann, Martin, 216, 217

Bowman, Byrne, 236–37

Bowman, Isaiah, 41

British Ministry of War Transport, 63

"Budapest Resolutions," 96, 106

Byrnes, James F., 37, 155, 268n67

Cadogan, Alexander, 75, 152, 198, 218, 221, 223

Cambodian crisis, 253

Chanler, William C., 93–99, 101, 102, 103, 105–7, 128, 131, 149, 215, 246, 254, 274n58, 276n25; "Can Hitler and the Nazi leadership be punished for their Acts of Lawless Aggression. . . ?," 95–96

China, Nationalist, 5, 154, 157

Churchill, Winston S., 13, 23, 34, 45–47, 88, 170, 178, 187, 201, 220, 254, 271–72n45; at Moscow Conference, 64; at Quebec Conference, 8, 24, 43–44, 51, 157, 175; at Yalta Conference, 118, 152, 153, 156, 157, 158, 159, 175

Clay, Lucius, 227

Clayton, William L., 157

Coldstream, G. P., 170, 171, 172, 178, 192

Cold War, 154, 229, 244, 248–49

Communists, 20, 276n25; German atrocities against, 18, 244; radical Right perception of, 77; *see also* Soviet Union

concentration camps, 26, 52–53, 161; Allied liberation of, 8, 202–5, 282n31; Allied reaction to, 203–4; congressional investigation of, 205–6; *see also* individual camps

conspiracy/criminal-organization issue, *see* Bernays, Murray C.

Control Council for Germany, 180

Coolidge, Calvin, 29

Cramer, Myron C., 33, 56, 68, 82–83, 84, 85, 100, 103, 121, 122, 128, 140–41, 236

Cripps, Stafford, 187

Crowley, Leo, 228

Cutter, R. Ammi, 56–57, 59, 66, 67, 68, 72, 79, 83–84, 85, 87, 99, 121, 125, 133, 135–36, 166, 167–69, 174, 175, 177, 178, 179, 180, 181–82, 185, 195, 196, 200, 216, 217, 224, 240, 242, 245, 276–77n45; "Memorandum of Proposals for the Prosecution and Punishment of Certain War Criminals and Other Offenders, A," 210–15, 216–17

Czechoslovakia, 96–97

Dachau, 201, 203, 205

Davies, Joseph E., 91, 108, 110, 121, 134, 136, 137, 138–40, 142, 145, 146, 147, 156, 160, 164–65, 168–69; access to FDR, 87, 88, 90, 129–30, 131–32, 149–50, 161–62, 164; accuracy and reliability questioned, 88–90, 118, 130–31; energy of, 88, 131, 133; *Mission to Moscow*, 88; pro-Soviet bias of, 88, 131–32

Dean, Patrick, 172, 181

de Gaulle, Charles, 190, 196
Democratic party, 88, 98; *see also*
    individual leaders
Donovan, William, 232; "Problems
    Concerning War Criminals," 58;
    see also Office of Strategic Ser-
    vices
Dorr, G. Harrison, 101–2, 103, 106
Dumbarton Oaks Conference, 63,
    76, 270*n*24

Eden, Anthony, 45, 64, 170, 178,
    196, 218, 219, 220, 221–22
Egleton, Clyde, 106
Eichmann, Adolf, 53, 248
Eisenhower, Dwight D., 14, 16, 19,
    44, 56, 159; *Crusade in Europe*,
    21; German policy, 21, 29, 40
Endlösung (Final Solution), 94–95;
    see also Germany; Hitler, Adolf;
    Jews; Nazi party; SS
English, B. M., 196
Erasmus, 256
European Advisory Commission, 13,
    63, 69
extermination camps, 204–5; *see*
    also Concentration camps

Faulkner, William, 255
Finlay, William, 170
forced labor, 166–67, 227–30, 231,
    250
Foreign Policy Association, 41
Forrestal, James, 30, 65, 72, 80,
    109, 147–48, 156
"Fortress America" concept, 154;
    see also Pax Americana
Four Freedoms, 154
France, 10, 15, 42, 154; confusion
    on conspiracy concept, 52; Nu-
    remberg role, 4, 133–34, 135, 148,
    165, 169, 171, 172, 173, 174,

179, 190, 192, 196, 221, 222,
    223, 224, 226, 240, 242, 244,
    245, 246, 248, 250
Frankfurter, Felix, 41, 44, 49, 50,
    54
Freeman, Alwyn Vernon, 103–6;
    "Is the Preparation and Launch
    ing of the Present War a Crime?,"
    103–6, 123

Gallup Poll, 229
Geneva Conventions, 101, 123–24,
    187–88, 201, 231
German Army, 14, 15, 17; *see also*
    SS; Wehrmacht
German Army High Command, 249
Germany: after World War I, 260;
    postwar (World War II) courts,
    250
Germany (Nazi): Allied invasion
    and occupation of, 11, 12–13, 15,
    16–19, 29, 31, 44, 55, 56, 105,
    257, 261; collective guilt of, 27,
    43, 51, 248; forced labor sug-
    gested, 166–67, 227–28, 229–30,
    231; in World War II, 10, 15,
    27, 153, 251–52; *see also* Con-
    centration camps; Nazi party; SS;
    specific battles
Germany (West), 268*n*67
Gestapo, 17, 32, 37, 51, 53, 65, 176,
    211; conspiracy/criminal-organi-
    zation charges against, 51–52, 57,
    184–85, 249–50; forced labor sug-
    gested for, 227–28, 229–30, 231;
    POW treatment by, 50; *see also*
    Nazi party
Gluck, Sheldon, 274*n*58
Goebbels, Joseph, 54, 179, 197, 217,
    237
Göring, Hermann, 3, 179, 219
Golunski, S. A., 222, 223
Grand Alliance, 3, 13; *see also* Al-
    lied powers; individual members

Great Britain: aides-mémoires to United States, 18, 20, 66–67, 68, 69, 73, 81, 134–35, 141, 265–66n8; Dominions, 10; Foreign Office, 46, 61, 64, 66, 69, 150, 198; legal systems and arguments, 45–46, 52, 58, 66–67, 68, 69, 70, 126, 133, 134, 150, 179, 180, 212, 217, 245, 265–66n8, 271–72n45; manuscript collections, 7; in Nuremberg planning, 162–89, 200, 220–21, 222, 226, 232, 246, 259; political gamesmanship of, 9, 10–11; postwar planning, 37, 43–44, 45, 47, 250; public opinion in, 10, 11, 202, 203, 204, 251, 252; United States aid to, 29, 45, 96; war crimes policy of, 18, 19, 34, 45–46, 47, 64, 66–67, 68, 69, 70, 134–35, 141, 144, 150, 162–89, 193–95, 217, 259, 265–66n8; in World War II, 54, 153, 157, 161; *see also* Allied powers; Churchill, Winston S.; Halifax (Lord); Simon, John A.

Grew, Joseph, 89, 161–62, 164–65, 207, 279n28

Gromyko, Andrei, 63

Gypsies: Nazi extermination of, 234

Hackworth, Green H., 19, 57, 69, 73, 80–82, 83, 85, 86, 108–9, 119, 125, 128–29, 133, 134–35, 136, 138, 145, 147, 148, 162, 163, 164, 166, 167, 215, 222, 240, 245–46, 254; criticism of Bernays draft by, 81–82, 84–85

Hague conventions, 4, 187–88; Hague III (declaration of war), 124, 140; Hague IV (*Rules of Land Warfare*), 123–24, 241–42, 243

Halifax (Viscount), 60–61, 76, 116, 162–63, 218, 271n35

Handy, Thomas T., 100

Harriman, Averell, 62, 155, 220, 228

Harrison, George L., 121, 121n

Harvard Law School, 132

Henry, Stephen G., 51, 68

Herodotus, 261

Hilldring, John H., 23, 34, 40

Himmler, Heinrich, 28, 46, 179, 202

Hiss, Alger, 155

Hitler, Adolf, 5, 16, 17, 19, 22, 32, 45, 46, 57, 64, 76, 78, 94, 96, 97, 101, 102, 115, 120, 129, 130, 153, 173–74, 175, 176, 186, 187, 188, 190, 197, 204, 233, 234, 239, 249, 251, 252, 258, 260; generals' plot on life of, 15, 28; suicide of, 8, 217, 219, 220, 222

Hitler Youth, 23

Hodges, Courtney, 8

Holland, *see* Netherlands

Holocaust, 202, 282n32; *see also* Jews; specific concentration camps

Hoover, Herbert, 29

Hopkins, Harry L., 5, 23, 25, 30, 36, 37, 38, 62, 86, 87, 118, 155, 156, 257, 268n62

House Foreign Affairs Committee, 96

Hull, Cordell, 19, 23, 24, 26, 30, 35, 36, 39, 40–41, 43, 44, 49, 55, 65, 72, 90–91, 157, 267n52, 270n15

Hyde, Charles C., 106

"Implementing Instrument," 148, 151, 168, 169, 177–78, 180, 200, 211

international law, 103, 123; absentia trials, 216–17, 244–45; accessories, 110; aggressive war charges, *see* Bernays, Murray C., Nazi party; arraignment proposals, 173–74, 175, 177, 179, 180–82, 183,

186–87, 188, 194, 196, 217; belligerent rights and status, 18, 96–97, 101, 103, 124, 241; burden of proof, 59; civil courts, 51, 165; civil liberties, 52; common law in, 165; conspiracy/criminal-organization charges, 91–92, 104; *see also* Bernays, Murray C., Nazi party; court "masters," 165, 167; due process, 34, 42, 150; evidence, 56, 71, 83, 166, 179, 233, 235, 239, 240, 249; ex post facto law, 18, 133, 168; extradition procedures, 19, 97; genocide, *see* Concentration camps, Jews, Nazi party; growth and flexibility of, 123, 130; hostages, execution of, 100; innovation in, 102, 106–7, 110, 130, 142, 145, 160, 169, 213–14, 225; international tribunals, 51, 68, 145; judicial independence, 179; judicial proceedings in, 102, 178, 179, 182, 186–87, 193, 210, 212, 218–19, 220, 223; military courts and tribunals, 51, 56, 130, 133–34, 197, 209; mixed military courts and tribunals, 66, 68, 73, 163, 173, 184–85, 193–94; neutrals' rights in, 96, 124; political asylum in, 19; presumption of guilt in, 52; right of appeal in, 56, 148, 149, 217; right to counsel in, 34, 148, 149, 217; right to counsel vs. political execution in, 45–46, 47, 54, 173–74, 182, 186, 190–91, 197–99, 200–201, 209; right to trial in, 37, 41, 54, 148, 149, 175–77, 178, 179, 217, 219; rules of war in, 18, 51, 58, 140, 214, 221; secondary proceedings in, 83, 84, 85, 122, 210–11, 250; self-incrimination in, 235; sentencing in, 56, 64, 149; state trials in, 57, 188; summary executions in, 33–34, 37, 47, 48, 60, 63, 76, 137, 186,

190–91, 193, 218–19, 220; treaty courts in, 72, 73, 81–82, 84, 85, 86, 122, 127, 128–29, 133–34, 135, 140–41, 143, 145–46, 188; trial plans and proceedings in, 37, 57, 58–59, 64, 98–99, 165, 197–99, 213, 215–16, 219, 221–22, 224, 225–26, 240, 247–48; war crimes, traditional and technical vs. extension of definition, 18, 19, 50–51, 56, 57, 59, 66, 67, 68, 69–70, 72, 91–92, 100–101, 140, 143, 238; *see also* Geneva Conventions; Gestapo; Hague Conventions; Kellogg-Briand Pact; Nazi party; SS; United Nations; individual leaders' and countries' war crimes policies
International Law Association, 96
International Legal System, 106
International Military Tribunal, 3
Irving, David, 251
isolationism, 29–30, 98, 252, 260
Italy, 5; Allied occupation of, 14–15; war crimes, 140, 141

Jackson, Robert H., 87, 145, 157, 165, 190, 196, 208–10, 212–13, 214, 216, 217–18, 221, 227, 228–30, 231–34, 236, 239–40, 242, 245, 246, 248, 253, 254, 276–77*n*45, 285*n*122, 286*n*10; administrative problems of, 238–39; Nazi aggression emphasized by, 215, 233–34, 243, 246
Japan, 5, 153; Manchurian invasion by, 93; war-crimes trials, 5
Jehovah's Witnesses: German atrocities against, 18
Jessup, Philip, 106
Jews: Allied war-crimes policy blamed on, 276*n*25; American "assimilationist," 22, 41; German atrocities against, 18, 35, 36, 42–

Jews *(continued)*
    43, 53–54, 56, 94–95, 173, 174,
    206, 234, 258; nationality of, as
    issue, 35; radical Right percep-
    tion of, 77
Jodl, Alfred, 224
Jones, Elwyn, 286n10

Kane, R. Keith, 80
Kaplan, Benjamin, 242
Kellogg, Frank, 98
Kellogg-Briand Pact, 70, 95–96, 98,
    107, 124; on lawful belligerency,
    101, 104, 106, 174, 274n58; Nazi
    violations of, 120, 128, 174, 213,
    215, 243; resolutions, 123
Kennan, George F., 3, 89
Keynes, John Maynard, 76
King, Archibald, 57–58
Knox, Frank, 29, 30

Lauterpacht, Hersch, 123, 276n25
Law, Richard, 219
League of Nations, 123; on aggres-
    sive war, 103; resolutions, 4
lend-lease, 45, 96, 269n100; *see also*
    Great Britain
London Charter, 4, 199, 242, 246,
    258
"Lublin mass murder," 33, 54

McCarthy, Joseph, 20
McCloy, John J., 23–24, 25, 32, 34,
    40, 53–54, 58, 60, 62, 73, 85,
    88, 101, 105, 156, 179–80, 234,
    254, 256, 281n23; personality,
    68–70, 97, 109, 128, 191; preju-
    dice of, 191; tactical problems
    and errors of, 86, 99, 100, 103,

107, 109–10, 121–22; war crimes
    policy of, 54, 56, 59, 66, 68–71,
    79–80, 82, 85–86, 87, 91–92, 93,
    94, 95, 100, 102, 107, 108, 110,
    112, 114, 121–23, 125, 128, 129,
    135, 136, 138, 142, 145, 147,
    162, 190–93, 195–96, 197, 198–
    200, 207, 208, 209–10, 225, 230,
    231, 236, 239, 245
Maidanek, 10, 33, 41, 54
Malkin, William, 169–70, 171, 172,
    178, 181, 221, 222
Malmédy massacre, 113, 114–18,
    125, 126, 237, 255, 257, 258
Manchuria: crisis of 1931, 29, 93;
    Soviet privileges in, 157
Manual of Military Law (British),
    58
Marshall, George C., 30, 32, 33, 38,
    41, 62, 94
Matthews, H. Freeman, 155
Molotov, Vyacheslav, 63, 141–42,
    221, 222
Montaigne, Michel de, 259
Moran (Lord), 152
Morgan, Edmund M., 132–33
Morgenthau, Henry, Jr., 30, 40, 43,
    44–45, 54, 62, 90, 114, 137, 143–
    44, 156, 157, 227, 238, 254, 256,
    258; deindustrialization policy of,
    20, 21, 24, 25–26, 28–29, 31, 35,
    36, 38, 41, 42, 271n27; person-
    ality, 22, 23, 26, 31–32; resigna-
    tion of, 232; war crimes policy of,
    20–28, 31, 34, 39–42, 54–55,
    102, 109, 146, 149, 230–31, 232
Morgenthau plan, 28–29, 36–37,
    38, 42, 43, 44–45, 46, 48–50, 55,
    56, 63, 77, 137, 151, 199, 228,
    249, 261n, 269n100; criticism of,
    38, 44–45, 49, 54–55; ethical
    merit of, 38
Moscow Conference, Moscow Dec-
    laration, 10, 46, 221, 267n52
Murphy, Robert, 37, 268n67
Mussolini, Benito, 179, 219, 220

Napoleon, 3, 45, 173
"Nazi Flying Corps," 17
Nazi party (NSDAP), members, 17,
32, 33, 36, 42, 63, 93, 110, 138,
141, 142, 150; absentia trials of,
244; "accessorial liability" of, 214;
aggressive war charges against, 91,
92, 93, 99, 102, 103–4, 107, 110,
120, 124–25, 130, 143, 144–45,
177, 180, 185, 199, 212, 215,
224, 233, 234, 236, 237, 243,
246, 252, 253; Allied and Axis
laws violated by, 215, 225; antitrust parallels to, 75–76, 230;
atrocities committed by, 94, 98,
105, 108, 110, 126, 130, 140,
144, 161, 165–66, 170, 176, 178,
180, 191, 199, 201, 202, 203–5,
221, 258, 265–66n8; burden of
proof issues, 226, 245; "common
enterprise" prosecution of, 181,
184–85, 206, 210, 233, 243,
244; Communists persecuted by,
244; complexity of, 234; conspir-
acy/criminal-organization charges
against, 62, 63, 69, 72, 75, 83–
84, 104–5, 109, 111, 112, 117,
118, 120, 125, 126–27, 130, 132–
33, 134, 140, 143, 144, 151, 161,
166, 172, 175–76, 188, 196, 205,
208, 210, 211, 215, 216, 219–20,
221, 224–25, 230, 233, 236, 237,
242, 243–44, 245, 249, 250, 252–
53, 254, 255–56, 258–59, 260;
crimes against German and Axis
nationals, 110, 126, 132–33, 139,
161, 170, 173, 185, 215, 217,
233, 244; crimes against humanity, 236, 253; crimes against Jews,
173, 174, 180; *see also* Nazi party:
atrocities; crimes against German
and Axis nationals; crimes against
minorities, 180, 221, 227; criminal liability of superiors, 170;
expropriations by, 233; forced
labor suggested for, 166–67, 227–
30, 231, 250; group-detention
provisions for, 36, 159; international law violated by, 191; interrogation of, 235; leaders of, 191,
193, 196, 197, 207, 208, 209,
210, 211, 214, 215, 218, 219,
220, 221, 224, 248, 249, 265–
66n8; Leadership Corps, 249–50;
legal defense of war crimes, 105;
major crimes committed by, 170,
172, 173, 174, 176, 178, 179,
182, 183, 186, 187, 188, 190;
mass trial suggested for, 221;
membership as proof of guilt of
war crimes, 178, 184–85, 216,
230–31, 249; neo-Nazi revival,
205; neutral rights attacked by,
251; POW treatment and reprisals by, 160, 161, 176, 201, 224,
237; prewar crimes and atrocities
committed by, 170, 172, 173,
176, 185, 199, 213, 215, 224,
225, 258; processing of, 218, 219;
revival feared, 221; rules of war
violated by, 140, 145, 176, 213,
221; summary execution proposed
for, 34, 45–46, 47, 63, 64, 76,
102, 150, 171, 173, 175, 176,
187, 192, 193, 197–98, 218, 219,
222, 271–72n45; superior orders
as defense by, 216, 244; traditional war crimes of, 236; treaty
violations by, 243; Yalta discussion of, 158–60, 162, 163, 171,
175; *see also* Gestapo; Hitler,
Adolf; SA; SD; SS
neo-Nazis, 205, 221
Netherlands, 27, 130, 140; government of, in exile, 9, 10; in World
War II, 54
Normandy invasion, 5, 14
Norway, 140; government of, in
exile, 9, 10
Nuremberg system and trial, 3–5,
18, 33, 51–52, 112, 146, 211,
234–53; development of, 7–8,

Nuremberg system and trial *(cont.)*
   166, 199–200; judicial vs. political
   procedures in, 33–34, 178, 179,
   182, 186–87, 193, 210; success
   of, 242–43, 247–48, 254; *see also*
   Nazi party; Summary execution;
   specific countries, leaders, issues

Office of Strategic Services (OSS),
   58, 232, 235–36, 271n27; *see
   also* Donovan, William
"Office of the Chief Counsel for
   the Prosecution of Axis Criminality," 227
OGPU, 61, 62
Okinawa invasion, 5
OSS, *see* Office of Strategic Services

Pacific theater of war, 118, 152, 153
Pact of Paris, *see* Kellogg-Briand
   Pact
Pan American Conference, 103–4,
   123
Papen, Franz von, 233, 248
Parliament, 187; *see also* Great
   Britain
Patterson, Robert, 201
Pauley, Edward W., 227–29, 231
pax Americana, 97–98, 251, 256–
   57, 259; *see also* United States:
   postwar policy
Pearl Harbor, 29
Pearson, Drew, 270n15
Pehle, John W., 35, 51
Peiper (*Obersturmbannführer*), 117
Pell, Herbert, 19, 91, 92, 119–20,
   161
Poland, 96–97, 118, 153, 250; con
   centration camps, 33, 53, 204; *see
   also* specific listings; government

of, in exile, 9, 10, 152; Nazi persecution of Poles, 206
POWs, 124; Allied, 64, 82, 160,
   161; German, 17, 236–37; Nazi
   treatment of Anglo-Americans, 9,
   46, 50, 116, 201–2; Nazi treatment of Soviets, 201
prisoners of war, *see* POWs
progressive politics (United States),
   77–78
Provisional French Republic, 190;
   see also France

Quebec Conference and agreement,
   8, 24, 43–47, 48–49, 51, 55, 64,
   157, 175

radical Right, 77, 276n25
Red Army, 61, 161; POWs, 201;
   see also Soviet Union
Remagen, 8, 161, 201
Republican party, 29–30, 98; *see
   also* individual leaders
revisionist historians, 32, 251
Ribbentrop, Joachim von, 179
Riddleberger, James W., 230
Roberts, Owen Josephus, 196
Robin Moor incident, 251
Roosevelt, Eleanor, 257
Roosevelt, Elliott, 271n45
Roosevelt, Franklin Delano, 5, 36,
   71, 72, 80, 90, 98, 116, 164, 165,
   175, 271n27; death of, 156, 172,
   182, 183, 188, 257; illness of, 42,
   78, 151, 155, 145, 171–72, 257,
   266n23, 273n12; personality of,
   42, 77–78; political gamesmanship of, 9, 13–14, 19–20, 24, 30,
   37, 42, 44, 55, 64, 76–79, 86–87,
   91, 118–19, 151, 155, 159, 161–
   62, 168, 195, 254, 255, 258–59,

273*n*12; at Quebec Conference, 43–44, 46–47, 51, 55, 64, 157; war crimes policy of, 13–14, 25, 26–28, 35, 37, 38, 42, 43, 48, 73, 76, 77–78, 86–87, 118–19, 120, 132, 258–59, 275*n*14; at Yalta Conference, 118, 137, 150, 151, 152–53, 154–57, 159
Roosevelt, Theodore, 29, 61, 75
Rosenman, Samuel I., 30, 87–88, 91, 108, 110, 119, 120, 121, 122, 125, 128, 129, 130, 133, 134, 135, 136, 137, 138, 142–44, 147, 148, 150–51, 156, 161, 164, 165, 166, 167–71, 195–96, 254, 275-*n*14; at London conference, 169–73, 174–82, 183, 184, 186, 188, 192, 193–94, 196, 280*n*59; at San Francisco Conference, 207–8, 209, 216, 217, 219, 220, 221–24
Royall, Kenneth C., 102–3, 106, 142, 160–61
Ruhr, 45, 55; *see also* Morgenthau plan
Rules of Land Warfare: Hague Convention (Hague IV), 123–24; U.S. War Department, 100
Rundstedt, Karl Rudolf Gerd von, 233

SA, 17, 28; conspiracy/criminal-organization charges against, 51–52, 249; political unimportance of, 53; *see also* Nazi party
Saar, 55; *see also* Morgenthau plan
Salter, Arthur, 63
Schacht, Hjalmar, 233, 248
SD, 17; *see also* Gestapo; Nazi party
Security Service, *see* SD
SHAEF, *see* Supreme Headquarters Allied Expeditionary Force
Shawcross (Lord), 286*n*10
Shea, Francis, 242

Sicily: invasion of, 14; *see also* Italy
Siegfried line, 14, 54
Simon, John A., 45–46, 64, 170, 171, 172–73, 174–75, 176, 177, 178–79, 180, 183, 184, 185, 186, 187, 188, 192, 193, 197–98, 212, 219, 254, 281*n*23
Slavs, 191, 203
Smith, Bradley F. (ed.), *American Road to Nuremberg: The Documentary Record, The,* 8*n*
Smuts, Jan, 187
Sobolev, S. S., 63
Somervell, Donald, 172, 176, 177–78, 181, 192, 198
Soviet Union, 88, 154–55, 167; forced-labor plans of, 166–67, 227–30, 231, 250; legal system of, 52, 131, 198, 219, 223–24; in Nuremberg planning, 131, 150, 160, 169, 173, 179, 190, 192, 196, 200, 220–21, 222, 223, 226, 232, 246; secret police, 61, 62; war crimes policy of, 9–10, 34, 49, 63–64, 71, 134, 141–42, 150, 160, 172, 186, 187, 190, 217, 219, 237; in World War II, 62, 118, 131, 152, 153, 229, 252; *see also* Allied powers; Red Army; Stalin, Joseph
Speer, Albert, 248–49
SS, 15, 26, 28, 65, 176, 211; atrocities committed by, 114–15, 117, 126; breakdown of, 203; common enterprise charge against, 184–85; conspiracy / criminal-organization charges against, 51–52, 159–60, 184–85, 238, 249–50, 258; enlisted ranks, 17, 159–60; First Panzer Regiment, 114, 116; forced labor suggested for, 227–28, 229–30; internment planned for, 159–60; in Malmédy massacre, 114–15; POW treatment by, 50; rules of war violated by, 115;

SS *(continued)*
  see also Gestapo; Hitler, Adolf;
  Nazi party
Stalin, Joseph, 13, 34, 47, 63–64,
  88, 271n45; at Yalta Conference,
  118, 152, 156, 158, 159
Stettinius, Edward, 88–89, 120,
  144, 167, 217, 218, 219, 220,
  221, 222; "three Secretaries' memorandum," 146, 147, 148, 150,
  151, 156, 159, 162, 164, 167,
  168, 169, 175, 193, 195, 197,
  200, 209, 257; weakness of, 89,
  90–91, 108, 109, 118, 120, 155,
  157, 171–72, 181–82, 207
Stimson, Henry L., 5, 23–24, 25–
  26, 44, 67, 93–94, 99, 101, 123,
  156, 157, 198, 253, 254, 256,
  257, 271n35; anti-Semitism of,
  31, 41; career of, 29, 75–76, 93,
  94; diary, 11, 24, 36, 38, 61,
  62, 76–77, 116, 147, 161, 266–
  67n30, 270n15; personality of,
  26, 31–32, 38, 39, 43, 44, 53, 62,
  63, 92–93, 94, 97, 143; show trial
  favored by, 61, 62, 63, 64–65;
  "three Secretaries' memorandum," 146, 147, 148, 150, 151,
  156, 159, 162, 164, 167, 168,
  169, 175, 193, 195, 197, 200,
  209, 257; war crimes policy of,
  12, 25, 26, 33–35, 36, 37, 41,
  42–43, 44–45, 48, 49–50, 53–54,
  60, 61–63, 64–65, 75–76, 79,
  86, 92, 95, 98, 108, 109, 112,
  116, 118, 122, 128, 136, 151,
  179, 182, 239, 245, 246; *see also*
  U.S. War Department
Storm Troopers, *see* SA
sugar trust conspiracy, 75–76
summary execution, 34, 45–46, 47,
  63, 64, 76, 102, 150, 171, 173,
  175, 176, 187, 192, 193, 197–98,
  218, 219, 222, 271–72n45
Supreme Headquarters Allied Expe-

ditionary Force (SHAEF), 115,
  224, 227

Taft, William Howard, 29
Taylor, A. J. P., 251
Taylor, Telford, 251
Teheran Conference, 34, 63
"three Secretaries' memorandum,"
  146, 147, 148, 150, 151, 156,
  159, 162, 164, 167, 168, 169,
  175, 193, 195, 197, 200, 209,
  257
Trainin, A. W., 123, 131, 276n25
Treblinka, 204
Truman, Harry S., 5, 182, 198,
  208, 223; personality, 195; presidential style, 195, 207, 257; war
  crimes policy of, 193, 194–95,
  207, 208, 218, 227, 228, 231,
  245, 257

United Nations, 17, 35, 63, 72, 81,
  85, 91, 97, 124, 133, 138, 148,
  154, 161, 165, 168, 169, 181,
  191, 199, 206, 214, 260; General
  Assembly, 157; San Francisco
  Conference, 200, 207–8, 209,
  210, 211, 216, 217, 218, 220–27,
  239, 242, 244, 245
United Nations Commission for the
  Investigation of War Crimes, *see*
  United Nations War Crimes
  Commission
United Nations War Crimes Commission (UNWCC), 10, 11, 18,
  19, 35–36, 66, 67, 69, 81, 91,
  104–5, 119, 120, 130, 134, 141,
  144, 161, 163, 170, 184, 188,
  208; Draft Convention, 135; *see
  also* Nazi party
United States: bureaucratic and interdepartmental tangles, 28–29,

30–31, 34, 39, 43, 48, 53, 54–56, 62; manuscript collections, 7; military-necessity policy of, 30–31, 39–40; political gamesmanship of, 9, 10–11; postwar policy of, 32, 40, 43–44, 154–55, 164, 231, 250, 252, 256–57, 259, 261; public opinion in, 10, 11, 19, 35, 54, 114–15, 117, 123, 139, 201–2, 203, 204–5, 251, 252, 259–60, 261; war crimes policy of, 18–19, 35, 70–71, 87, 90–91, 156, 157–59, 160–61, 162–89, 190, 193–95, 213–21, 229–30, 259, 261; war crimes policy drafts and redrafts, 224–27, 239–46, 258; see also Bernays, Murray C., McCloy, John J.; Roosevelt, Franklin D.; Truman, Harry S.; U.S. legal system; individual leaders, cabinet departments, Secretaries, officials

U.S. Army, 14, 17–18, 42; First, 8; German occupation, 16–18, 23, 24, 27, 28–29, 34, 40, 41, 56, 159–60, 227; on hostage executions, 100; Italian occupation, 14–15; 106th Infantry Division, 236; screened from political controversy, 30; see also U.S. War Department; individual leaders

U.S. Cabinet Committee on Germany, 24, 26–27, 34–38, 40, 42, 44

U.S. Congress, 9; concentration-camp investigation, 205–6; see also U.S. Senate; specific House and Senate committees and members

U.S. Justice Department, 108, 109–10, 111, 112, 121, 182; see also Biddle, Francis

U.S. legal system, 52, 145–46; conspiracy concept in, 52, 77, 124; evidence in, 83; judicial independence in, 179; transferability of judgments between courts in, 59–60, 82–83, 85, 127, 128, 141, 145; see also specific lawyers and scholars

U.S. Navy Department: conspiracy/criminal-organization position of, 80; war crimes policy of, 65–66, 67–68, 69, 70–71, 80, 133, 147–48

U.S. Senate: on treaty ratification, 83; treaty-ratification problems of, 81, 82, 110, 136, 145

U.S. State Department, 12–13, 14, 18, 26, 63, 121, 129, 155, 162, 164, 171, 192, 207–8, 276n25; additions to "three Secretaries' memorandum" by, 167, 168; conspiracy/criminal-organization position of, 159, 166; German memorandum, 36; German policy, 36, 40, 55; opposition to War Refugee Board by, 22; "Report on Reparation, Restitution, and Property Rights—Germany," 20; war crimes policy of, 19, 35, 36, 66–68, 69, 70–71, 80, 92, 105, 108; weakness of, 90–91, 108–9, 112, 119, 156, 157, 158, 171–72, 181–82, 196, 209, 215; see also Hull, Cordell; Stettinius, Edward

U.S. Treasury Department, 21, 27–28, 143–44; British policy, 44, 45; factionalism in, 137; German policy, 28–29, 30–31, 34, 36–37, 38, 40, 43; war crimes policy of, 148–49, 160, 227–29, 231; and War Department conflicts, 28–29, 30–31, 34, 38, 40, 43, 53, 54–56, 62, 109, 112, 136–37, 164, 227–28; and War Department rapprochement, 65; see also Morgenthau, Henry, Jr.; Morgenthau plan

U.S. War Department, 11, 16, 26, 41, 149, 164, 165, 199, 206,

U.S. War Department *(continued)*
261n; on acts against German
nationals, 161; on aggressive war
as crime, 91–93, 103–4, 108, 109,
122–23, 124–26, 127–28, 129,
135, 140, 142, 143, 161, 215; on
atrocities, 161; Civil Affairs Division, 12–13, 23, 50, 51, 93,
100; conspiracy/criminal-organi-
zation position of, 80, 103, 107,
108, 110, 112, 116–17, 120, 121,
122, 125, 127, 129, 132, 135,
136–37, 140, 141, 142–43, 144,
161, 168, 169, 175, 176, 178,
184, 200, 215; factionalism in,
85–86, 93, 94, 95, 99, 100–101,
107, 112, 121–23, 125, 128, 132,
136, 160–61, 200, 206, 254; G-1
(personnel branch), 50, 51, 58,
65, 91–92, 99, 100, 107, 122–23,
127–28; *Handbook of Military
Government for Germany*, 16–
17, 20, 21, 25–28, 32, 40; "Interim Committee," 121n; *Interim
Directives on Occupation Procedures*, 16, 17, 20, 21, 28–29, 44;
Joint Chiefs of Staff, 30, 39, 66,
155–56, 227; Joint Chiefs of Staff
Order number 1067, 16, 79;
Judge Advocate General's office
role, 50, 53, 54, 57–58, 59–60,
61, 66, 67, 82–83, 86, 92, 100–
101, 102, 103–6, 107, 108, 121,
122–23, 124, 125, 126, 128, 129,
131–32, 134, 136, 137, 140–43,
144–45, 160, 200, 206, 236, 237,
254; lawyers' role in Nuremberg
system, 33, 43, 49–54, 57–62, 65–
68, 75, 98–99, 102, 104, 116–19,
121–29, 131–40, 147, 255; POW
concern on, 116; on prewar persecution by Nazis, 161; *Rules of
Land Warfare*, 100; satirical
memo, 49; soft German policy of,
20, 25; and Treasury Department
conflicts, 28–29, 30–31, 34, 43,
48, 53, 54–56, 62, 136–37, 164,
200, 227–28; and Treasury Department rapprochement, 64–65;
war crimes planning group, 206–
7, 209; war crimes policy, 20, 24–
25, 28–29, 30–31, 33–34, 38, 40,
43, 48, 53, 54–62, 66, 75, 80, 86,
91–113, 116–17, 120, 121–29,
134, 136, 138, 140, 142–47, 150–
51, 160–61, 164, 175–76, 178,
181–83; *see also* Bernays, Murray
C.; McCloy, John J.; Stimson,
Henry L.

VE Day, 12, 214, 227, 240, 245

war crimes, war crimes policy, *see*
International law; Nazi party; specific countries and leaders
War Refugee Board, 22, 35, 57, 64,
258
Ward, J. G., 218, 219
Warsaw: fall of, 153
Wechsler, Herbert, 109–10, 111–
12, 116, 125, 126–27, 128, 129,
130, 136, 138, 145, 147, 195,
210, 216, 217, 220, 224, 240,
241, 242, 246, 254
Wehrmacht, 15, 17, 63; *see also*
Nazi party
Weir, John, 69, 103, 121, 132, 137,
138, 142, 143, 147, 162, 163,
164, 165, 166, 167–69, 178, 179,
181–82, 185, 188, 196, 206, 236,
237
White, Harry Dexter, 20, 21, 23,
34, 63, 269n100
Wiener, Frederick Bernays, 50, 54,
69
Wilhelm (kaiser of Germany), 19
Willkie, Wendell, 30
Wilson, Woodrow, 61, 81

Winant, John G., 63, 69, 70, 196
Winthrop, Stimson, Putnam, and Roberts, 94
Wood, Edward F. L., *see* Halifax (Lord)
World Court, *see* Hague Conventions
World War I: as influence on World War II, 8, 13, 19, 260; U.S. international commitments after, 260
World War II, 93, 104; rightist consequences of, 205; two-front

aspect of, 153; war-making system, 203–4; *see also* individual armies, battles, countries, leaders
Wright, Quincy, 106

Yalta Conference, 113, 118, 125, 137, 138, 142, 148, 150, 152–63; unrepresentative nature of U.S. staff, 155, 156; war crimes discussed at, 158–60, 162, 163, 171, 175